Minds Unveiled

This book demonstrates how generative artificial intelligence (AI), a form of sophisticated AI technology, is transforming our knowledge of how the human mind functions in relation to business leadership and decision-making. It describes the most recent findings and applications of generative AI in psychology. The book explains the relationships between language, thinking, and behavior as well as how AI may aid in our understanding of learning, decision-making, and problem-solving. In addition, it discusses the significance of applying AI properly and ethically. This book provides a comprehensive overview of how AI is increasing our understanding of the mind and how it impacts each of us professionally.

Minds Unveiled
Exploring the Effects of Generative AI on Business Behavior

Edited by
Raul V. Rodriguez and Hemachandran K

Routledge
Taylor & Francis Group

A PRODUCTIVITY PRESS BOOK

First published 2025
by Routledge
605 Third Avenue, New York, NY 10158

and by Routledge
4 Park Square, Milton Park, Abingdon, Oxon, OX14 4RN

Routledge is an imprint of the Taylor & Francis Group, an informa business

ISBN: 978-1-032-71501-8 (hbk)
ISBN: 978-1-032-71107-2 (pbk)
ISBN: 978-1-032-71108-9 (ebk)

DOI: 10.4324/9781032711089

Typeset in Garamond
by KnowledgeWorks Global Ltd.

Contents

Preface

In the dynamic landscape of contemporary business, the emergence of generative artificial intelligence (AI) stands as a transformative force, promising unprecedented opportunities and challenges alike. This book presents a collection of insightful contributions that delve deep into the sophisticated relationship between generative AI and business dynamics.

We aim to provide an understanding of how generative AI influences various facets of business behaviour, and how businesses can harness its potential to thrive in an increasingly digitized world. The chapters in this volume cover a wide array of topics, each shedding light on different dimensions of the symbiotic relationship between generative AI and business operations. From the foundational principles of generative AI to its profound impact on consumer behaviour, marketing strategies, and personalised customer experiences.

Additionally, this book also addresses the ethical implications inherent in the deployment of AI technologies. With chapters dedicated to exploring the convergence of generative AI and ethical considerations, as well as navigating the ethical landscape of simulated intelligence, we endeavour to foster a responsible approach to AI implementation in business contexts.

Moreover, this volume goes beyond theoretical discourse to offer practical insights into leveraging generative AI for innovation and competitive advantage. From innovative product design to enhancing decision-making through human-AI collaboration, the chapters in this book provide actionable strategies for businesses aiming to stay ahead in an AI-driven world.

Importantly, the contributions in this volume do not confine themselves to theoretical speculation; rather, they draw from real-world examples and case studies across diverse sectors such as retail, finance, healthcare, and more. By examining the tangible impact of generative AI in these domains, we offer readers a comprehensive understanding of its potential to revolutionise various industries.

Furthermore, we hope that this book provides a comprehensive overview of generative AI in business applications, and how it is transforming different sectors. We believe that this book will be a valuable resource for academics, researchers, professionals, and policymakers who are interested in understanding the potential of generative AI in the business world.

We would like to thank all the contributors who have made this book possible, and we hope that readers will find it informative and thought-provoking.

Contributors

Mir Aadil
Woxsen School of Business,
  Woxsen University, India

Adil Abdhul
Woxsen University, Hyderabad,
  India

Gomathy Annamaneni
Woxsen University, Hyderabad,
  India

Ezendu Ariwa
Professor, University of Warwick,
  Coventry CV4 7AL, United
  Kingdom

MNS Ram Kumar Babu
Woxsen University, Hyderabad,
  India

Bidisha Banerji
Amity University, Noida, India

Akoparna Barman
Jain (Deemed-to-be) University,
  Bengaluru, India

Vinay Kumar Bodepu
Woxsen University, Hyderabad,
  India

Shruti Choudhary
Woxsen University, Hyderabad,
  India

Palagudi Venkata Deepak
Woxsen University, Hyderabad,
  India

Vegi Dharshini
Woxsen University, Hyderabad,
  India

Darla Dheeraj
Woxsen University, Hyderabad,
  India

Sri Durga
Woxsen University, Hyderabad,
  India

Ravali Gogula
Woxsen University, Hyderabad,
  India

Shravya Goud Godishela
Woxsen University, Hyderabad,
India

Rahul Kumar Gupta
Woxsen University, Hyderabad,
India

Abu Bakar Abdul Hamid
Infrastructure University Kuala
Lumpur (IUKL), Malaysia

Zahid Hussain
Khadim Hussain Shah Institute of
Technology, Karachi, Pakistan

Rishabh Jaiswal
Woxsen University, Hyderabad,
India

Christian Kaunert
Dublin City University, Ireland &
University of South Wales UK

Arman Khan
Shaheed Benazir Bhutto University,
Pakistan

Paduru Rama Krishna Reddy
Woxsen University, Hyderabad,
India

**Puvvaladasu M. Sai Subramanya
Krishna**
Woxsen University, Hyderabad,
India

Pokala Pranay Kumar
University of Maryland, Baltimore
County, United States

Praveen Kumar T
Woxsen University, Hyderabad,
India

Sathwika Manthena
Woxsen University, Hyderabad,
India

Ajay Midimalapu
Woxsen University, Hyderabad,
India

Purushottam Patnaik
Woxsen University, Hyderabad,
India

Anish Reddy Peddi
Woxsen University, Hyderabad,
India

Anjali Perla
Woxsen University, Hyderabad,
India

Parth Prakash
Woxsen University, Hyderabad,
India

Abbu Pravalika
Woxsen University, Hyderabad,
India

Kamalraj R.
Jain (Deemed-to-be) University,
Bengaluru, India

Khant Mayank Rameshbhai
Woxsen University, Hyderabad,
India

Deepthi Reddy
Woxsen University, Hyderabad,
India

Ravuri Venkata Trinadh Reddy
Woxsen University, Hyderabad,
India

Revanth Reddy Regalla
Woxsen University, Hyderabad,
India

Shashanka Reddy
Woxen University, Hyderabad, India

Suraj Reddy
Woxsen University, Hyderabad,
India

S. A. Mokhtar Rizvi
Amity University, Noida, India

Anirudh Sai Vallabhaneni
Woxsen University, Hyderabad,
India

Riya Sham
Woxsen University, Hyderabad,
India

J. Shanti
Amity University, Noida, India

Anusha Siddadapu
Woxsen University, Hyderabad,
India

Bhupinder Singh
Sharda University, Greater Noida,
India

Akhilesh Sunkara
Woxsen University, Hyderabad,
India

Teja Swarup R
Woxsen University, Hyderabad,
India

V. Vishnu Vardhan
Woxsen University, Hyderabad,
India

Chapter 1

Introduction to Generative AI and Business Behaviour

Mir Aadil, Vinay Kumar Bodepu, Vegi Dharshini, and
Durga Lakamsani

1.1 Introduction

The convergence of behavioural assessment and generative artificial intelligence (AI) is a key point of intersection inside the present-day employer panorama, where it is propelling modern breakthroughs in the course of a couple of industries. The motive of this creation is to define the essential thoughts and vital realisations that resource the utility of generative AI to the sector of enterprise behaviour evaluation.

Designed to simulate, synthesise, and generate records, generative AI contains a wide variety of computational techniques that help businesses assume consumer alternatives, extract actionable insights, and optimise operational techniques. Complex algorithms like reinforcement learning (RL), variational autoencoders (VAEs), and generative adversarial networks (GANs) are the inspiration for generative AI. These algorithms enable corporations to provide sensible outputs, version elaborate styles, and navigate unpredictable environments with formerly unheard-of accuracy and performance [1].

A new technology of innovation and disruption is being ushered in via the emergence of generative AI, which is absolutely redefining the manner business behaviour evaluation is performed in an entire lot of industries, which incorporates advertising, finance, delivery chain control, and customer courting control. Businesses can discover hidden insights and hidden interior massive datasets, decorate decision-making techniques, and capture new

DOI: 10.4324/9781032711089-1

opportunities in dynamic marketplace environments by using the power of generative AI-pushed algorithms.

But as agencies include the revolutionary capacity of generative AI, they face a huge style of limitations, along with felony compliance, ethical troubles, and technological constraints. The notable use of deepfake technology, algorithmic biases, and problems about statistics privateness spotlight how crucial it is to put into effect generative AI interior enterprise ecosystems in a responsible and ethical manner.

In moderate of this, the research delves deeply into the sector of generative AI and examines the way it influences commercial organisation behaviour evaluation. This chapter aims to make clear the essential mechanisms, developing styles, and destiny commands influencing the changing panorama of generative AI in enterprise contexts via the usage of synthesising theoretical frameworks, empirical research, and actual worldwide programmes [2].

1.2 Literature Evaluation

Generative AI and commercial enterprise behaviour constitute a burgeoning area of studies and practical application that has garnered sizable interest from teachers, practitioners, and enterprise leaders alike. This intersection presents a unique possibility for both studies and sensible utility. This literature evaluation gives a complete review of the present-day panorama and future ability of generative AI to shape enterprise behaviour with the aid of synthesising key findings and insights from a diverse range of studies, papers, and courses. The motive of this evaluation is to offer complete statistics.

Foundations of Generative AI: It is essential to gain an understanding of the foundational ideas of generative AI in an effort to understand the impact that it has on the behaviour of businessmen. Generative AI strategies, which include GANs, VAEs, and RL, have emerged as effective gear for generating sensible facts, synthesising novel insights, and optimising choice-making techniques. These techniques have currently won a great deal of interest.

Generative AI has packages in commercial enterprise behaviour analysis. It gives modern answers and transformative talents across a number of commercial enterprise behaviour analysis domain names. The application of generative synthetic intelligence in marketing makes it viable to generate customised content, centred advertisements, and predictive analytics models, all of which enhance patron engagement and boom conversion charges.

Furthermore, generative AI also permits predictive call for forecasting, optimisation of inventory stages, and mitigation of operational dangers in the context of supply chain control.

Generational synthetic intelligence performs a pivotal function in reshaping the dynamics of patron experience and engagement. This is a sizeable advantage for businesses. Companies are able to acquire more profound understandings of the preferences, emotions, and styles of behaviour in their clients by way of using techniques inclusive of natural language processing (NLP), image reputation, and sentiment analysis. Personalised experiences, expecting client wishes, and cultivating lengthy time-period loyalty are all matters that can be completed by organisations via the utilisation of generative artificial intelligence-pushed chatbots, virtual assistants, and advice systems.

Regulatory and Ethical Considerations: As the use of generative AI is increasing across industries, issues regarding ethics, privateness, and regulatory compliance have reached the leading edge of the communique. The situations where generative AI could be abused to provide deepfake content, to disseminate false facts, and to violate the privacy rights of people highlight the importance of establishing robust moral frameworks, governance mechanisms, and responsibility standards.

Despite the reality that it has the potential to be transformative, generative synthetic intelligence (GSI) is faced with a number of demanding situations that pertain to generation, ethics, and society. These challenges require, in addition, research and mitigation. The development of trust, reliability, and duty in generative synthetic intelligence systems calls for troubles regarding statistics bias, version interpretability, and algorithmic transparency to be addressed. The advancement of studies in explainable AI (XAI), fairness, and algorithmic equity is also critical for ensuring equitable effects and mitigating the results of unintended results [3].

1.2.1 Discovering New Opportunities and Trends

In the future, the trajectory of generative artificial intelligence in enterprise behaviour analysis is going to be formed by using some of the rising traits and opportunities. The convergence of AI-driven robotics and automation and the combination of generative AI and the blockchain era are two examples of unconventional programmes and synergistic approaches that agencies are investigating. These tactics promise to liberate new cost propositions, force innovation, and beautify aggressive gain [4].

1.3 Understanding Generative Artificial Intelligence

In the sector of AI, generative AI is a paradigm shift that emphasises the introduction, synthesis, and technology of the latest information as opposed to simplest analysing preexisting information or making selections totally based on preset guidelines. Gaining a know-how of generative AI necessitates familiarity with its centre thoughts, techniques, and packages in diverse fields.

Fundamentally, the intention of generative AI is to simulate and model the innate variability and complexity found in actual-world information distributions. Generative AI models create new statistics samples that carefully resemble the education facts they had been exposed to, in contrast to traditional AI fashions that paint on discriminative ideas—classifying information into predefined categories or making predictions totally based on found patterns.

Among the primary strategies underlying generative AI are:

GANs: GANs, which were first offered with the aid of Ian Goodfellow and pals in 2014, are made from a generator and a discriminator neural community. The discriminator assesses the validity of generated samples, whereas the generator tries to create synthetic information samples, which can be indistinguishable from actual facts. GANs iteratively beautify the discriminator's capacity to differentiate among actual and generated samples, in addition to the generator's capacity to generate realistic facts through opposed training [4].

VAEs: VAEs are a subset of the autoencoder version family. The encoder network compresses the input statistics right into a latent area that is lower-dimensional, and the decoder network makes use of the latent representation to reconstruct the original information. By sampling from the learned distributions, VAEs—in contrast to traditional autoencoders—introduce probabilistic distributions over the latent area, allowing for the introduction of recent information samples. The underlying structure and variability of complicated information distributions are in particular nicely captured by using VAEs [5].

Transformer Models and Recurrent Neural Networks (RNNs): Additionally, transformer fashions and recurrent neural networks have been modified for generative obligations, especially in the areas of sequence era and NLP. Because RNNs can process records sequentially, they may be beneficial for generating textual content, song, and time-series records. Transformer models use self-attention mechanisms to seize long-variety dependencies and convey coherent data sequences. One instance of such an architecture is OpenAI's generative pre-skilled transformer (GPT) collection.

Generative AI has applications in many specific fields, along with:

- Image and Video Generation: Deepfake motion pictures, practical avatars, and high-decision pics can all be produced with the aid of generative AI models.
- Text and Language Generation: Generative AI powers a wide variety of language-related duties, such as dialogue structures, content material introduction, herbal language era, and gadget translation.
- Drug Discovery and Molecular Design: To create new compounds with preferred properties, generative AI algorithms are increasingly getting used in drug discovery and molecular design.
- Creative Content Generation: Generative AI stimulates creativity in domain names like track, artwork, and design by way of producing unique and varied consequences on its own [6].

1.3.1 Fundamentals of Generative AI

Within the field of AI, generative synthetic intelligence (GSI) is a paradigm that focuses on generating new text, images, information, and other types of content material. Generative AI seeks to mimic human creativity and imagination by way of producing particular outputs that resemble actual records, in contrast to standard AI strategies that focus on classification or prediction primarily based on already-current facts.

The following are the fundamental thoughts that power the operation of generative AI:

- Data Generation: Generative AI's principal goal is to produce sparkling statistics samples that closely resemble the schooling units of statistics it has been uncovered too. This system includes figuring out the fundamental systems and patterns discovered within the schooling facts and developing new statistics factors that observe these styles.
- Probabilistic Modelling: To constitute the uncertainty and variability present in actual-world statistics distributions, generative AI regularly makes use of probabilistic fashions. Generative AI models are able to produce samples that accurately constitute the diversity of the schooling

information with the aid of mastering possibility distributions across the input area.

■ Adversarial Training: One of the principal methods in GANs is the training procedure, which consists of a competition among neural networks, a discriminator, and a generator. Whereas the discriminator seeks to determine between generated and real samples, the generator seeks to offer practical samples. Both networks gain higher overall performance through iterative education, which ends in the advent of more sensible data samples [6].

1.3.1.1 Fundamental Algorithms and Mechanisms

Depending on the unique method used, exceptional generative AI fashions have unique underlying mechanisms and algorithms. Nonetheless, routine themes encompass:

■ Neural Networks: Convolutional neural networks (CNNs) are usually used in generative AI fashions for image generation, while RNNs are usually used for sequence technology.

■ Techniques for Optimisation: Instruction Optimisation algorithms like stochastic gradient descent (SGD) or its variations, which iteratively replace version parameters to minimise a loss feature, are frequently used in generative AI models.

■ Probability Distributions: To constitute the uncertainty and variability found in the information, generative AI fashions make use of possibility distributions. These distributions are sampled and discovered using methods like variational inference and maximum likelihood estimation (MLE).

1.3.2 Applications in Business Behaviour Analysis

Business behaviour analysis is undergoing a revolution way to generative AI, which is supplying sparkling views and facilitating information-pushed decision-making in lots of industries, such as advertising and marketing, supply chain management, purchaser dating management (CRM), and finance [7].

■ Function in Marketing: Personalised content material advent, ad marketing campaign optimisation, and stepped forward customer engagement are all made viable by way of the usage of generative AI in advertising and marketing. By using sophisticated techniques like picture technology and NLP, generative AI permits entrepreneurs to personalise messages and visuals to every man or woman's preferences, increasing purchaser satisfaction and conversion fees. For example, chatbots pushed via generative AI are capable of having interaction with customers immediately, imparting tailored guidelines and efficaciously answering their questions. Additionally, generative models can compare client sentiment from social media facts, supporting marketers in spotting developments and changes in sentiment that could guide their technique.

- Function in Supply Chain Management: Generative AI allows with demand forecasting, stock optimisation, and predictive analytics in supply chain management. Generative AI fashions can forecast demand fluctuations, expect supply chain disruptions, and optimise inventory stages to minimise fees and maximise performance by means of analysing ancient statistics and external factors. In order to simulate distinctive supply chain situations, for instance, generative AI algorithms can generate artificial information. This permits businesses to discover ability risks and create backup plans. Additionally, generative models can optimise scheduling and routing picks, ensuring on-time delivery and reducing transportation expenses.

- Function in Customer Relationship Management (CRM): Businesses can use generative AI to examine client behaviour, section audiences, and personalise interactions at scale, which improves CRM efforts. Generative AI assists businesses in identifying high-fee clients, waiting for their needs, and customising verbal exchange tactics to build enduring relationships. It does this by producing insights from client information. Recommendation engines driven by generative AI, for example, can investigate browsing behaviour and past purchases to make applicable product and service tips to customers. Furthermore, tailor-made electronic mail campaigns and promotional offers can be produced by way of generative models, which increases client engagement and retention prices.

- Function in Finance: Risk assessment, fraud detection, and portfolio control are all being revolutionised in the finance enterprise via generative AI. Generative AI models can decorate regulatory compliance and decision-making tactics by means of identifying patterns, detecting anomalies, and mitigating dangers in actual-time through analysing considerable amounts of financial statistics. To educate fraud detection fashions, for example, generative AI algorithms can produce synthetic information that mimics specific fraud scenarios, growing the accuracy of the model. Moreover, with the aid of producing plenty of funding techniques and mimicking marketplace conditions to assess chance publicity, generative models can help with portfolio optimisation.

1.4 Leveraging Generative AI for Business Insights

By the use of generative AI for commercial enterprise insights, organisations can better apprehend marketplace trends, expect consumer behaviour, and offer greater individualised experiences. Generative AI exactly forecasts call for, segments clients, and identifies rising developments by analysing huge datasets through predictive analytics. Businesses can boost client engagement and loyalty by imposing generative AI-powered recommendation systems, chatbots, and digital assistants. These systems provide personalised interactions that speak to man or woman preferences. By making use of the strength of generative AI, organisations can quickly adapt to changing market dynamics and take an advantage of an aggressive edge in the trendy customer-centric landscape by turning facts into actionable insights.

1.4.1 Customer Behaviour and Predictive Analytics

Predictive analytics is revolutionised by means of generative AI, which makes use of current methods to predict customer behaviour and pinpoint new marketplace tendencies with formerly unheard-of precision and detail. Generative AI enables agencies to attain actionable insights into customer preferences, shopping patterns, and sentiment shifts through the usage of state-of-the-art algorithms and massive datasets.

■ Predicting Consumer Behaviour and Market Trends: Generative AI fashions look for underlying styles and correlations that point to future customer behaviour by way of analysing historic information, social media interactions, and online browsing styles. Businesses can expect shifts in client options, marketplace demands, and competitive dynamics by way of growing synthetic facts points and modelling feasible eventualities.

■ Customer Segmentation and Trend Analysis: Businesses can divide their clientele into discrete companies consistent with psychographic profiles, buying patterns, and demographics thanks to generative AI. Businesses can efficaciously target particular segments with their pricing, product services, and advertising and marketing techniques with the aid of figuring out styles and clusters within the records. Additionally, via recognising new developments, patron options, and market possibilities, generative AI makes trend evaluation less complicated and empowers corporations to innovate and adapt early.

■ Demand Forecasting: To correctly expect the demand for items and offerings, generative AI models make use of beyond income records, economic indicators, and out of doors variables. Businesses can optimise inventory management, manufacturing scheduling, and supply chain logistics to fulfil consumer demand while minimising fees and stockouts by forecasting future fluctuations in demand and seasonality styles.

1.4.2 Customer Experience and Personalisation

By offering customised interactions and offerings that talk to everybody's unique needs and possibilities, generative AI-driven personalisation transforms patron experiences and engagement. Generative AI enables organisations to create customised stories across more than one touchpoints, increasing purchaser pleasure and loyalty through sophisticated algorithms and real-time information processing.

■ Improved Customer Experiences: Recommendation engines, chatbots, and digital assistants that tailor interactions and services according to person options, ancient activity, and contextual cues are powered via generative AI. These structures dynamically regulate content material, product tips, and communication channels to enhance engagement and pride by way of evaluating user information and feedback.

■ Recommendation systems: Personalised tips for goods, facts, and services are produced by means of generative AI algorithms, which have a look at consumer behaviour, past purchases, and product attributes. Recommendation structures decorate sales growth, improve cross-promoting opportunities, and optimise product discovery by comprehending man or woman options and consumption patterns.

■ Chatbots and Virtual Assistants: Generative AI-powered chatbots and virtual assistants provide customers with tailor-made assistance, guidance, and pointers through quite a few channels, together with messaging apps, cell apps, and websites. These conversational interfaces improve client delight and loyalty by offering clean, tailored reports that imitate human interaction by comprehending herbal language inputs and context-unique queries [8].

1.5 Ethical and Regulatory Considerations

When deploying generative AI, moral and regulatory issues are important. Because of its potential to produce realism in content and to govern records, privacy, bias, and misuse worries the floor. It's important to strike a stability between responsibility and innovation. To lessen the risks of incorrect information and manipulation, express pointers governing facts utilisation, algorithmic transparency, and person consent are necessary. Regulatory frameworks should alternate to satisfy new issues, preserve accountability, and prevent ethical transgressions. In order to build acceptance as true, hold integrity, and responsibly and ethically harness the transformative strength of generative AI within the digital age, cooperation among enterprises, policymakers, and ethicists is vital.

1.5.1 Overcoming Ethical Obstacles

When the usage of generative AI for commercial enterprise behaviour analysis, ethical issues keep in mind some of the issues, which include algorithmic bias, statistics privacy, and decision-making transparency.

- Data Privacy: Generative AI frequently works with sizeable datasets that include private records. Ensuring strong facts privacy measures is important to defensive consumer information and upholding privacy rights. These measures encompass encryption, anonymization, and access controls.
- Algorithmic Bias: It is feasible for generative AI fashions to unintentionally give a boost to biases discovered in the schooling set, that could bring about discriminatory and unfair consequences. Careful training facts choice, steady commentary, and model performance assessment are vital for mitigating algorithmic bias a good way to find and accurate biases.
- Transparency: Questions of trust and duty are raised by means of the opacity of generative AI algorithms. Encouraging accountability and bolstering stakeholder confidence is executed through promoting

transparency in AI-driven selection-making procedures, encompassing version architectures, data assets, and decision criteria.

1.5.2 Compliance and Regulatory Frameworks

Different nations and industries have one of a kind regulatory frameworks in place governing the use of AI in business settings, so cautious navigation and compliance techniques are required.

- Data Safety Laws: Strict recommendations are positioned on information series, processing, and garage via laws like the California Consumer Privacy Act (CCPA) inside the US and the General Data Protection Regulation (GDPR) in the EU. Getting clean person consent and putting in region sturdy statistics governance processes are necessary to make sure compliance with these policies.
- Industry-Specific Regulations: The application of AI and facts analytics is ruled by way of zone-precise guidelines in a number of industries, along with finance and healthcare. Adherence to enterprise quality practices and specialised expertise are important for compliance with regulations which includes the Basel Committee on Banking Supervision (BCBS) recommendations and the Health Insurance Portability and Accountability Act (HIPAA).
- Ethical Standards and Guidelines: To promote the moral software of AI in enterprise, professional institutions and enterprise firms create moral requirements and suggestions. Respecting ethical requirements like equity, openness, and duty indicates a willpower to moral behaviour and encourages public self-belief in AI structures [8].

1.6 Future Trends and Opportunities

Future traits in generative AI hold the ability to completely rework the take a look at of enterprise behaviour and gift formerly unheard-of probabilities for growth and creativity. The competencies of generative AI may be progressed with the aid of trends in deep studying architectures, along with transformer fashions and reinforcement mastering, a good way to permit for greater complex content introduction, customised reports, and predictive analytics. The mixture of part computing and blockchain era with generative artificial intelligence will open up new avenues for safe records sharing and on the spot decision-making. Furthermore, as generative AI equipment and systems emerge as extra widely available, businesses of all sizes will be capable of taking advantage of AI-pushed insights, which leads to raise their competitiveness, agility, and capacity to create price within the digital economy.

1.6.1 New Developments in Generative AI Trends

New tendencies in generative AI have the capacity to transform enterprise behaviour analysis and spur innovation in a lot of sectors.

- Future Developments in Generative AI Will Centre on Improving Deep Learning Architectures: GANs and VAEs are examples of deep studying architectures with the intention to be further evolved to be able to produce extra numerous and sensible outputs in regions which include textual content, audio, and photograph era.
- Unsupervised and Self-Supervised Learning: Generative AI models will be able to analyse unlabelled data due to advancements in unsupervised and self-supervised learning techniques. This will reduce the need for big annotated datasets and boom scalability and generalisation.
- Multidisciplinary Uses: As generative AI becomes greater incorporated with other domain names like pc vision, reinforcement studying, and natural language processing, it's going to open up new possibilities for interdisciplinary uses in content material advent, drug development, and self-sufficient structures.

1.6.2 Prospects for Originality

Companies have quite a few probabilities to be creative and use generative AI to gain an aggressive edge.

- Personalised Customer Experiences: Businesses can improve engagement and loyalty with the aid of implementing interactive interfaces, personalised content, and product pointers way to generative AI.
- Predictive Analytics and Forecasting: Businesses can expect market tendencies, spot new opportunities, and improve useful resource allocation and selection-making processes via using generative AI for predictive analytics and forecasting.

- Content Creation and the Creative Industries: Media, enjoyment, and advertising sectors can now automate content material advent, optimise production methods, and offer audiences with immersive and charming experiences way to generative AI.
- Supply Chain Optimisation: Demand forecasting, stock control, and logistics optimisation are a number of the methods that generative AI enables corporations optimise their supply chains. This effects in lower prices, less waste, and multiplied productivity.
- Strategic making plans and sizeable idea are essential while integrating generative AI into organisational techniques.
- Data Quality and Governance: To effectively train generative AI models and reduce the danger of bias, mistakes, and moral worries, organisations have to ensure information satisfactory, integrity, and governance.
- Talent and Expertise: To fully utilise generative AI technology and spur innovation inside companies, investments in expertise development and understanding are critical.
- Cooperation and Partnerships: Knowledge sharing, getting right of entry to ultra-modern technologies, and cooperative innovation in generative AI can all be facilitated by means of participating with AI studies establishments, generation companies, and industry companions [9].

1.7 Conclusion

In conclusion, the incorporation of generative synthetic intelligence into business behaviour analysis ushers in a brand new era of innovation, agility, and competitiveness for individuals and companies operating in a whole lot of sectors. In the course of this research, we've witnessed the transformative capacity of generative synthetic intelligence in terms of predicting the behaviour of purchasers, personalising the reviews of clients, and optimising operational approaches. Nevertheless, these opportunities come with some demanding situations, inclusive of moral concerns, regulatory obstacles, and the necessary requirements for responsible deployment.

When it involves the utilisation of generative synthetic intelligence technology, groups want to make transparency, responsibility, and moral stewardship their pinnacle priorities as they navigate this panorama. Businesses can leverage generative synthetic intelligence to drive sustainable growth, improve customer satisfaction, and keep an aggressive edge in a digital economy that is rapidly evolving. This may be accomplished via embracing emerging tendencies, seizing possibilities for innovation, and fostering collaboration.

Generative artificial intelligence, in its essence, is not only the most effective tool for commercial enterprise transformation but also a catalyst for shaping a future in which innovation and moral issues coexist harmoniously. This will pave the way for an extra inclusive, obvious, and accountable method to commercial enterprise behaviour analysis in the future years.

References

1. Antoniou, A., Storkey, A., & Edwards, H. (2017). Data augmentation generative hostile networks. ArXiv preprint arXiv:1711.04340. 2017 Nov 12.
2. Aydın, Ö., & Karaarslan, E. (2022). OpenAI ChatGPT generated literature review: Digital twin in healthcare. Available at SSRN 4308687.
3. Chiriac, I. (2021). The impact of economy on mergers & acquisitions in European markets. Journal of Financial Studies & Research, 2021, 1–8.
4. Cho, S., & Chung, C. Y. (2022). Review of the literature on merger waves. Journal of Risk and Financial Management, 15(10), 432.
5. Clark-Murphy, M., & Soutar, G. N. (2004). What man or woman buyers value: Some Australian proof. Journal of Economic Psychology, 25(4), 539–555.
6. Jeblick, K., Schachtner, B., Dexl, J., Mittermeier, A., Stüber, A. T., Topalis, J., & Ingrisch, M. (2023). ChatGPT makes medicine smooth to swallow: An exploratory case have a look at on simplified radiology reviews. European Radiology, 1–9.
7. Mesatania, C. P. (2022). Factors influencing online buying behavior: A case of shopee customers. Management Science and Business Decisions, 2(1), 18–30.
8. Källström, J., & Heintz, F. (2019, December). Reinforcement mastering for laptop generated forces the use of open-source software program. In Interservice/Industry Training, Simulation, and Education Conference (pp. 1–11).
9. Lindholm, A., Wahlström, N., Lindsten, F., & Schön, T. B. (2022). Machine studying: A primary path for engineers and scientists. Cambridge University Press.

Chapter 2

Evolution of Generative AI

Ravali Gogula, Teja Swarup R, Paduru Rama Krishna Reddy, and Pokala Pranay Kumar

2.1 Introduction

"Artificial Intelligence (AI) is not a mystical phenomenon but rather a system based on rational reasoning." Mathematics and statistics are fundamental components of any AI algorithms and need a comprehensive understanding of approaches to effectively address various real-world situations. There are over 50 AI algorithms and heuristics. Although many AI approaches are based on models, the majority depend on data and need huge training datasets. The quality of the data and its attributes, such as dimensionality, distributions, and the 5-Vs of data, often have an impact on classification, identification, and prediction tasks.

For more than a decade, AI-based apps have been developed for numerous applications, including controversial ones. For example, picture morphing techniques like Face2Face and Face App can automatically alter a person's face by adding a grin, making them seem younger or older, or even changing their gender. Such apps may deliver "beautifying" benefits that include smoothing out wrinkles and, more controversially, whitening the skin.

AI-powered technologies are simplifying the process of creating authentic movies and imitating individuals, ensuring that the facial expressions of the imitated person align with those of the individual being monitored by a depth-sensing camera [1]. Additional AI techniques, such as Lyrebird, are used to mimic the voice of someone else and modify the perception of reality [2]. Furthermore, there has been a surge in the popularity of large language models (LLMs) since they possess the capability to

DOI: 10.4324/9781032711089-2

generate responses to queries that closely resemble human-like replies. Simultaneously, there are lingering concerns over the dissemination of false or misleading information via these models, as well as the extensive influence these models may have on the future learning and growth of students [3].

The capacity to accomplish these technological revolutions is enabled by breakthroughs in hardware and software, such as enhanced processing capabilities and exponential growth in storage capacities. Although AI-based tools provide significant benefits, there is a legitimate risk that many self-proclaimed AI industry experts may use these powerful technologies without fully comprehending their inner workings and limitations [4].

2.2 Reflections on Historical Events

Search and optimisation are essential components of any AI system. These algorithms use many similarity criteria, such as pattern matching, to aid in targeted search inside the representation or problem domain. To achieve the desired objective, many methodologies including guidance, selection schemes, fitness function, loss function, transfer function, and matching functions have been used. Most AI algorithms are probabilistic and need the transformation of discoveries into a decision or recommendation domain [5]. The efficiency of AI algorithms is largely dependent on optimising many control parameters, including both internal and external factors such as mapping functions, encoding techniques, distance measures, recognition thresholds, and meta-heuristics. For attaining algorithmic success via hybridisation in a specific application, it is necessary to combine AI methodologies with data pre-processing techniques like sampling and dimensionality reduction, as well as post-processing methods like output filtering and visual interpretation.

2.2.1 2023: GPT-4 Is Launched

OpenAI's GPT-4 is cutting-edge technology, generating replies that are both safer and more valuable. GPT-4 exhibits enhanced accuracy in tackling intricate issues due to its extensive breadth of general knowledge and advanced problem-solving capabilities. It outperforms GPT-3.5 in terms of its creativity, ability to process visual data, and capacity to handle longer context.

2.2.2 2023: The Launch of Falcon

Falcon LLM is a fundamental LLM consisting of 40 billion parameters that were trained using 1 trillion tokens. Falcon has the highest position on the hugging face open LLM leaderboard. The team prioritised the enhancement of data quality on a large scale [5]. The developers exercised meticulous attention in constructing a data pipeline to get superior online material by using thorough filtering and deduplication techniques.

2.2.3 2023 Marks the Debut of Bard

Google introduced Bard as a direct rival to ChatGPT. It is an AI chatbot developed by Google that engages in conversation with users. Bard engages in conversational interactions, using the PaLM foundation paradigm. It responds to follow-up queries, acknowledges errors, challenges faulty assumptions, and rejects improper requests.

2.2.4 2023: Music Gen Launch

Music Gen is an advanced auto-regressive Transformer model that can produce excellent music samples based on written descriptions or audio instructions [5]. The frozen text encoder model processes the text descriptions to generate a succession of hidden-state representations.

2.2.5 2023 Marks the Debut of Auto GPT

Auto-GPT is a trial open-source programme that demonstrates the functionalities of the GPT-4 language model. This programme uses GPT-4 to connect LLM "thoughts" in a sequential manner, enabling it to independently accomplish any desired objective. Auto-GPT, being among the first instances of GPT-4 operating in a completely self-governing manner, pushes the limits of AI capabilities.

2.2.6 2023 Marks the Launch of Long Net

The need to adjust the length of sequences has become crucial in the age of extensive language models. Nevertheless, current techniques encounter difficulties due to the computational cost or limited model expressivity, which imposes constraints on the maximum sequence length. LongNet, a variation of the Transformer model, has the ability to handle sequence lengths of over 1 billion tokens without compromising its performance on shorter sequences [6].

2.2.7 2023: The Launch of Voice Box

Meta AI has unveiled Voice box, a revolutionary advancement in generative AI specifically designed for voice. The researchers created Voice box, an advanced AI model that can carry out voice creation tasks, such as editing, sampling, and stylizing, using in-context learning, without the need for special training.

2.2.8 2023: The Launch of LLaMA

Meta AI has unveiled LLaMA, a compilation of foundational language models with parameter sizes ranging from 7 billion to 65 billion [5]. They demonstrated the feasibility of training cutting-edge models using just publically accessible datasets, without relying on private or unavailable datasets. LLaMA-13B exhibits superior performance compared to GPT-3 (175B) across the majority of benchmarks.

2.3 Principles of Generative Artificial Intelligence

The principles behind generative AI may be partly ascribed to evolutionary computing models. The significant progress in big data and the increased capabilities of technology, such as GPUs, have been the main drivers behind the significant impact of deep neural networks (DNNs) in this domain. DNN generative models have made substantial progress in complex domains like computer vision and natural language processing (NLP).

2.3.1 Generative Artificial Intelligence in Natural Language Processing

Generative models have significantly transformed the field of NLP and have attained the most advanced outcomes in many tasks. Previously, traditional techniques used linguistic knowledge-based approaches [2]. However, in recent years, statistical/probabilistic generative language models have been the dominant approach owing to the availability of large amounts of unlabelled text data. In the field of generative language modelling, DNNs are specifically trained to calculate the likelihood of the next word or phrase in a series of words in a text. This enables us to produce new text. Generative language models have achieved significant advancements in several areas of NLP. These include question answering, the ability to compose essays or tales based on given prompts, sentence completion, reading comprehension, natural language inference (which involves inferring links between phrases), and machine translation. Generative language models, such as BERT and Elmo, have made significant advancements in NLP. These algorithms have been successfully used in a range of tasks, including question interpretation and response. Likewise, the OpenAI research group has shown the capabilities of its widely discussed GPT algorithms, which have proven that generative language models can produce text that closely resembles human writing with little guidance. Simultaneously, we must exercise caution over the use of these models, since the same algorithms employed may be exploited for harmful purposes. For instance, they can be employed to create deceptively genuine fake news stories using just a little amount of information about the desired narrative [2]. Therefore, it seems that the regulation of the use of these models is an urgent need. Following this, we provide a concise summary of many influential DNN generative models, including variational autoencoders (VAEs), generative adversarial networks (GANs), and transformers.

2.3.2 Training Generative Models Before Their Main Training Phase

An essential component for the exceptional performance of GPT is the generative pre-trained transformer. More precisely, the transformer model undergoes pre-training using vast and varied collections of unlabelled text. As an example, the third iteration of the generative pre-trained transformer (referred to as GPT-3) is trained using data collected by systematically searching the internet, books, Wikipedia, and other sources. This enables the model to acquire knowledge about the overall structure of language.

The GPT-3 model is very large, with over 175 billion parameters. Hence, pre-training on extensive datasets enables the model to optimise its parameters based on overarching patterns seen in various scenarios. Following pre-training, the model may be further optimised for various tasks without requiring task-specific architectures. This can be achieved using guidance from a smaller number of labelled samples. Curiously, GPT-3 does not use the technique of fine-tuning. Specifically, it has been shown that fine-tuning has a detrimental effect on performance when attempting to apply the learned model to out-of-distribution test data [7]. The objective of GPT-3 is to possess task-agnostic capabilities and exhibit generalisation abilities in few-shot, one-shot, and zero-shot scenarios.

In the few-shot scenario, the model is presented with a limited number of demonstrations of a NLP job and thereafter tasked with solving a new instance. For instance, the model is presented with K examples of translating text from one language to another, and it is then required to translate a new piece of text. In the scenario where only one attempt is allowed, a task is described using plain language, accompanied by a solitary demonstration. This is also strongly linked to the process of human learning, which does not need a large number of instances for the same activity.

Zero-shot learning involves providing the model with simply a plain language description of the job, without showing any examples. Subsequently, the model is anticipated to successfully complete the job for a novel case.

Undoubtedly, this is the most challenging and almost comparable to the level of performance anticipated from people. Figure 2.1 is a schematic representation of GPT-3. Empirical evidence has shown that GPT-3, as well as subsequent iterations used in ChatGPT, have exhibited remarkable performance in all of these contexts. Consequently, this progress has brought

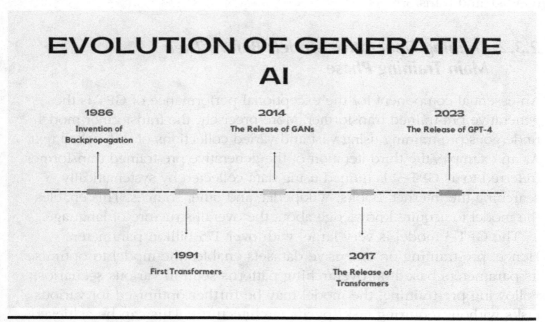

Figure 2.1   Evaluation of generative AI.

us closer to achieving general intelligence [7]. The remarkable ability of ChatGPT to produce replies that are almost indistinguishable from those given by humans has profound technical, social, and ethical consequences. Here, we provide a theoretical sequence of steps for generative AI applications.

2.4 A Pipeline for Generative Artificial Intelligence

2.4.1 Preprocessing

The inputs to a generative AI pipeline may be either homogenous, meaning they are of the same sort, or heterogeneous, meaning they are a blend of diverse kinds. Input types include several kinds of data, including numerical data, categorical data, text, speech, images, or multimodal data.

Data may be structured in a systematic manner, as in the form of tabular data. However, when it comes to generative AI models, it is more common for the data to lack organisation or structure. Research done by MIT's Sloan School indicates that around 80–90% of the world's data is classified as unstructured. Prior to loading unstructured data, pre-processing procedures may be necessary, depending on its characteristics. This job might be challenging, particularly for large models [7]. For language models such as GPT-3, the Common Crawl dataset used to train the model has an original size of 45 terabytes before pre-processing. After applying the filtering method, the data is then reduced to a size of 570 gigabytes. Big data solutions like Cloudera, Apache Spark, AWS, and Google Cloud are often used to manage the pre-processing of large-scale data, a process known as ETL (Extract, Transform, and Load).

2.4.2 Tokenization

Tokenization translates unstructured data to structured data. The choice of tokenization method depends on the characteristics of the data. Within the field of NLP, there exists a wide range of tools available for the purpose of tokenization, including Stanford's natural language toolkit (NLTK). More sophisticated tokenization includes converting between data formats. The process described in Speech2Text involves generating text tokens from voice signals. For multimodal applications that include text as well as other forms of input such as pictures or videos, it is necessary to align the text tokens with the corresponding characteristics in the image or video.

2.4.3 *Establishing Object Libraries*

Language models are crucial to AI pipelines that create text-based content and associate words with generated objects or components. The interpretation of these components is often not easily understandable in the context of DNN models. DNNs use a sub-symbolic distributed representation, in which information is spread among interconnected units within the network. Therefore, symbolic notions such as words are represented as vectors inside the DNN. Crucially, the embedding preserves semantic information, meaning that ideas that are closely related in the actual world are also closely related in the embedding space.

Pre-trained embeddings enable the transfer or reuse of DNNs in downstream tasks, even without access to the original datasets that produced these embeddings, which may be huge in size. Embeddings may be seen as a collection of items that can be used by various subsequent operations.

It is important to translate these embeddings into a format that can be easily understood by humans in order to employ them in subsequent activities.

One common approach in text-based models is to generate output tokens, such as words, by sampling from a probability distribution determined by the embedding. Nevertheless, in this particular period, it may be necessary to rely on external information in order to guarantee the significance of the generation. For instance, an educational question-answering system must include knowledge of fundamental principles governing the physical universe, including gravity, motion, and other related concepts. In order to create a computer code generation system, it is necessary to record the syntax and semantic knowledge of programming languages. Embedding commonplace information into DNN libraries is a difficult undertaking and an area of continuous investigation.

Although pre-training using extensive datasets might help mitigate some of these difficulties (provided that common knowledge can be derived as patterns from these datasets), it is nevertheless acknowledged as a notable constraint in generative AI.

2.4.4 *Subsequent Tasks*

Common uses of generative AI include question-answering, machine translation, reading comprehension, natural language inference, and language completion tasks like sentence completion and paragraph building.

Both BERT and GPT models are suitable for the bulk of these future tasks. In multimodal settings that integrate verbal and visual representations, additional goals include producing visuals from text using methods such as stable diffusion.

2.5 Emerging Patterns That Will Influence the Trajectory of Generative AI in the Future

- The capacity of generative AI to generate distinctive material via NLP will profoundly transform the procedure of creating text-based content, influencing many domains such as creative writing, entertainment, marketing, and customer support [8].
- As organisations accumulate vast quantities of data, there will be a growing need for domain-specific and self-hosted LLMs, resulting in the development of specialised generative AI models tailored to particular business requirements.
- The strategic allocation of corporate investments towards AI will prioritise customer experience, revenue growth, and productivity, ultimately resulting in the targeted adoption of generative AI.
- The mastery of "Prompt Engineering" will be crucial in maximising the effectiveness of generative AI solutions, perhaps emerging as a pivotal job function.
- Generative AI has the potential to revolutionise important industrial procedures [8]. For instance, it might facilitate the development of new drugs by generating unique chemical structures based on patterns identified in current medication compositions. Additionally, it can aid in reducing financial risks by identifying irregularities in transactional data.
- Rising apprehensions over ethical implications pertaining to intellectual property rights, information precision, and privacy will result in formulating policies to enhance oversight and regulation.

2.6 Potential Applications of AI Generative Models in Certain Industries

With the advancement of deep learning in AI, there will be a growth in specialised applications of generative AI tools tailored for various corporate businesses.

2.6.1 Health Care

Recurrent neural networks in generative AI may use extensive case histories and medical data to detect patterns, assisting in the prediction and diagnosis of diseases. This enables early, precise, and efficient therapy for patients.

Considerable efforts are already being allocated to AI-driven drug research applications, with generative models projected to spearhead more than 30% of novel drug development by 2025.

2.6.2 Marketing & Advertising

Presently, AI solutions for natural language processing are already enhancing marketing activities such as performing research, generating customer-facing content and outbound messages, and planning campaigns. Future advancements in AI will enhance deep learning language models' comprehension of human psychology, enabling them to provide emotionally captivating and relevant material for specific clients [9].

2.6.3 Design

Generative design enhances the design process in several fields by speeding up the creation of prototypes via the generation of patterns that minimise waste and by recommending materials that are lighter, less expensive, or more durable. Generative design AI will automate a substantial chunk of the design process in the automotive, industrial, and aerospace sectors.

Designers will need to feed material and product feature requirements into future generative AI tools. These tools will then produce more sophisticated design outputs and engineering specifications.

2.6.4 Financial Management

Recurrent neural networks, when applied to financial data analysis, are highly suitable for transforming into personalised wealth managers. These models gather fragmented financial information and portfolios from customers, merging them into a unified customer profile with a customised financial goal. By streamlining and integrating areas such as taxes, financial institutions will have the ability to provide value-added services to their consumers.

A sophisticated deep learning architecture specialised in anomaly detection will enhance fraud detection efforts, while the development of synthetic data will provide generative models with abundant training data to construct resilient fraud models.

2.6.5 Software Development

In the future, AI will enhance programming by using machine learning methods in generative models to automate laborious activities like code creation, translation, optimisation, and debugging.

Generative AI will assist in updating old code in the near future, while AI is projected to produce around 15% of new apps by 2027.

2.6.6 Media & Entertainment

GANs in generative AI models have the ability to produce highly realistic visuals. Additionally, NLP may assist in content production. Consequently, AI is expected to play a crucial role in the entertainment business.

The integration of AI-generated songwriting and unique compositions will enhance the creative process for artists. Additionally, AI voice synthesis and speech recognition will enable automatic real-time dubbing, translations, and voiceovers.

Dall-E, an AI tool, utilises a fusion of transformer neural network and generative adversarial network to produce extremely innovative AI art by generating pictures. According to some calculations, the bulk of the material in popular films will be created by AI by the end of this decade.

2.6.7 Virtual Reality/Augmented Reality and Gaming

The use of generative AI will enhance the pace of creating immersive 3D settings in video games and virtual reality areas such as the Metaverse. These AI systems will have the capability to create detailed pictures of 3D environments and realistic moving virtual actors using computer vision. Additionally, they will enable real-time interactions with non-player characters that can adapt and respond without being limited by pre-written scripts.

2.6.8 Retail

It refers to the sale of goods or services to consumers, typically through physical stores or online platforms. The retail industry may derive several advantages from incorporating generative AI into its operational processes. AI models will enable interactive customer service, enhance personalised products, and optimise demand planning, forecasting, and inventory management.

2.6.9 *Advantages of Generative AI for Businesses*

The use of generative AI, which is taught on company data, will revolutionise the internal access and utilisation of information inside enterprises. Extracting and structuring data to produce replies based on prompts would significantly improve decision-making and empower the workforce across various business areas.

2.7 Generative AI Benefits for Enterprises

Integrating conversational AI with domain-specific LLMs that have been optimised to handle unstructured data will result in the development of very effective retrieval systems. Within a span of two years, almost 30% of organisations are expected to adopt an AI-augmented strategy. This approach aims to eliminate information biases, enhance data privacy, and simulate future business situations.

- **Customer Experience**
  The use of generative AI is expected to grow in order to improve the customer experience, provide customised suggestions, and create interactive engagements with consumers, particularly via the combination of sentiment analysis and natural language AI chatbots.
- **Brand Marketing and Content**
  Strategic promotion and creation of compelling material to enhance brand visibility and engagement.

  In addition to managing consumer data, a machine learning algorithm specifically designed for marketing may assist organisations in performing more effective marketing research and providing valuable insights that can influence overall marketing plans.

  Tools like Dall-E and Jasper will have a significant influence on brand creation and content planning [10]. They will provide AI-generated material, either in the form of text or images, that aligns with brand rules and can be personalised.

  In the near future, NLP has the potential to generate the first versions of many types of content, such as blogs, social media posts, reports, and emails. This would allow content writers and marketers to allocate more time towards developing strategies.

■ **Productivity**

The integration of generative AI into workflows has significantly reduced the time required for tasks and automated repetitive jobs, enabling humans to concentrate on their primary activities. In the next five years, more than 100 million workers will use AI to enhance their productivity.

■ **Human Resources**

While generative AI transforms workers' expertise in information management, employees will collaborate with AI to carry out their responsibilities [10]. The automation of talent acquisition will be facilitated by AI, which will assist in finding the most suitable personnel to fill roles. Additionally, AI-powered models will provide immediate performance evaluations of workers based on historical data and current key performance indicators (KPIs).

■ **Compliance**

Enterprises may use generative AI to ensure compliance with rules pertaining to risk reduction and sustainability. Computer vision, a kind of deep learning, utilises visual analysis to identify fraudulent activities and patterns.

2.8 Challenges and Regulations Around Generative Artificial Intelligence

Like all emerging technologies, generative AI presents issues and obstacles, particularly with security and ethical implementation.

2.8.1 Concerns

■ Generative AI lacks the need of obtaining agreement from authors of input works, resulting in the production of new data that often bears resemblance to original copyrighted works.

■ Identity misappropriation, whether it occurs to persons or brands, may result in fraudulent activities or the dissemination of misleading information, which can be detrimental to the affected parties.

■ The absence of legal frameworks for intellectual property raises doubts and ambiguity over ownership rights.

- The general data protection regulation (GDPR) does not provide protection for AI systems that are trained using public data. Consequently, any sensitive data from businesses that are inputted into tools such as ChatGPT may be at danger of becoming publicly accessible information.
- Since the tools lack references or credits to the original work, it is not possible to verify or get approval from the sources.
- Deepfakes, which are very authentic media produced by AI, provide a challenge in distinguishing between AI-generated content and genuine material.
- LLMs, when trained on input data, will reproduce any biases or discriminatory patterns present in the data in the resulting output.
- "Hallucination" is a significant issue in generative AI, when the system produces false or invented data that it claims to be true due to a lack of relevant knowledge [11].

2.8.2 Regulation Mechanisms

- To mitigate cybersecurity fraud, it is essential for cyber insurance providers to provide comprehensive coverage within their plans.
- By confining sensitive data to the internal systems of the organisation, self-hosted LLMs will effectively address privacy issues.
- Implementing watermarking on AI-produced artefacts is a method to regulate the proliferation of fraudulent or counterfeit visuals, however, more stringent measures will be necessary.
- Consistently testing models through the process of verifying exact outcomes and rejecting mistakes will enhance the model's ability to provide precise results.
- Frameworks for ensuring ethical use of generative models and enhancing accountability must be established [12].

2.9 Conclusion

Although generative AI has a very brief history, its influence on the future is extensive. The emergence of generative AI has led to significant transformations in companies and creative expression. However, the absence of sufficient governance and regulatory frameworks poses a hazard to both organisations and people, making them vulnerable to fraud, disinformation, identity theft, and theft of AI-generated property.

Gaining insight into the potential value enhancement that generative AI offers to businesses will enable organisations and individuals to effectively respond to issues and explore its many advantages, some of which are yet unknown.

References

1. Whittaker M, Crawford K, Dobbe R, Fried G, Kaziunas E, Mathur V, Schwartz O. The contested terrain of generative AI. Proceedings of the ACM on Human-Computer Interaction. 2023;7(CSCW1):1–35.
2. Smith AM. The generative AI revolution: How companies can prepare. MIT Sloan Management Review. 2023;64(3):1–8.
3. Daugherty PR, Wilson HJ. Generative AI: Toward participatory human-machine co-creation. MIT Sloan Management Review. 2022;63(4):20–28.
4. Fleming N. How generative AI will transform marketing. Harvard Business Review. 2023;101(1):40–51.
5. Johnson M, Gupta A. Generative AI and the future of work. McKinsey Quarterly. 2022;4(4):84–95.
6. Laxmi S, Rudra NS, Hemachandran K, Santosh KN. Machine learning techniques in IoT applications: A state of the art. InIoT Applications, Security Threats, and Countermeasures. 2021: 105–117.
7. Hemachandran K, Alasiry A, Marzougui M, Ganie SM, Pise AA, Alouane MTH, Chola C. Performance analysis of deep learning algorithms in diagnosis of malaria disease. Diagnostics. 2023;13(3):534.
8. Peysakhovich V, Lavin J, Lanphier C. Responsible development of generative AI models. Nature Machine Intelligence. 2022;4(12):991–998.
9. Buchanan BG. Artificial intelligence in marketing and communications. Journal of Marketing Research. 2022;59(5):963–980.
10. Ng A. The societal implications of generative AI systems. Communications of the ACM. 2023;66(3):31–35.
11. Chen Y, Cai Y. The rise of generative AI: Opportunities and challenges for business innovation. California Management Review. 2023;65(2):54–73.
12. Floridi L, Cowls J. Generative AI: A threat model and governance framework. AI & Society. 2023;38(1):53–68.

Chapter 3

Generative AI and Consumer Behavior

Khant Mayank Rameshbhai and Parth Prakash

3.1 Introduction

In the current global market, AI was brought into being quite some time ago; however, generative AI can be considered as a new branch of AI. Consider a virtual bookstore in which all shelves speak only to you, providing recommendations. Visualize news feeds presenting pieces reflecting your deepest desires, based on the transformation of thought. This is the core example of personalized content production, which can be characterized as a connection between the knowledge of consumer behavior and AI generative magic. In the traditional world, content makers aim for a broad appeal with themes that would be liked by all and most. However, the modern-day consumer is smarter today and they crave deeper connections with their true selves. The creation of personalized content meets this demand, making the universal form into an individually tailored pattern based on individual preferences and behavior. Among the various traditional market research instruments are surveys, focus groups, and data. Here comes generative AI, a revolutionary solution that processes extraordinary levels of data in milliseconds, ranging from social media banter to order history. However, it goes into digital traces we leave behind to expose elaborate patterns and revelations invisible on the face of things.

Common method of market research involves the use of surveys, focus groups, and data analysis – all pretty effective but slow and unwieldy tools that are very prone to human bias. Then comes generative AI, which

DOI: 10.4324/9781032711089-3

processes data at light speed and derives patterns from large datasets as social media "chatter" and previous purchases. It goes into the dark side of our digital footprint to find the hidden relationships that evade bare-eye interpretation. However, it is about much more than numeric calculus – its primary aim is to search for narrative using numbers. Social media applications allow AI to evaluate the sentiment and read consumer passions, dreams, frustrations, and changing values. As it is capable of creating life-like exercises that mirror the way consumers will act through their natural behavioral patterns, firms have an opportunity to test new products and marketing concepts within a digital sandbox before venturing into reality otherwise referred as the real world.

Today, businesses use historical data and gut feelings to predict consumption patterns. They tossed a coin, crossed their fingers, and hoped for the best. However, in the present data-driven era, predictive analysis is a more precise methodology. Consider colossal databases filled with purchase histories, Facebook chats, and website clicks flooding complex algorithms. Machine learning and statistical algorithms analyze data like digital sleuths finding the underlying patterns that predict future behaviors, with eerie accuracy.

The ability to foresee further behavior can open a rich mine of benefits. The targeted provision of highly relevant services, because companies can tailor their products and approaches to particular consumer segments. Think about personalized customer discounts for loyal customers, recommendations based on previous purchases, or individual messages that speak to each person.

Generative AI can accumulate big data sets of personal information which includes purchase histories as well as social media footprints. This brings into question the collection, storage, and usage of this data. However, the risk of data breaches and unauthorized access is high which may lead to exposure of sensitive details or decline in customers' trust. Consider, a private content creation engine accidentally revealing your medical history as a result of a data breach that jeopardizes health and privacy.

3.2 Literature Review

The use of generative AI in the fashion sector can revolutionize many aspects of business including design, marketing, and customer interaction. With the close of fashion weeks worldwide, brands are researching ways in which generative AI as represented by ChatGPT and GPT-3.5 technologies can increase creativity levels and efficiency respectively. McKinsey expects a conservative enhancement of $150 billion to $275 billion in the operating profit [1] for apparel, fashion, and luxury sectors over the next three-to-five years due to generative AI. These early use cases include co-designing, speeding up content production, and hyper-personalizing customer engagements. Generative AI traverses the entire fashion value chain, from turning sketches into 3D designs to honing store configurations. Key applications appear in the realm of product innovation, marketing, sales, and consumer experience. While these promises are enticing, it is necessary to proceed with caution since legal uncertainties persist; AI can have biases that need addressing and a workforce needs upskilling. Fashion leaders, therefore, are advised from a strategic vantage point to evaluate the value and address risk for their teams through generative AI partnerships on this transformational path [1].

Some researchers are focused on generative AI for marketing at a macro level. For example, new studies documented that generative AI, including LLM, can attain productivity in writing works and search engine advertising such shifts how businesses relate with business concerns in a commercially acceptable way for customer service results. Research shows some marketing processes generate the changes of generative AI.

Personalization in marketing communication is one of the closely related research lines. Tucker (2014) indicates that personalized advertisements are much more effective than nonpersonal ones. It means that the personalization is resulting in marketing effectiveness. But privacy concerns, particular and general AI-led personalized video ads rejection can be viewed as consumers' strategies towards AI driven personalized video advertisements. Therefore, it is hypothetically questionable whether the generative AI-introduced personalized video ads work.

Thus, despite the fact that the literature in terms of what could possibly make generative AI-produced personalized video ads work effectively for some contexts of marketing communication is by no means abundant yet current findings reveal rather positive outcomes with such an approach. However, privacy concerns or disagreement with the algorithm may lead to a different reaction of consumers toward AI-based personalized video advertisement [2].

3.3 Methods

Generative AI has been the latest disruption in an ever-changing environment of consumer behavior. The term refers to a series of technological innovations that have dramatically transformed our lives and how we interact with each other, including content creation, market research and insights, chatbots, virtual assistants, predictive analytics, and automatic production systems for product delivery. This abstract focuses on the paradigm shift that generative AI has brought to these aspects, highlighting the interplay between revolutionary technological changes and human psychology.

3.3.1 Current Stand of Generative AI and Consumer Behavior

Generative AI has made great progress, and the impact of its influence on consumer behavior cannot be denied. The generative models, especially the deep learning ones, have done remarkably well in producing meaningful text as well as images and videos. There have been advancements in multiple areas of use including content creation, design, and customization. In the realm of consumer behavior, generative AI has affected consumers by how they engage with new digital content and goods. Customers' preferences and decisions on purchase have been swayed by the spreading of generative algorithms that facilitate personalized recommendations. Besides, the application of generative AI to virtual assistants and chatbots has made possible user interactions that are more conversational having a better fit with context. However, ethical concerns as well as matters related to personal information protection along with issues concerning inappropriate usage of generated material play a significant role in the development and proliferation of industries focused on consumers. The scenery might have changed even more, and you should refer to recent sources in order to acquire the most updated data [3].

3.3.2 Ethical Considerations While Using Generative AI for Consumer Behavior

Fairness and nondiscrimination should also be a matter of commitment. Practicing bias mitigation is important to make AI accessible for all segments of the population. This demands the right teams that proactively detect and respond to potential biases, enabling reasonable development and application. Consider various AI developers integrating different datasets and feedback loops to prevent their algorithms from continuing societal prejudices. We should never forget that human monitoring and control are constantly indispensable. The power of AI should never be unaccounted for. The role of humans must be to define ethical standards, create a set of responsible guidelines, and control how AI is developed and used in an approach that reflects our values. Imagine an ethics committee reviewing AI-generated content creation to ensure that it fosters inclusivity and rejects the typecast.

The intersection of generative AI and consumer behavior is a fascinating ethical terrain. However, we need to handle it with care, avoiding personalization without losing the foundation of fairness, privacy, and human control. With transparency, bias reduction, and human oversight the benefits of AI can be realized without endangering its potential to do good in this world – creating a future where technology works for us instead. So, in the right hands of creators and users, generative AI can become a beneficial tool for improving our lives and creating an even better world to live in [4].

3.3.3 The Challenges in the Implication of Generative AI and Consumer Behavior

If generative AI presents a panoply of challenges in understanding and manipulating consumer behavior. A key issue here is the ethical component; people are concerned about how AI can be used to violate privacy, seek consent, and even control people. The generation of personalized content by generative AI highlights the possibility that advertisers may use it to develop targeted advertising and manipulative messaging aimed at influencing consumer choices. Also, maintaining transparency and accountability within the algorithms that drive generative AI systems presents a problem because of how intricate these models are in the sense that consumers become unable to understand decision bases. In addition, the development of AI technology is developing at a breakneck speed and may overtake regulatory frameworks, requiring continuous efforts to adjust and establish safeguards. With organizations continuing to use generative AI to predict and shape consumer preferences, balancing innovation with ethical application becomes a key component in ensuring public trust that works against unintended consequences arising from those changes [5].

3.4 Research and Development Models

3.4.1 Personalized Content Creation

Personalized content creation is not only about satisfying an individual's whims. It looks deeper into the psychological causes that drive consumer behavior. The tendency to seek confirmational information, susceptibility, and hunger for novelty within the familiar are analyzed by AI models. They use these insights to create content that feels like a chat with someone we trust, gently pushing us toward new explorations while assuring our familiar surroundings. But this brave new world has its own challenges. However, there are many ethical concerns that must be addressed because AI algorithms tend to reinforce biases as a result of their data learning. The two key aspects are transparency and user control, meaning that users have to know how their data is applied while being able to influence a higher personalized experience. In addition, the human touch is incomparable. AI could come up with a perfect recipe, but an experienced chef knows the finesse and excitement of departure from it.

AI algorithms operate like a genius detective identifying patterns, predicting future trends, and profiling consumer groups with incredible accuracy. What they can find is not that specific factors influencing purchasing decisions are as subtle emotional triggers, subconscious social cues, and so on. Assume that not only would you be able to know what consumers purchase but also why they buy it, which makes them desire for something and leaves cold. But this effective tool must be used carefully. Although there are various ethical considerations, the AI algorithms can perpetuate biases toward discrimination. The consumers should be able to know the method used in using his or her data and also have control over opting out of personalized experiences [6].

3.4.2 *Market Research and Insights*

In the past, providing customer service meant navigating through never ending phone menu's, putting up with hold music which was robotic and hoping to talk to a human being that understood your problem. Both chatbots and virtual assistants overturn this setup, providing round the clock assistance with a digital smile. Employing linguistic processing powered by AI, they can answer your queries, address your problems, and even suggest products via an interface as natural as a text message. Without the power of generative AI, this level of personalization wouldn't be possible. Machine learning algorithms utilize the data generated from your past chats and purchase history to formulate a clear perspective of your interests, traits, as well as emotions that initiate triggers. With this information, chatbots can personalize their responses with the appropriate tone of voice and notes to encourage a connection [7].

3.4.3 Content Creation and Marketing

Content creators have long slaved writing messages delivered to the general public, hoping that at least a few will click with them all. Marketing campaigns were scattergun blasts, covering the area in anticipation of scoring a bulls-eye. So, here is generative AI – a revolutionary tool that makes sense of an ocean of data – purchase histories or social media clicks to learn the hidden desires in each person. It involves them with the trail of digital data that are left by us, deciphering their difficult definition and what drives us deep into our minds. Armed with this information, generative AI can create content that seems like a personal discussion. Having personalized blog posts replicating the depth of your hidden questionings, product descriptions exposing unspoken necessities and advertisements revealing solutions to unsolved issues. AI can create images that represent your style, compile eclectic soundtracks that embody the journey of emotions you inhabit within, and write stories based on what only would popularize your suppressed dreams. But, along with this brave new world, there come great obstacles. With these in mind, ethical issues are everywhere as AI algorithms could reinforce biases instilled within the data they learn from. Transparency and more user friendly are crucial to consumers and how their resources are being used, and they are more entitled to choices about how and what personalized experiences they want. Additionally, the human factor is untouchable. AI may create the ideal recipe, but a professional chef knows all about taste subtlety and the thrill of inventiveness [8].

3.4.4 Chatbots and Virtual Assistants

Regular shopping entailed negotiating the poorly organized aisles, reading illegible product labels, and pleading for moments with an employee. This process is completely reversed by virtual shop assistants who can offer a 5-star service at any time of the day or night with an electronic smile. Powered by advanced language processing and image recognition, they can provide answers to your questions and recommendations based on products you like or even virtual fitting rooms without losing their human touch as SMS conversations. However, virtual shopping assistants are much more than just smart salesmen. They become smart companions, evolving with you and changing their reactions if necessary. For example, consider a personal assistant who knows your size and details and recommends similar products based on previous purchases or current fashion, even one's own body type.

Now consider a stylist who studies the closet and comes up with suitable ensembles not just for official events, but seemingly in accordance with your impressions or mood. Still, as with any highly developed technology, there are numerous issues. From an ethical perspective, virtual assistants that have been trained using biased data can disseminate discriminatory activities. It is vital since consumers are aware, of what services utilize their data and can revert from personalized negotiations if desirable. Furthermore, there is no alternative for the human element. Although virtual assistants can perform relatively simple tasks and provide general information, they mostly fail in terms of empathy, wit, or nuanced emotional cues. Human knowledge and AI sustainability are the future, where virtual assistants only serve as helpers or pals who never replace humans [3].

3.4.5 Ethical Considerations

One of the significant ethical landmines is manipulation and exploitation. The power of AI to learn human intentions is so great that it can be used forcefully against people, thus ensuring a profitable business. Personalized ads and recommendations seem to address our needs exactly, yet they might abuse our weaknesses by prompting us into quick purchases or another subscription we don't really need. Consider an AI-driven intelligent shopping assistant pulingly modifying your wish list due to recent financial hardships, driving you into unwary debt. Yet, this ethical labyrinth is not an excuse to lose hope. They can and should be accepted as principles that ensure AI functions for human beings rather than serving itself. Transparency and user control are essential. At the same time, consumers should know how their data is utilized and be able to reject personalized services. The logic behind algorithm decisions should be understandable and auditable, enabling us to audit the algorithms. Imagine a virtual shopping assistant that explicitly specifies the data it uses to generate recommendations and allows users to either anonymize or restrict its access [9].

3.5 Discussions

This individualized attention results in significant benefits. Statistics show that content addressed to consumers is 80% likely for them to interact with it, leading to increased clicks, conversions, and brand preference. Multi-perspective suggestions may allow us to escape the echo chamber, broaden our horizons, and get acquainted with positions other than ours. It is a great tool for creators, helping them gain access to many small niches where they can share their passions with those who really care [10].

Secondly, the human factor remains incomparable. AI might identify a trend, but only human insight and imagination can transform that recognition into effective products or campaigns. AI teams up with human expertise to create the market research field of tomorrow, where data insights are combined with creative and strategic thinking to drive innovation and success. However, just like with any strong technology, the issues surface. On the one hand, ethical concerns emerge as chatbots programmed on biased data have a tendency to carry over discriminatory behaviors. Providing transparency and user control is the focus, assuring that consumers are aware of how their data would be utilized and can opt-out of customized interplays [11].

But with great power comes even greater responsibility. As biased data is likely to cause discrimination, considerations of ethics take the front seat. Despite this, transparency and user control are essential since consumers need to understand what happens with their data if they want a chance of not receiving personalized experiences, as well as all the human element remains irreplaceable. A trend may be predicted by AI, but only human intuition and imagination can transform such insight into a successful product or campaign. The actual magic is in the balance between AI and human knowledge, where intuition informs data-driven insights for creative decisions, generating redefined outcomes from analysis.

This is the major impact brought about by this AI-powered content and marketing. It is reported that consumers are 80% more likely to interact with content, which goes beyond the personalization barrier and seems made especially for them; delivering greater click-through rates, conversions as well as brand loyalty. All echo chambers are broken with the help of individual recommendations, which allow us to see other's views and mindsets. For creators, it provides opportunities to reach out to a selective audience who love their work.

Finally, virtual shopping assistants provide us with a taste of how the next stage could be where technology is embedded in our retail environment and helps meet our needs at every turn through personalization. Through careful use of generative AI, these digital companions will be more than just tools; they will be trusted guides, stylists, and even friends who lead future shopping journeys as a joyful dance to savor the discovery but satiate hunger.

In the end, we should not forget about human control in processes and decision-making. However good AI can be, it should never work in isolation. As a result, humans have to define the ethical framework, provide responsible standards, and check in with AI development's rollout process so that it remains consistent with our principles. Consider an ethics committee scrutinizing AI-driven content creation with the aim of promoting inclusion while eliminating unwarranted stereotypes.

3.6 Conclusion

To sum up, the fast development of generative AI in consumer behavior has established a revolutionary time in personalized content production; advanced market research and insights; chatbots, interactive virtual assistants etc. This abstract has discussed the drastic changes, owing to generative AI in these dimensions showing that technology is interdependent with human nature.

Personalized content creation perfectly reflects this aspect of generative AI, as customized stories, music playlists, and pictures are not produced according to any conventional one-size-fits-all scheme. Market research and insights will adopt a new paradigm as generative AI quickly programs comprehensive databases to forecast trends, partition populations, and reveal the human narrative behind figures. Customer interactions are redefined by chatbots and virtual assistants, which provide personalized support transforming into complicated companions that keep satisfaction, creation of loyalty to the brand, and increase conversion rates.

Predictive analytics works as a digital magic ball, gearing consumer behavior understanding to the point where business enterprises can design strategies using unnervingly accurate forecasts. On the other hand, ethical aspects emphasize that its use should be responsible, transparent, and have human supervision to avoid discriminatory practices. Content production and promotion are then a combination of art with science, as the personalized messages appeal to consumers in an emotional way.

Integrating virtual shopping assistants makes a smooth transition between digital and physical platforms, providing personalized advice and suggestions. Although improving customer satisfaction, issues related to bias and transparency as well as the human hand's necessity remain in focus which highlights ethical AI implementation significance.

This last part considers ethical issues related to generative AI and consumer behavior, including bias, manipulation, and privacy. Transparency, user control, fairness, and human oversight are stressed because responsible AI due to humanity, is deployed ethically.

In other words, the combination of generative AI and consumer behavior creates a world full of opportunities along with challenges. Navigating this terrain is a careful balancing act between the advantages of personalized experiences and principles such as fairness, privacy, and human mastery. By promoting transparency, eliminating bias, and emphasizing human control, we can harness the power of generative AI, which improves our lives by driving us forward into a future in which technologies enhance without degrading fundamental values. Such responsible creation and consumption of generative AI can help us build a future where innovation exists alongside ethics, creating an even brighter world that is more inclusive for everyone.

References

1. Sohn, K., Sung, C. E., Koo, G., & Kwon, O. (2020). Artificial intelligence in the fashion industry: Consumer responses to generative adversarial network (GAN) technology. International Journal of Retail & Distribution Management, 49(1), 61–80.
2. Kumar, M., & Kapoor, A. (2023). Generative AI and Personalized Video Advertisements. Available at SSRN 4614118.
3. Rane, N. (2023). Role and challenges of ChatGPT and similar generative artificial intelligence in business management. Available at SSRN 4603227.
4. Gao, B., Wang, Y., Xie, H., Hu, Y., & Hu, Y. (2023). Artificial intelligence in advertising: Advancements, challenges, and ethical considerations in targeting, personalization, content creation, and ad optimization. SAGE Open, 13(4), 1–20.
5. Rane, N. (2023). ChatGPT and similar generative artificial intelligence (AI) for smart industry: Role, challenges and opportunities for industry 4.0, industry 5.0 and society 5.0. Challenges and Opportunities for Industry, 4, 1–12.
6. Ooi, K. B., Tan, G. W. H., Al-Emran, M., Al-Sharafi, M. A., Capatina, A., Chakraborty, A., & Wong, L. W. (2023). The potential of generative artificial intelligence across disciplines: Perspectives and future directions. Journal of Computer Information Systems, 1–32.
7. Jain, V., Wadhwani, K., & Eastman, J. K.. (2023). Artificial intelligence consumer behavior: A hybrid review and research agenda. Journal of Consumer Behavior, 1–22.
8. Yoo, S. C., & Piscarac, D. (2023). Generative AI and its implications for modern marketing: Analyzing potential challenges and opportunities. The International Journal of Advanced Smart Convergence, 12(3), 175–185.

9. Hussain, K., Khan, M. L., & Malik, A. (2024). Exploring audience engagement with ChatGPT-related content on YouTube: Implications for content creators and AI tool developers. Digital Business, 4(1), 1–14.

10. Hartmann, J., Exner, Y., & Domdey, S. (2023). The power of generative marketing: Can generative AI reach human-level visual marketing content?. Available at SSRN.

11. Eickhoff, F., & Zhevak, L. (2023). The consumer attitude towards AI in marketing: An experimental study of consumers attitudes and purchase intention.

Chapter 4

AI and Social Impact: A Business Perspective

Rishabh Jaiswal, Rahul Kumar Gupta, and
Chinna Swamy Dudekula

4.1 Introduction

4.1.1 AI and Social Impact: A Business Perspective

The inexorable rise of artificial intelligence (AI) in recent years has ignited a global discourse about its implications, encompassing not only economic and technological advancements but also its profound impact on the very fabric of society. While the potential benefits of AI for business are widely acknowledged and eagerly pursued, the ethical considerations and social consequences of its implementation pose significant challenges that demand careful attention and responsible action.

For management and IT students poised to enter the ever-evolving professional landscape, understanding AI's social impact is not merely an academic exercise; it is a critical imperative. Equipping yourselves with the necessary knowledge and foresight to navigate the complex ethical dilemmas and potential social consequences arising from AI adoption within organizations is essential. This awareness empowers you to become informed and responsible decision-makers, capable of leveraging AI's remarkable capabilities for both business success and positive societal contributions.

DOI: 10.4324/9781032711089-4

4.1.2 The Transformative Power of AI for Social Good

AI's potential to address some of the most pressing global challenges, from poverty and healthcare to environmental sustainability, is undeniably transformative. Imagine intelligent systems that can analyze vast datasets to predict and prevent natural disasters, personalize education for children in underserved communities, or develop innovative solutions for clean energy and climate change mitigation. These are just a glimpse of the possibilities that AI holds for social good, promising to alleviate human suffering and improve the lives of millions worldwide.

4.1.3 The Ethical Considerations of AI Implementation

However, the potential benefits of AI are not without their accompanying risks. Concerns regarding biases embedded within algorithms, the potential for algorithmic discrimination, and the opaque nature of decision-making processes raise ethical concerns that demand careful consideration. Businesses implementing AI solutions must actively address these issues by ensuring transparency and accountability, employing diverse datasets to train algorithms, and developing robust frameworks for ethical AI development and deployment.

4.1.4 The Impact of AI on the Workforce

As AI automates routine tasks and disrupts traditional industries, anxieties regarding job displacement and the future of work naturally arise. While some jobs may be lost, it is important to recognize the potential for AI to create new opportunities and augment human capabilities across various sectors. The key lies in preparing the workforce for a future where human and machine collaboration is paramount. Reskilling and upskilling initiatives become crucial, equipping individuals with the skills and knowledge necessary to thrive in the changing landscape.

4.1.5 The Role of Businesses in Fostering Positive Social Impact

Businesses are uniquely positioned to leverage AI's capabilities for positive social impact. By integrating social responsibility into their AI strategies and actively seeking opportunities to address societal challenges, businesses can contribute to a more equitable and sustainable future. This may involve partnering with NGOs to develop AI-powered solutions for healthcare or education, prioritizing responsible data collection and usage practices, or promoting diversity and inclusion within AI teams to ensure fairer outcomes.

4.1.6 Shaping the Future with Responsible AI Leadership

As future leaders in management and technology, the onus is upon you to harness the transformative potential of AI while mitigating its potential risks. By critically examining the social impact of AI, you can contribute to the development and deployment of responsible AI solutions. This necessitates a proactive approach that involves continuously learning, engaging in open dialogue with diverse stakeholders, and actively advocating for ethical AI practices within your organizations and beyond.

4.1.7 A Call to Action

The journey toward a future where AI serves as a force for positive social change requires collective effort and unwavering commitment. By embracing AI with a critical and responsible lens, prioritizing ethical considerations, and actively seeking opportunities to leverage its power for social good, we can harness its transformative potential to create a more just and sustainable world for generations to come. Let us embark on this journey together, united by a common vision and a shared responsibility to shape a future where technology serves humanity and unlocks its full potential for positive social impact.

This chapter has merely scratched the surface of the complex and multifaceted relationship between AI and social impact. As you delve deeper into this domain, remember to:

■ Remain inquisitive and constantly update your knowledge about the evolving landscape of AI and its social implications.
■ Engage in critical thinking and dialogue, challenging assumptions and actively seeking diverse perspectives on the ethical considerations of AI.
■ Develop your skills in identifying and evaluating AI solutions that address social challenges and contribute to a more equitable and sustainable future.

■ As future leaders, take responsibility for shaping the development and deployment of AI in a way that maximizes its positive impact on society.

By embracing these principles, you can become a powerful force for positive change, ensuring that AI serves as a tool for progress and empowers us to build a better future for all.

4.2 Positive Social Impacts of AI

4.2.1 Healthcare

■ Improved Diagnosis and Treatment Planning: AI-powered diagnostic tools leverage advanced algorithms and machine learning to analyze medical data swiftly and accurately. This not only expedites the diagnostic process but also enhances the precision of identifying diseases at early stages. Early detection often leads to more effective treatment plans and improved prognosis for patients.

■ Personalized Medicine: AI enables the development of personalized treatment plans by analyzing vast datasets, including genetic information, patient history, and lifestyle factors. This approach tailors medical interventions to individual characteristics, optimizing the effectiveness of treatments and minimizing adverse effects.

■ Drug Discovery and Development: AI algorithms expedite drug discovery by analyzing large datasets to identify potential drug candidates and predict their efficacy. This accelerates the research and development process, potentially bringing life-saving medications to market more quickly.

■ Enhanced Resource Allocation: AI-driven analytics assist healthcare providers in optimizing resource allocation, predicting patient admission rates, and managing inventory. This efficiency contributes to cost reduction and ensures that resources are allocated where they are most needed.

The integration of AI in healthcare is a testament to its positive social impact, fostering a change in basic assumptions towards more efficient, personalized, and accessible medical care.

4.2.2 Educations

AI is making significant contributions to the field of education, ushering in a new era of personalized and accessible learning experiences.

- Personalized Learning Systems: AI-driven personalized learning systems analyze individual student performance, preferences, and learning styles. These systems adapt and tailor educational content in real-time, providing customized lessons and exercises to meet the specific needs of each student. This fosters a more engaging and effective learning environment.
- Accessibility and Inclusivity: AI technologies contribute to the creation of inclusive learning environments by addressing diverse learning needs. For example, AI-powered tools can assist students with disabilities by providing tailored support, such as text-to-speech functions, adaptive interfaces, and customized learning materials, thereby breaking down traditional barriers to education.
- Efficient Resource Allocation: AI assists educators and institutions in optimizing resource allocation. By analyzing data on student performance and engagement, AI systems can help identify areas that require additional resources or intervention. This data-driven approach enhances the efficiency of educational systems, ensuring that resources are directed where they are most needed.
- Adaptive Learning Paths: AI enables adaptive learning paths that cater to the pace at which individual students grasp concepts. By continuously assessing a student's performance and understanding, AI systems can dynamically adjust the difficulty and progression of lessons. This ensures that students are neither overwhelmed nor bored, promoting a more effective learning experience.
- Global Access to Quality Education: AI facilitates remote and online learning, breaking down geographical barriers and providing access to quality education for individuals in remote or underserved areas. Virtual classrooms, AI-driven educational platforms, and digital resources enhance educational opportunities for students worldwide, contributing to a more equitable distribution of knowledge.
- Teacher Support and Professional Development: AI assists educators by automating administrative tasks, allowing teachers to focus more on personalized instruction and mentorship. AI tools can also analyze teaching methods, provide feedback, and offer tailored

resources for professional development, thereby enhancing the overall quality of teaching.

The integration of AI in education holds promise for creating a more inclusive, personalized, and effective learning experience for students, contributing positively to societal development.

4.2.3 Environment

AI is emerging as a valuable tool in addressing environmental challenges, offering innovative solutions for monitoring, conservation, and sustainable resource management.

■ Environmental Monitoring and Protection: AI technologies, such as satellite imagery analysis and sensor networks, enable real-time monitoring of environmental changes. This includes tracking deforestation, detecting pollution levels, and monitoring wildlife populations. By providing timely and accurate data, AI enhances our ability to respond to environmental threats, enabling more effective conservation efforts.

■ Optimized Resource Management: AI algorithms are applied to optimize the use of resources in various sectors, including agriculture and energy. In agriculture, AI assists in precision farming by analyzing data on soil health, weather patterns, and crop conditions, allowing for more efficient resource allocation. In the energy sector, AI helps optimize power distribution, reducing waste and promoting sustainability.

■ Sustainable Solutions and Climate Modeling: AI plays a crucial role in developing sustainable solutions to address climate change. Machine learning models are employed to analyze large datasets related to climate patterns, helping scientists and policymakers make informed decisions. AI-driven climate models contribute to our understanding of environmental changes and support the development of strategies to mitigate the impacts of climate change.

■ Wildlife Conservation and Anti-Poaching Efforts: AI-powered systems, including drones and camera traps, are employed for wildlife conservation. These technologies assist in monitoring and protecting endangered species by detecting and preventing poaching activities. AI algorithms can analyze large datasets of images and sensor data, helping conservationists better understand and safeguard biodiversity.

■ Waste Management and Recycling Optimization: AI is utilized to optimize waste management processes. Smart waste bins equipped with sensors and AI algorithms can monitor and manage waste levels, enabling more efficient collection routes. Additionally, AI contributes to the identification and sorting of recyclable materials, reducing the environmental impact of waste disposal.

■ Climate-Resilient Agriculture: AI assists farmers in adapting to changing climate conditions. Machine learning models analyze climate data to provide insights into optimal planting times, crop choices, and irrigation strategies. This helps farmers make informed decisions, enhance crop resilience, and improve overall agricultural sustainability.

4.2.4 Social Justice

AI has the potential to play a transformative role in promoting social justice, fostering fairness, and empowering marginalized communities.

■ Fairness and Bias Mitigation: AI tools can be designed to identify and mitigate biases in decision-making processes, helping to ensure fair treatment across diverse populations. Techniques such as algorithmic auditing and fairness-aware machine learning contribute to reducing discrimination in areas such as hiring, lending, and law enforcement.

■ Criminal Justice Reform: AI applications in criminal justice can contribute to reform efforts by providing more accurate risk assessments and aiding in predictive policing. Fair and transparent AI models can assist in reducing bias in legal decisions, ensuring that individuals are treated equitably within the criminal justice system.

■ Inclusive Access to Information: AI-driven language translation and accessibility tools improve communication and information access for individuals with diverse linguistic backgrounds and abilities. These technologies contribute to breaking down language barriers, promoting inclusivity, and ensuring that information is accessible to a broader audience.

■ Enhanced Civic Participation: AI technologies, such as chatbots and virtual assistants, can engage citizens in civic activities by providing information, facilitating communication with government agencies, and encouraging participation in public decision-making processes.

This enhances democratic practices and ensures a more informed and engaged citizenry.

▪ Education Equity: AI technologies contribute to education equity by providing personalized learning experiences, adapting to individual needs, and addressing learning gaps. Virtual tutors and AI-assisted educational platforms can support students in underserved communities, offering them access to high-quality educational resources and opportunities.

4.3 Negative Social Impacts of AI

AI has undoubtedly revolutionized various aspects of our lives, bringing convenience, efficiency, and innovation. However, its rapid advancement also raises concerns about its potential negative social impacts.

4.3.1 Job Displacement

▪ Job Losses and Economic Disruption: The implementation of AI-driven automation in industries such as manufacturing, customer service, and transportation can lead to the displacement of human workers. This shift may result in economic disruptions, with workers facing unemployment and the need for retraining to acquire new skills suitable for an evolving job market.

▪ Inequality and Wage Disparities: AI may exacerbate existing socio-economic inequalities by impacting different job sectors unevenly. High-skilled jobs requiring creativity and complex problem-solving may see growth, while lower-skilled jobs susceptible to automation may experience declines. This can contribute to wage disparities and create challenges for workers in certain sectors.

▪ Skills Gap and Retraining Challenges: The rapid evolution of AI may create a skills gap, where the existing workforce lacks the necessary expertise for emerging roles. Retraining programs and education initiatives become crucial to equip workers with the skills needed for the changing job landscape, but implementing effective retraining measures poses significant challenges.

▪ Psychosocial Impact on Workers: Job displacement and the fear of automation can have profound psychosocial effects on workers. Anxiety, stress, and uncertainty about the future of work can contribute to mental health challenges within the workforce. Addressing the psychosocial impact is crucial for maintaining the overall well-being of individuals affected by AI-driven job changes.

■ Challenges in Job Creation: While AI may lead to the creation of new jobs in emerging fields, the pace and nature of job creation may not match the rate of job displacement. The shift in the job market could result in challenges related to job scarcity, requiring initiative-taking measures to ensure a smooth transition for the workforce.

4.3.2 Algorithmic Bias

AI algorithms, if not carefully designed and monitored, have the potential to perpetuate and even exacerbate existing biases in society, leading to unfair outcomes in various domains.

■ Bias in Hiring and Employment: AI-powered tools used in recruitment processes may inadvertently incorporate biases present in historical hiring data. If the historical data reflects gender, racial, or socioeconomic biases, the algorithms may perpetuate these biases, leading to discriminatory hiring practices.

■ Criminal Justice Disparities: AI algorithms used in predictive policing may inherit biases from historical crime data, leading to the over-policing of certain communities and reinforcing existing disparities. This can result in discriminatory law enforcement practices and exacerbate social inequalities.

■ Unfair Loan and Credit Decisions: AI systems used in assessing creditworthiness may inadvertently perpetuate biases related to race, gender, or socioeconomic status present in historical lending data. This can result in unfair loan or credit decisions, further marginalizing certain groups and hindering financial inclusion.

■ Reinforcement of Gender and Racial Stereotypes: AI algorithms that process and analyze vast amounts of data may inadvertently perpetuate gender and racial stereotypes present in the training data. This can result in biased recommendations, advertisements, and content moderation decisions, reinforcing harmful stereotypes.

■ Ethical Considerations and Lack of Transparency: The lack of transparency in AI algorithms and decision-making processes raises ethical concerns. Users and affected individuals may not fully understand how decisions are reached, leading to a lack of accountability and challenges in addressing biased outcomes. Transparency is crucial for maintaining public trust in AI systems.

4.3.3 Privacy and Surveillance

The deployment of AI for surveillance and data collection introduces significant concerns regarding individual privacy, raising apprehensions about potential misuse and threats to civil liberties.

■ Mass Surveillance and Intrusion: AI-powered surveillance systems, equipped with facial recognition and behavior analysis capabilities, can enable mass surveillance on a scale previously unseen. This extensive data collection raises concerns about the invasion of individuals' privacy, as it allows authorities and entities to monitor and analyze activities in public and private spaces.

■ Algorithmic Profiling and Discrimination: The use of AI algorithms in surveillance can lead to the profiling and targeting of individuals based on their characteristics, behavior, or associations. This raises concerns about discriminatory practices, where certain groups may be disproportionately targeted or face bias in decisions made by automated surveillance systems.

■ Data Breaches and Security Risks: The extensive collection and storage of data for AI applications increase the risk of data breaches and unauthorized access. Inaccurate or inappropriate use of surveillance data can lead to serious privacy violations, and compromised security measures can expose individuals to identity theft and other cyber threats.

■ Chilling Effects on Free Expression: Widespread surveillance, especially when coupled with advanced AI analytics, may create a chilling effect on free expression and dissent. Individuals may alter their behavior or refrain from expressing certain opinions due to the fear of being monitored, leading to a potential stifling of open discourse and democratic participation.

■ Lack of Accountability and Oversight: The rapid advancement of AI in surveillance has outpaced regulatory frameworks and oversight mechanisms. The lack of clear regulations and accountability measures increases the risk of misuse and abuse of surveillance technologies.

Establishing robust legal and ethical frameworks is essential to ensure responsible deployment and usage of AI in surveillance.

4.3.4 Weaponization

The development and deployment of AI in autonomous weapons raise significant ethical and safety concerns, posing the risk of unintended harm and potentially exacerbating conflicts.

- Autonomous Weapons and Ethical Dilemmas: The use of AI in autonomous weapon systems raises profound ethical questions. The delegation of lethal decision-making to machines introduces concerns about accountability, moral judgment, and adherence to international humanitarian law. Autonomous weapons may lack the ability to differentiate between combatants and civilians, leading to severe ethical dilemmas in warfare.
- Unintended Consequences and Lack of Control: The use of AI in weapons introduces the risk of unintended consequences due to the complexity and unpredictability of real-world scenarios. The lack of human oversight and control in autonomous systems may result in unforeseen actions, posing dangers to civilians and escalating conflicts beyond the intended scope.
- Arms Race and Proliferation: The development of AI-powered weapons has the potential to trigger an arms race, with nations vying to enhance their military capabilities. The proliferation of autonomous weapons raises concerns about their accessibility to non-state actors, increasing the risk of conflicts and posing challenges for global security and stability.
- Erosion of Human Dignity in Warfare: The deployment of autonomous weapons may contribute to the erosion of human dignity in armed conflicts. Removing the human element from decision-making in warfare can devalue the importance of empathy, compassion, and ethical considerations, potentially leading to a dehumanizing effect on the conduct of warfare.
- Public Perception and Acceptance: The public perception and acceptance of AI-powered weapons play a crucial role in shaping societal attitudes toward autonomous systems in warfare. Concerns about accountability, safety, and ethical implications may lead to public resistance, impacting the legitimacy and responsible deployment of AI in military contexts.

4.4 Addressing Social Concerns and Ensuring Responsible AI Development: A Balancing Act

As AI continues to evolve at an unprecedented pace, its impact on society grows increasingly significant. While the potential benefits of AI are vast, ranging from personalized healthcare to revolutionizing industries, concerns about its potential misuse and negative societal consequences have also emerged. Striking a balance between harnessing the power of AI and mitigating its risks demands a proactive approach to addressing social concerns and ensuring responsible development.

One of the primary social concerns surrounding AI is the potential for bias and discrimination. AI algorithms trained on biased data can perpetuate and amplify existing social inequalities, leading to unfair outcomes for certain groups. Research by [1] highlights this issue in her analysis of algorithms used in criminal justice systems, which disproportionately target individuals from marginalized communities. Similarly, [2] expose gender and racial bias in commercially available facial recognition technology. Addressing these concerns requires careful attention to data collection and curation, employing diverse and representative datasets to train AI systems.

Another significant concern is the potential for job displacement due to AI automation. As AI automates tasks previously performed by humans, fears of widespread unemployment have emerged. While some job losses are inevitable, [3] argue that the impact will likely be unevenly distributed, with certain sectors and occupations facing greater disruption than others. To mitigate the negative impacts of job displacement, comprehensive reskilling and upskilling initiatives are crucial, enabling individuals to adapt to the changing job market and acquire the skills necessary to thrive in the AI-driven economy.

Furthermore, the opaque nature of AI decision-making processes raises concerns about transparency and accountability. The lack of public understanding of how AI algorithms arrive at their decisions can undermine trust and fuel concerns about bias and manipulation. To address this issue, researchers like [4] advocate for explainable AI, where AI systems are designed to be transparent and provide explanations for their decisions in a way that is understandable to humans.

Ensuring responsible AI development requires a multi-pronged approach. Governments play a crucial role in establishing ethical guidelines and regulations for AI development and deployment. Initiatives like the European Union's General Data Protection Regulation (GDPR) and the

Asilomar AI Principles offer frameworks for addressing ethical concerns and promoting responsible AI development. Additionally, industry leaders have a responsibility to implement robust ethical frameworks within their organizations, ensuring that AI is developed and used in a way that aligns with human values and societal well-being.

Finally, it is essential to foster open dialogue and public engagement with AI development. By encouraging public education and awareness, promoting diverse representation in the field of AI, and actively engaging with stakeholders from various backgrounds, we can build trust in AI and ensure that its development serves the interests of all members of society.

4.5 Case Studies of AI's Social Impact: Positive and Negative Implications

The potential of AI to impact society in profound ways is undeniable. While the potential benefits are vast, encompassing advancements in healthcare, education, and environmental sustainability, concerns about its negative societal consequences, such as job displacement and algorithmic bias, have also emerged. Examining real-world case studies provides valuable insights into the multifaceted impact of AI on society and helps us understand its potential benefits and risks.

- AI for Social Good: The Case of Early Childhood Development in Ecuador
  In Ecuador, a project titled "The Listening Book" leverages AI technology to address the critical issue of early childhood development. This initiative utilizes AI-powered chatbots that engage parents and caregivers through interactive storytelling and educational content, fostering crucial early language and cognitive development in children. The project has shown promising results, with children participating in the program exhibiting significant improvements in language skills and cognitive development compared to those in the control group. This case study demonstrates the potential of AI to address social challenges and improve the lives of vulnerable populations.
- AI-powered Healthcare: Revolutionizing Diagnosis and Treatment
  AI is revolutionizing the healthcare landscape by enabling more accurate diagnoses, personalized treatment plans, and improved clinical decision-making. One example is the use of AI in cancer diagnosis and

treatment. Deep learning algorithms can analyze medical images with exceptional accuracy, leading to earlier and more precise diagnoses. Similarly, AI-powered chatbots are being used to provide personalized support to patients and address mental health challenges on a large scale. These advancements illustrate the potential of AI to improve healthcare outcomes and access for all.

■ AI and Environmental Sustainability: Optimizing Resource Management and Combating Climate Change
AI plays a crucial role in combating climate change and promoting environmental sustainability. One example is the use of AI in smart grids, which optimize energy distribution and consumption, leading to reduced carbon emissions. Additionally, AI-powered sensors are being deployed to monitor environmental conditions, detect pollution sources, and predict natural disasters. These applications demonstrate the potential of AI to contribute to a more sustainable future.

■ Algorithmic Bias and Discrimination: The Case of Facial Recognition Technology
Despite its potential benefits, AI can also exacerbate existing social inequalities and perpetuate discrimination. A notable example is facial recognition technology, which has been shown to exhibit racial and gender bias, leading to false identifications and disproportionate negative impacts on marginalized communities. This case study highlights the critical need for responsible AI development and deployment, ensuring fairness and inclusivity in all applications.

■ Job displacement: The Impact of AI Automation on the Workforce
While automation driven by AI has undoubtedly improved efficiency and productivity across various industries, concerns about widespread job displacement remain valid. One example is the automation of tasks in the manufacturing sector, leading to job losses in certain regions. This case study underscores the need for proactive measures to mitigate the negative impacts of job displacement, including reskilling and upskilling initiatives to equip individuals with the skills necessary to thrive in the evolving job market.

These case studies provide a glimpse into the multifaceted impact of AI on society. By understanding both its potential benefits and its risks, we can ensure that AI is developed and implemented in a responsible manner that promotes positive social change and benefits all members of society.

4.6 Future Directions and Opportunities: Glimpsing the AI Horizon

As we stand poised on the precipice of a new era, the future of AI shimmers with a kaleidoscope of possibilities. Fueled by advancements in deep learning, natural language processing, and computer vision, the capabilities of AI are poised to transcend the realms of science fiction and become an inextricable part of our daily lives. However, navigating this frontier demands careful consideration of not only the opportunities but also the challenges that lie ahead.

■ Expanding the Canvas of AI Capabilities: The future promises AI systems with abilities that currently resemble the stuff of futuristic dreams. Deep learning algorithms will crack the code of complex reasoning, enabling machines to tackle intricate problems and make nuanced decisions previously reserved for human minds. Imagine AI systems crafting groundbreaking scientific discoveries, composing symphonies that stir the soul, or even writing novels that rival the works of literary giants. The boundaries between human and machine intelligence will continue to blur, ushering in a new era of creative collaboration.

■ Harnessing AI for Social Good: The potential of AI to address global challenges and improve lives is undeniable. Personalized education tailored to individual needs could revolutionize learning, making quality education accessible to all corners of the globe. In healthcare, AI algorithms can analyze vast medical data to predict disease outbreaks, personalize treatment plans, and assist in diagnoses, democratizing access to quality healthcare. From optimizing resource management to combatting climate change and developing sustainable energy solutions, AI can be a powerful tool for creating a more equitable and sustainable future.

■ Human-AI Collaboration: A Symbiotic Future: The future of work will not be characterized by machines replacing humans, but rather by humans and machines working together in a symbiotic partnership. Instead of fearing job displacement, humans will increasingly collaborate with AI, focusing on tasks where their unique strengths shine: Creativity, critical thinking, social intelligence, and ethical decision-making. AI will handle the heavy lifting of routine tasks and data analysis, freeing humans to pursue innovation, solve complex problems, and forge meaningful connections. This human-AI synergy is crucial for maximizing the potential of both to achieve groundbreaking outcomes.

■ Navigating the Ethical Landscape: Responsible AI Development: As AI's power and influence grow, the need for ethical development and responsible deployment becomes paramount. We must address issues like algorithmic bias, data privacy concerns, and the potential for misuse of AI technology. Frameworks like the Asilomar AI Principles and the European Union's GDPR offer valuable guidance for ensuring ethical and accountable AI development. Transparency, explainability, and robust oversight mechanisms are crucial for building trust and ensuring that AI serves the best interests of society.

■ Explainable AI: Demystifying the Machine Mind: With increasingly complex AI systems, understanding how they arrive at their decisions becomes crucial for trust and accountability. Explainable AI (XAI) initiatives aim to demystify the black box of AI algorithms, providing insights into their reasoning processes. This is particularly important in areas like healthcare, finance, and law, where AI decisions can have significant consequences for individuals and society. By making AI more transparent, we can foster trust, address concerns, and ensure responsible deployment.

■ AI Governance: Building a Robust Framework: As AI becomes more pervasive, establishing a comprehensive framework for governance is essential. This involves setting clear regulations and guidelines for development, deployment, and use, ensuring responsible AI practices across all sectors. International collaboration and knowledge-sharing are crucial for addressing global challenges and ensuring consistent AI governance frameworks. By working together, we can shape an AI future that benefits all.

References

1. Eubanks, V. (2018). Automating inequality: How high-tech tools profile, police, and punish the poor. St. Martin's Press.
2. Buolamwini, J., & Gebru, T. (2018). Gender shades: Intersectional accuracy disparities in commercial gender classification. Proceedings of the Machine Learning Research, 81, 1–15.
3. Frey, C. B., & Osborne, M. A. (2013). The future of employment: How susceptible are jobs to computerization? Technological Forecasting and Social Change, 80(7), 1725–1748.
4. Mittelstadt, B. D., Allo, P., Taddeo, M., Wachter, S., & Floridi, L. (2019). The ethics of algorithms: Mapping the debate. Big Data & Society, 6(2), 1–21.

Chapter 5

Customer-Centric AI Solutions

Puvvaladasu M. Sai Subramanya Krishna, Praveen Kumar T, Ravuri Venkata Trinadh Reddy, and Ezendu Ariwa

5.1 Introduction

In the fast-paced realm of contemporary business, the integration of artificial intelligence (AI) has become a pivotal force in reshaping the dynamics between consumers and organizations. At the forefront of this transformative journey lies the concept of customer-centric AI solutions, a paradigm that goes beyond mere transactional exchanges to redefine the very essence of customer-business interactions.

Customer-centric AI solutions represent a departure from conventional approaches, where businesses cater to broad demographics. In this era of heightened connectivity and data-driven insights, the spotlight is now on tailoring experiences to meet the unique needs and preferences of individual customers. This chapter endeavors to unravel the intricacies of this revolutionary phenomenon, exploring the intersection of AI and customer-centricity and its profound implications for businesses across diverse industries.

At its core, customer-centric AI solutions leverage advanced technologies such as machine learning, natural language processing (NLP), and predictive analytics to decode patterns and anticipate customer behaviors. This proactive approach enables businesses to customize their offerings, communications, and overall engagement strategies in real-time, aligning seamlessly with the ever-evolving expectations of their diverse customer base.

The journey into the world of customer-centric AI solutions commences with an exploration of the technological foundations that underpin this paradigm shift. This includes an in-depth examination of machine learning

DOI: 10.4324/9781032711089-5

algorithms that empower predictive modeling, allowing businesses to forecast customer needs and trends with unparalleled accuracy. Additionally, the role of NLP is elucidated, showcasing how it facilitates the development of conversational AI, transforming customer interactions through chatbots, virtual assistants, and voice-activated systems.

However, the successful implementation of customer-centric AI solutions extends beyond technological prowess. It necessitates a cultural shift within organizations, emphasizing a customer-centric mindset that permeates every facet of the business. This cultural transformation is a key aspect explored in this chapter, underscoring the imperative for businesses to embrace agility and adaptability in response to evolving customer expectations.

To illustrate the tangible impact of customer-centric AI solutions, the chapter incorporates a series of case studies. These real-world examples demonstrate how various industries have successfully navigated challenges and harnessed the benefits of this transformative approach. From personalized shopping experiences in e-commerce to AI-driven patient care in healthcare, these case studies serve as inspiring benchmarks for organizations venturing into the realm of customer-centric AI.

While celebrating the potential of customer-centric AI solutions, it is crucial to acknowledge challenges, ethical considerations, and the delicate balance between automation and maintaining a human touch. As the chapter progresses, it will delve deeper into practical strategies for implementation, ethical considerations, and the evolving landscape of regulations guiding the responsible use of AI in customer-centric endeavors.

Together, we embark on a journey into the heart of innovation, where the fusion of AI and customer-centricity propels businesses toward unprecedented heights of success in meeting the unique and dynamic needs of their valued clientele.

5.1.1 Purpose of Chapter

In the present-day panorama of business and generation, the integration of AI has emerged as an effective catalyst for trade, redefining the dynamics between agencies and their customers. This chapter aims to illuminate the reason and importance of customer-centric AI solutions, delving into their transformative capability and the profound effect they can have on the way agencies engage with and serve their purchasers.

At its core, the purpose of this chapter is to demystify the concept of customer-centric AI solutions and shed light on how it transcends the traditional paradigms of consumer-business interactions. The overarching aim is to provide readers with a complete understanding of the ideas, programs, and implications associated with infusing AI technology into purchaser-centric techniques.

One primary goal is to explore the technological foundations that empower customer-centric AI solutions. The chapter endeavors to get to the bottom of the intricacies of machine mastering algorithms, NLP, and predictive analytics. By doing so, it aims to clarify how these technologies work in concert, permitting organizations to decipher styles, count on consumer behaviors, and dynamically adjust their offerings to align with character alternatives. Through this exploration, readers will advantage insights into the capability of AI to revolutionize patron stories and foster true, personalized connections.

Moreover, the chapter seeks to emphasize the cultural shift required inside companies to absolutely include a consumer-centric mindset. The motive is to underscore that customer-centric AI solutions increase beyond technological implementations; they necessitate a holistic organizational approach that places the patron on the middle of selection-making and operational techniques. By examining real-international examples and case research, the chapter aims to showcase how groups have successfully navigated this cultural transformation, fostering agility and flexibility in response to evolving purchaser expectancies.

The chapter serves as a sensible manual for businesses looking to leverage customer-centric AI solutions to decorate client delight and loyalty. It aims to offer actionable insights and techniques for implementation, empowering agencies to navigate the demanding situations related to the adoption of AI technologies in a consumer-centric context. By addressing ability pitfalls and providing first-rate practices, the chapter aims to equip readers with the information needed to embark on their very own journeys of innovation and transformation.

Ethical concerns represent an important aspect of the chapter's purpose, as it delves into the responsible use of AI in patron-centric endeavors. By exploring the delicate balance between automation and the human touch, the chapter aims to provoke a considerate discourse on the moral considerations that accompany the integration of AI into purchaser interactions. This discussion is essential for making sure that groups leverage AI technologies ethically and responsibly, fostering belief and transparency with their consumer base.

In summary, the motive of this chapter is multifaceted. It aims to demystify customer-centric AI solutions, discover their technological foundations, highlight the cultural shift required within groups, offer practical guidance for implementation, and deal with ethical considerations. Through this comprehensive exploration, the chapter aims to empower organizations to harness the transformative electricity of AI in creating purchaser-centric reports that no longer only meet but exceed the specific and dynamic expectancies of their customers.

5.2 Literature Review

The integration of AI into client-centric strategies has witnessed a surge of interest in recent years, as businesses are searching for progressive approaches to cater to the evolving expectancies of their purchasers. This literature assessment aims to explore and synthesize the existing frame of knowledge surrounding customer-centric AI solutions, losing light on key themes, tendencies, and insights that have fashioned this transformative intersection of era and customer engagement.

A foundational element of the literature on customer-centric AI solutions revolves around the evolution of customer expectancies in the virtual age. As highlighted by authors including Pine and Gilmore (2013) in their seminal work on the experience financial system, clients are more and more searching for personalized and remarkable interactions with manufacturers. The literature underscores how traditional, transactional procedures are not sufficient in a panorama where customers call for tailored, immersive reviews.

Machine learning, a central issue of AI, takes the middle level inside the literature as an era that permits predictive modeling and customization. Davenport et al. (2007) emphasize the strength of predictive analytics in expertise purchaser conduct and alternatives, heralding a paradigm shift from reactive to proactive patron engagement. The literature converges on the notion that machine gaining knowledge of algorithms empower corporations to count on and satisfy person client wishes, fostering a greater profound connection between the logo and the client.

NLP emerges as some other pivotal aspect in the literature on customer-centric AI solutions. Authors such as Jurafsky and Martin (2019) delve into the position of NLP in allowing conversational AI, reworking customer interactions through chatbots, virtual assistants, and voice-activated systems. This functionality now not simplest complements the performance of customer support but additionally contributes to a greater natural and personalized communication channel.

Customer-centricity, a routine topic inside the literature, transcends technological elements to encompass organizational tradition. Pine and Gilmore (2013) emphasize the shift from a product-centric to a revel-in-centric mindset, underscoring the want for businesses to orient their strategies across the specific needs and goals of man or woman customers. This cultural transformation, as echoed by numerous authors, is portrayed as a prerequisite for the successful implementation of customer-centric AI solutions.

Real-world case research comes to be treasured contributions to the literature, imparting tangible examples of companies that have effectively embraced customer-centric AI solutions. For instance, Zhang et al. (2006) discover how e-commerce giants leverage AI to customize buying experiences, while Topol (2019) delves into the healthcare area, illustrating the impact of AI on customized patient care. These case research serve not only to validate the theoretical underpinnings but also as sources of notion for groups considering the mixing of AI into their patron-centric techniques.

Ethical concerns, a growing issue in the literature, encompass problems together with privacy, transparency, and bias in AI algorithms. Mittelstadt et al. (2016) emphasize the significance of accountable AI use, urging agencies to navigate the moral complexities associated with purchaser records and algorithmic choice-making. The literature underscores the need for a balanced method that prioritizes purchaser well-being and trust.

The literature on customer-centric AI solutions paints a dynamic photograph of a transformative landscape in which generation, consumer expectancies, and organizational culture converge. From predictive analytics to conversational AI, the literature provides a comprehensive understanding of the multifaceted additives shaping the adoption and impact of customer-centric AI solutions. As agencies navigate this panorama, the synthesis of present knowledge serves as a treasured guide, providing insights and issues essential for informed selection-making and successful implementation.

5.3 Understanding Customer Behavior

Understanding client conduct is an essential element of growing powerful purchaser-centric AI solutions. In this phase of the book chapter, we are able to delve into the significance of comprehending patron behavior, the position of AI in this context, and the impact of such knowledge on business techniques.

Customer conduct encompasses the movements and choice-making procedures of people as they interact with merchandise, services, and brands. By gaining insights into consumer behavior, agencies can tailor their services, advertising techniques, and patron studies to better meet the desires and options of their audience.

AI plays a pivotal function in information consumer behavior by way of reading extensive amounts of statistics to discover patterns, trends, and correlations. Through superior information analytics, gadget getting to know algorithms, and predictive modeling, AI can discover treasured insights regarding patron preferences, shopping for behavior, and engagement inclinations.

One of the essential ways AI allows the information of customer conduct is through predictive analytics. By studying ancient information and ongoing interactions, AI can forecast future purchaser moves and choices with an excessive diploma of accuracy. This capability allows companies to anticipate consumer needs, customize advertising efforts, and optimize product services.

Moreover, AI-pushed sentiment evaluation allows companies to recognize consumer feelings, sentiments, and feedback throughout numerous channels consisting of social media, patron reviews, and support interactions. By gauging patron sentiment, agencies can proactively cope with concerns, become aware of regions for improvement, and beautify ordinary consumer pleasure.

In the context of e-commerce, AI-powered recommendation systems play a vital position in understanding and influencing client behavior. By reading beyond buy records, surfing styles, and demographic data, these systems can advise customized product suggestions, thereby increasing purchaser engagement and riding income.

Furthermore, AI enables the knowledge of purchaser conduct through consumer journey analysis. Businesses can make use of AI to map the numerous touchpoints and interactions that customers have with their emblem, allowing a holistic view of the client experience. This expertise enables identifying pain points, optimizing touchpoints, and handing over an unbroken customer adventure.

The impact of knowledge customer conduct through AI transcends marketing and income efforts; it extends to product development and innovation. By leveraging AI-generated insights, organizations can become aware of emerging developments, unmet purchaser wishes, and opportunities for product enhancements, leading to more customer-centric services.

In summary, the knowledge of client behavior facilitated with the aid of AI is instrumental in shaping customer-centric techniques across industries. By harnessing the power of AI for customer insights, businesses can pressure customized experiences, enhance client pride, and ultimately foster long-term loyalty. This transformative effect underscores the importance of integrating patron conduct understanding with AI-powered solutions in present-day business operations.

5.4 Implementation and Integration

Implementation and integration of purchaser-centric AI solutions are critical aspects that corporations need to recall to leverage the entire capacity of AI in enhancing client experiences and using commercial enterprise boom. In this segment of the ebook chapter, we will explore the numerous facets of enforcing and integrating AI solutions in the context of patron-centric techniques.

The first step in implementing consumer-centric AI solutions entails defining clean targets and identifying key performance indicators (KPIs) to measure the effect of AI tasks on purchaser-centric dreams. This ought to encompass objectives together with enhancing patron delight rankings, enhancing personalization efforts, or growing purchaser retention charges. Setting tangible dreams is crucial for aligning AI implementation with commercial enterprise consequences.

Once the objectives are defined, organizations want to evaluate their current information infrastructure and skills. AI-powered purchaser-centric answers rely upon sturdy information collection, garage, and processing mechanisms. Therefore, it's far imperative to assess the readiness of the agency's information structure to assist AI tasks efficaciously. This may additionally include consolidating disparate information assets, imposing statistics governance practices, and making sure records best quality and integrity.

Selecting the right AI technology and structures is a crucial choice in the implementation phase. Businesses want to evaluate diverse AI solutions consisting of predictive analytics gear, system getting to know frameworks, NLP engines, and personalization engines to align with their consumer-centric goals. Additionally, considerations associated with scalability, interoperability, and compliance with facts privacy guidelines should be taken into consideration for the duration of the choice manner.

The integration of AI solutions within existing patron-centric frameworks requires a strategic approach. Seamless integration of AI technologies with customer relationship management (CRM) systems, marketing automation platforms, and e-commerce programs is essential to ensure that AI-generated insights and recommendations are successfully applied across touchpoints. Furthermore, integrating AI into customer service structures can enhance the performance and personalization of patron interactions.

Organizational readiness and change management play a pivotal position in successful AI implementation and integration. Businesses need to spend money on education and upskilling their workforce to harness the abilities of AI answers correctly. Additionally, fostering a tradition of statistics-pushed selection-making and purchaser-centric questioning throughout departments is instrumental in ensuring the successful adoption of AI-powered techniques.

The dimension and non-stop optimization of AI-powered purchaser-centric initiatives are critical for long-term fulfillment. Businesses want to establish comment loops and iterative improvement methods to refine AI fashions, algorithms, and techniques based on actual-time client feedback and overall performance records.

In conclusion, the implementation and integration of client-centric AI solutions require a strategic and holistic approach. By aligning AI tasks with clean targets, comparing records infrastructure, deciding on suitable AI technology, and fostering organizational readiness, businesses can correctly harness the transformative strength of AI to enhance consumer stories and power sustainable business growth. This phase of the book chapter emphasizes the sensible concerns and quality practices for enforcing and integrating AI in client-centric techniques.

5.5 Future Trends and Innovations

Future tendencies and improvements in customer-centric AI solutions are shaping the way companies interact with and serve their clients. In this section of the ebook financial disaster, we will explore growing technology and tendencies which is probably poised to transform consumer-centric strategies and redefine the purchaser experience panorama.

Conversational AI, such as chatbots and digital assistants, is at the forefront of reworking client interactions. These AI-powered conversational interfaces enable corporations to supply customized help, proactive pointers, and seamless critiques across diverse touchpoints. As NLP and AI algorithms evolve, conversational AI is increasingly becoming human-like and powerful in expertise and addressing patron inquiries.

Predictive analytics powered with the aid of way of the usage of AI is some extraordinary outstanding future fashion. Advanced device getting to know algorithms permit companies to count on customer wishes, behaviors, and opportunities with high-quality accuracy. By studying wealthy datasets, predictive analytics can forecast customer movements, permitting agencies to proactively customize offers, look forward to churn, and optimize pricing techniques.

The integration of augmented truth (AR) and virtual fact (VR) with purchaser-centric AI solutions is on the horizon as well. AR and VR technology provides immersive and interactive reports, permitting customers to visualize products in actual global settings, participate in virtual strive-ons, and engage with producers in cutting-edge strategies. AI can beautify those studies by personalizing AR/VR content fabric based totally on man or woman options and behaviors.

Furthermore, the utility of emotion AI is gaining traction in client-centric techniques. Emotion AI leverages facial recognition, voice evaluation, and biometric facts to determine consumer emotions and sentiments. By facts client feelings, agencies can tailor studies, adapt messaging, and offer manual processes that resonate with customers on a deeper level.

Hyper-personalization is an evolving frontier that entails leveraging AI to deliver mainly individualized evaluations based mostly on real-time patron context. AI-powered personalization engines can dynamically tailor offerings, content material, cloth material, and communication primarily based on customer conduct, interactions, or even emotional states, leading to greater proper and impactful engagements.

The convergence of AI with Internet of Things (IoT) era is redefining consumer-centric strategies. IoT devices generate wonderful quantities of client behavioral records, and AI can extract actionable insights from this information to customize critiques, decorate product hints, and facilitate predictive preservation, thereby enhancing everyday client pleasure.

Innovations in explainable AI (XAI) are paramount for building genuine and transparency in patron-centric AI solutions. XAI aims to make AI algorithms and preference-making strategies more interpretable and comprehensible to people. This transparency is essential, mainly in regulated industries, because it lets corporations offer a reason behind the purpose at the back of AI-generated guidelines and predictions to clients and regulatory authorities.

In essence, the future tendencies and innovations in customer-centric AI solutions preserve tremendous promise for redefining client recollections and the use of enterprise fulfillment. As organizations encompass conversational AI, predictive analytics, AR/VR integration, emotion AI, hyper-personalization, IoT convergence, and XAI, they may be better located to supply genuinely purchaser-centric evaluations that anticipate and fulfill individual dreams and opportunities. This segment of the ebook financial ruin sheds moderate on the transformative functionality of these rising eras and tendencies in shaping the future of patron-centric techniques.

5.6 Conclusion

The evolution of AI has revolutionized the manner agencies engage with and cater to their customers. In this financial ruin, we have delved into the numerous factors of using patron-centric AI solutions to create a more personalized, efficient, and pleasant experience for purchasers.

Understanding customer needs and pain factors is crucial to developing powerful AI solutions. By leveraging information, agencies can gain worthwhile insights into client conduct, choices, and tendencies. This data-pushed approach permits agencies to assume, in choice to react to, customer dreams, thereby fostering a deeper sense of knowledge and reference to the client base.

Personalization is at the heart of consumer-centric AI solutions. By the usage of AI algorithms, businesses can tailor products, offerings, and marketing efforts to man or woman customer opportunities, thereby growing a more proper and tasty experience. The capacity to provide custom designed hints and solutions now not only most effectively complements client pride but also additionally cultivates prolonged time period loyalty and advocacy.

Transparency and trust are vital additives of purchaser-centric AI solutions. As businesses integrate AI into patron interactions, it is imperative to preserve transparency regarding record usage, algorithmic selection-making, and privacy measures. By doing so, organizations can instill trust and self-warranty in their AI-pushed tactics, thereby fortifying consumer relationships and logo credibility.

Furthermore, the AI era has transformed customer support by permitting speedy, accurate, and personalized assistance. Chatbots, digital assistants, and AI-powered analytics have streamlined customer service tactics, resulting in more potent responsiveness and backbone costs. This no longer augments the consumer experience but also optimizes aid allocation and operational efficiency for organizations.

Effectively measuring the achievement of consumer-centric AI solutions is paramount. Key metrics, which encompass purchaser pleasure, retention expenses, conversion costs, and consumer lifetime rate, provide corporations with tangible insights into the impact of their AI responsibilities. These metrics function as benchmarks for universal performance assessment and manual iterative improvements to ensure sustained patron-centricity.

Despite the numerous blessings of patron-centric AI solutions, demanding situations persist in their implementation. Ethical concerns, data privacy guidelines, technological barriers, and the capability for algorithmic biases necessitate a careful and responsible technique. Addressing those annoying conditions is critical to maximize the effective impact of AI on patron relationships and business agency outcomes.

Looking in advance, the destiny of customer-centric AI solutions is marked by using thrilling opportunities. Advancements in NLP, system gaining knowledge, and predictive analytics will further augment the capabilities of AI in understanding and serving clients. Additionally, the aggregate of AI with emerging generations, which incorporates augmented reality and the IoT, holds promise for creating immersive, context-aware patron opinions.

Customer-centric AI solutions represent a paradigm shift in how groups interact with and cater to their customers. By harnessing the energy of AI to apprehend, personalize, and guide clients, groups can domesticate stronger, more proper relationships while driving sustainable boom and differentiation in an increasingly aggressive marketplace. Embracing client-centric AI isn't always just a technological imperative but a strategic imperative for businesses searching to thrive within the technology of client enjoy-driven economies.

References

Davenport, T. H., Harris, J. G., Jones, G. L., Lemon, K. N., Norton, D., & McCallister, M. B. (2007). The dark side of customer analytics. *Harvard Business Review*, 85(5), 37.

Jurafsky, D., & Martin, J. H. (2019). Vector semantics and embeddings. *Speech Language Process*, 1–31.

Mittelstadt, B. D., Allo, P., Taddeo, M., Wachter, S., & Floridi, L. (2016). The ethics of algorithms: Mapping the debate. *Big Data & Society*, *3*(2), 2053951716679679.

Pine, B. J., & Gilmore, J. H. (2013). The experience economy: past, present and future. In *Handbook on the experience economy* (pp. 21–44). Edward Elgar Publishing.

Topol, E. J. (2019). High-performance medicine: the convergence of human and artificial intelligence. *Nature Medicine*, *25*(1), 44–56.

Zhang, L. M., Zhang, Z. P., Li, J., Abe, K., Abe, K., Adachi, I., ... & Tsuboyama, T. (2006). Improved constraints on D-0-(D)over–bar(0) mixing in D-0→ K+ π(-) decays from the belle detector. *Physical Review Letters*, *96*(15), 151801.

Chapter 6

Unveiling the Impact of AI in Customer Touchpoints: A Review and Research Agenda

Arman Khan, Abu Bakar Abdul Hamid, and Zahid Hussain

6.1 Introduction

Interactive marketing refers to a marketing process in which value is created and influenced by both the marketer and the customer through dynamic linkages, involvement, active participation, and reciprocating interaction (Wang, 2021). The emergence of artificial intelligence (AI) has significantly transformed the way consumers interact with brands and their buying experiences (Chintalapati and Pandey, 2022). AI, or artificial intelligence, encompasses the use of computer equipment to replicate human capabilities, such as executing physical or mechanical actions, cognitive processes, and emotional experiences (Huang and Rust, 2021). Diverse AI tools are used to enhance consumer interaction at every step of the buying process, such as the use of hotel robots for customer check-ins and virtual assistants for managing customer complaints. In this environment, improving the effectiveness of AI tools in interactive marketing from the perspective of customers is an important issue for academics, professionals, and marketers.

Furthermore, there has been a significant surge in the body of literature that expressly examines the application of AI in marketing, with a particular emphasis on the consumer's perspective. This study offers significant findings on how to optimize interactions between consumers and AI tools. Nevertheless, the existing literature is disjointed and encompasses

DOI: 10.4324/9781032711089-6

a broad spectrum of subjects and AI implementations. Although there are assessments available regarding the utilization of AI tools in marketing, two unresolved challenges persist in implementing them in interactive marketing. It is important to mention that certain studies have thoroughly investigated AI research in the marketing field. Nevertheless, the main focus of these studies was around operational and strategic topics or revolved around technical AI algorithms specifically designed to address marketing challenges (Huang and Rust, 2021). Moreover, prior assessments frequently fail to consider the unique characteristics inherent in the interactions between consumers and AI. Their presentation of pertinent information lacked a cohesive structure, which impeded the development of a comprehensive and logically coherent knowledge system. While Chintalapati and Pandey (2022) categorized AI marketing into five unique functional divisions, Mariani et al. (2022) identified eight distinct topic groups. Regarding the application of AI to interactive marketing, however, knowledge remains limited.

The inception of the customer journey model can be attributed to the prevailing circumstances, wherein clients engage with businesses through multiple touchpoints distributed across diverse platforms and mediums (Lemon and Verhoef, 2016). The model conceptualizes customer-brand interactions in three distinct stages: Pre-buy, purchase, and post-purchase. This enables more efficient monitoring and administration of each interaction. AI apps provide fresh touchpoints spread throughout customer experiences. This model provides a novel method for incorporating and analyzing existing data on customer interactions with AI tools by assessing the differences and linkages between different stages of the buying process.

The customer journey theory serves as the conceptual framework for this systematic review, which looks into the following research questions:

1. What are the specific points of interaction with AI and what are their specific objectives at each point of the customer journey?
2. What criteria or circumstances drive customers to choose AI touchpoints?
3. Which characteristics have a substantial impact on the efficacy of interactions between customers and AI?
4. What strategy should be employed to effortlessly include customers and AI in the customer journey?

The systematic review, carried out using a well-organized framework, produces four different contributions. To begin with, it organizes the disorganized literature on customer and AI interaction, extending the theory of the customer journey. This method, which outlines AI's three primary stages, creates a foundational framework for a thorough knowledge of the technology's application in interactive marketing. Furthermore, the present analysis emphasizes future research areas that have the potential to improve our understanding of the interaction between customers and AI throughout the entire customer journey. In addition, we augment the current customer journey theory by integrating AI touchpoints to showcase the potential of this coming technology in improving the whole customer experience. Moreover, the evaluation provides professionals in the industry with advanced insights on effectively utilizing AI for consumer engagement.

6.2 Customer Journey Analysis Using AI-Powered Touchpoints

The framework suggested by Lemon and Verhoef (2016) is used to examine and present the data methodically. This framework highlights the careful identification of important features in each phase of the customer journey model. This entails identifying distinct touchpoints encountered during the journey and determining the factors that influence customers' decisions to either continue or discontinue their purchasing journey. Moreover, customer actions at various phases of the purchase experience are utilized to classify brand touchpoints, including product and service attributes, pricing, and ease of use. AI apps that operate as brand touchpoints are categorized according to consumer engagement behaviors and their roles within the marketing mix.

This study aims to investigate the precise characteristics that drive customers to interact with AI contact points, seeing them as essential variables in the process of adoption. The literature has identified and categorized these elements based on the AI touchpoints they represent and subsequently grouped them accordingly. The following sections provide a more comprehensive examination of these AI applications and components within the customer experience.

6.3 The Structure and Function of AI Touchpoints

The following piece is an overview of AI applications that have been extensively examined in academic research. These applications are regarded as novel methods for engaging with consumers, and their ability to interact with consumers throughout the customer journey is assessed. The marketing industry has shown considerable interest in the implementation of AI in certain domains such as virtual assistants, chatbots, and service robots. These programs can be used during the full process of interacting with clients. Chatbots are AI programs created to imitate human conversations using voice instructions or text-based chats. They are computer programs specifically designed to interact with humans. Service robots are regarded as the tangible manifestation of AI. Choi et al. (2021) define them as physical entities in the sphere of information technology that may offer personalized services by carrying out both physical and non-physical tasks with a significant level of independence.

Throughout the customer journey, one can obtain specialized chatbots and support robots to offer customized services, such as Amazon's Alexa. However, specific robots, like Edward from Edwardian Hotels, function as substitute staff members for delivering services. Consumers assess the integration of AI services before making a purchase, which impacts their decision to either acquire the amenities or adhere to buy recommendations suggested by AI-driven chatbots or frontline service robots. Chatbots facilitate consumers' engagement in virtual shopping during the purchasing stage. The delivery of basic services to customers and the provision of supplementary services to improve vital goods after purchase are made possible by chatbots and service robots. AI influencers are virtual entities that gain popularity on the internet and employ software and algorithms to perform duties resembling those performed by people (Choi et al., 2021).

There is a lack of research on the use of digitally generated human models as brand endorsers instead of celebrities during the pre-purchase phase. The AI-enhanced contextual retail setting is regarded as a unique type of marketing that operates on the premise that the medium itself serves as the content (Longoni et al., 2019). AI may be a powerful tool for in-store marketing, providing an inimitable purchasing experience that entices customers to visit and make purchases during the pre-purchase period. The shopping systems of AI at storefronts assist customers in shopping, hence decreasing reliance on human labor and fostering a more autonomous shopping experience. The arrival of Amazon Go heralds a fresh and innovative paradigm shift in retail checkout. Customers can have a seamless and uninterrupted purchasing experience by using an AI-powered checkout system (Mariani et al., 2022). This demonstrates the utilization of AI in many areas of the entire purchasing process to get a diverse range of interactive functionalities. Nevertheless, there were two discrepancies. Prior research has predominantly concentrated on the domains of mechanical and cognitive intelligence, which pertain to the capacity of AI to perceive, evaluate, and resolve issues. However, the examination of emotional intelligence in AI systems has been limited. Furthermore, it is imperative to perform an exhaustive examination of the configuration of AI touchpoints and their function in exchanges, including the implementation of AI in the retail distribution of products to customers.

6.4 Consumer Preferences for AI Touchpoints: Influential Factors

The objective of customer journey analysis is to comprehend the various touchpoints available to customers and their decision-making process throughout different stages of the purchasing process (Lemon and Verhoef, 2016). Before examining the interaction process, it is essential to ascertain the elements that influence the selection of AI touchpoints across the customer journey.

6.4.1 Factors Affecting Consumer Adoption of Service Robots and Chatbots

Consumers have three primary reasons to either accept or reject AI touchpoints during the pre-purchase stage. Consumers' perspectives on chatbots and robots encompass a range of opinions, covering elements such as their functionality, enjoyment, social implications, and value. Consumers express concern that AI is characterized by its mechanistic and homogeneous nature, which may lead to disdain for its unique qualities and circumstances. This aspect hinders their acceptance of AI in healthcare (Longoni et al., 2019). Moreover, in the context of relationships, crucial elements include trust, rapport, and affinity that are oriented toward the robot. Simultaneously, consumer characteristics encompass self-efficacy, subjective societal standards, habitual behaviors, individual innovativeness, and perceived control over behavior.

6.4.2 Factors Affecting the Willingness to Embrace AI Channels

In the buying phase, five specific criteria influence the tendency to utilize AI purchase channels. An important thing to take into account is the channel characteristics of AI assistants, which encompass elements such as the level of media content and the ability to create a sense of one-sided social engagement. Customer perception of AI channels is the second factor. The widespread use of automated shopping systems is motivated by factors such as the perception of control and independence, the experience of significant interactions, individuality, and identity (Longoni et al., 2019). Mariani et al. (2022) found that consumer optimism, innovativeness, and insecurity had an impact on the shopping intentions of AI-powered automated retail outlets. Moreover, social culture refers to the elements of social interconnectedness and cultural customs (Lemon and Verhoef, 2016). The last aspect is related to the category of the product. Mariani et al. (2022) found that consumers demonstrate a predilection for acquiring items that require little effort through utilizing virtual assistants. The study examined the impact of different variables on customer satisfaction and acceptance of AI offerings or AI purchasing gateways in the pre-purchase and buying stages. Each of these variables related to various points of interaction can be cross-referenced. Interpersonal considerations can impact the choice of an AI platform, while the characteristics of the service can indicate if AI is suitable as a digital service provider. These relationships might be verified further in future investigations. The factors that drive consumers to seek help or file complaints through AI platforms after making a purchase have not been thoroughly explored.

6.4.3 Elasticities That Affect Consumer-AI Interactions

This section outlines the aspects that impact the efficiency of customer and AI interactions, organized according to the different stages of customer engagement. The initial two subsections primarily address the pre-purchase phase, which includes consumer activities such as identifying needs, conducting searches, and evaluating options (Lemon and Verhoef, 2016). Customer and AI interactions encompass the utilization of AI to suggest products to consumers and influence them to make purchases or develop loyalty toward a brand. The third component relates to the purchasing process and includes actions such as choosing, placing an order, and completing a transaction (Lemon and Verhoef, 2016). Interaction between AI and customer involve the use of AI to provide automated shopping assistance and enable voice-activated purchasing. The next two subsections of the study center on the post-purchase phase, which encompasses activities such as utilizing and consuming the purchased goods, engaging in post-purchase interactions, and making service inquiries (Lemon and Verhoef, 2016). The interactions between consumers and AI encompass AI providing services, collecting feedback, and implementing service recovery.

6.4.4 Factors That Impact the Persuasive Skills of Artificial Intelligence

To determine what influences AI's persuasive capabilities while making suggestions, the study looked at pre-purchase characteristics. Three primary categories were used to classify the factors.

6.4.4.1 Structure of the Persuasive Communication

The promotion of products can be effectively achieved through the use of suggestive guidance and communication strategies that focus on social aspects. Additionally, accurate information formats, financial portfolios, and funny scripts are useful in conveying the message about products (Longoni and Cian, 2022).

6.4.4.2 Structure for Displaying Artificial Intelligence Recommendation Systems

The success of AI recommenders in persuading individuals in different contexts is influenced by their physical appearance, gender, design of automated social presence, and level of cuteness, as demonstrated by studies conducted by Longoni et al. (2019) and Mariani et al. (2022).

6.4.4.3 Consumer Characteristics and Viewpoints Regarding Artificial Intelligence

Consumer characteristics include elements such as the consumer's product knowledge and their inclination toward seeking pleasure and satisfaction. Additionally, consumers consider apparent personalization, simplicity of use, improved usefulness, and wide accessibility among other aspects when assessing AI recommendation systems. According to Longoni and Cian (2019), customers tend to have higher trust in AI when it comes to evaluating practical elements rather than pleasant qualities. The user's text is straightforward and precise.

6.4.5 Factor Influences on Alternative AI-Based Promotion Methods

The literature has provided limited attention to the role of AI as an endorser and as a tool for in-store promotion. The involvement of AI influencers in breaches, such as making discriminatory statements, leads to a deterioration in the brand's reputation that they endorse (Choi et al., 2021). To mitigate the adverse effects, one can replace an AI influencer with a celebrity endorsement. AI functions as a promotional instrument within brick-and-mortar establishments, integrating AI-infused mixed reality and humanoid robots. The efficacy of this promotional strategy is impacted by various crucial factors, including the caliber of AI, as elucidated by Mariani et al. (2022). These in-store promotional strategies successfully fascinate a larger number of individuals to visit a business, participate in more transactions, and eventually, boost their spending.

6.5 Key Factors in the AI-Driven Retail Shopping Experience

AI can offer verbal and automated in-store shopping experiences during the buying process. The virtual buying process is impacted by the functionality and responsiveness of chatbots, as well as the consumer's personality. There has been limited study on the aspects influencing the automated offline purchasing experience. Research has clearly shown the advantages of AI-powered checkouts, such as improved assessments of store ambiance, buying inclination, shopping convenience, and willingness to become a return customer.

6.6 Factors Influencing the Interaction of AI Services

Service robots and chatbots serve as the primary interfaces between consumers and service providers during the post-purchase phase. The elements that influence AI-driven service interactions can be categorized into four distinct components.

6.6.1 Characteristics of AI-Driven Chatbots and Service Robots in Consumer Interaction

The aspects can be categorized into two distinct types: Visual attributes, encompassing anthropomorphic and robot-like displays, and engaging qualities, encompassing humanistic roles, interactivity, and engagement. The most extensively researched aspects of AI are its anthropomorphic characteristics, which encompass its look, capabilities, and linguistic style. Humanoid service robots lead to compensatory consumption, as demonstrated by Choi et al. (2021). According to Lemon and Verhoef (2016), the anthropomorphism of chatbots has a detrimental impact on customer happiness and corporate ratings, particularly among disgruntled customers.

6.6.2 Consumer Attributes

Attitudes, emotions, and behavioral inclinations toward chatbots and service robots are influenced by consumers' fundamental psychological demands (Mariani et al. (2022), technological anxiety for human interaction, and style of apprehensive attachment (Pillai et al., 2020).

6.6.3 How Customers View Chatbots and Service Robots

Customer perception elements can be categorized into two separate categories. The initial category focuses on the assessment of AI's skills and principles, including factors like self-awareness (Huang and Rust, 2021), user-friendliness (Lemon and Verhoef, 2016), and integration (Pillai et al., 2020). Secondly, the perception of consumers regarding the role of AI in their daily lives encompasses functions such as serving, befriending, commanding, entertaining, facilitating social interactions, and mentoring (Belanche et al., 2020). Consumer well-being and future usage might be influenced by perceived roles.

6.6.4 Environmental Aspects for Consideration

The deployment of chatbots and robots is associated with COVID-19 (Lemon and Verhoef, 2016), commercial attributes (Pillai et al., 2020), organizational dependability (Huang and Rust, 2021), and implications for society (Longoni and Cian, 2019).

6.7 Drivers Influencing AI Feedback Solicitation and Service Recovery Strategies

The responsibilities of service failure and subsequent recovery are critical in the context of post-core service interactions. It is essential to become proficient in effectively using AI to gather customer feedback and provide appropriate responses to achieve the desired service outcome. A study conducted by Pillai et al. (2020) investigated the efficacy of employing the humanistic design and foot-in-the-door technique to enhance user adherence to service feedback requests made by a chatbot.

The consumer's viewpoint highlights various factors contributing to AI service failures, such as concerns regarding functioning, challenges related to cognition, issues about emotions, problems with authenticity, and conflicts during integration (Huang and Rust, 2021). Belanche et al. (2020) found that consumers mainly attribute responsibility to the companies providing AI services for their behavior. There are two classifications of methods that can be employed to alleviate or avert the adverse outcomes of AI service failure. One specific domain of concentration pertains to the construction of chatbots and robotics. They may possess a visually appealing design, unique voice traits, and a certain typology of language (Pillai et al., 2020). The next component involves engaging with consumers in a proactive manner, which includes offering further information (Huang and Rust, 2021), issuing regret and justifications (e.g. Choi et al., 2021), and educating clients that their preference predictions are derived from their previous behavioral patterns (Longoni and Cian, 2019). As a result, there has been a shift toward prioritizing research on AI-driven product recommendations and service interactions. The existing literature lacks a comprehensive comprehension of the entire buying journey and the interdependence among its many phases.

6.8 Agenda for Future Research

This section provides a comprehensive and significant compilation of research inquiries to provide direction for future research endeavors. Lastly, we offer recommendations about research methodology. AI-driven interactions during the pre-purchase phase offer useful product insights that aid in making well-informed purchasing decisions. For instance, AI may guide the person in charge of product design or pricing decisions. AI design is a pioneering and creative method of fostering innovation. Lately, there has been a surge in the quantity of "AI architectures" that employ analytics to create unique artworks. This occurrence has sparked inquiries about the underlying nature of creativity and the significance of human ingenuity in influencing the future of civilization (Longoni and Cian, 2019). Subsequent inquiries may prioritize the examination of customers' perspectives on AI-generated items and the underlying data sources utilized by the AI design system. This study has the potential to enhance customers' impression of aesthetic or artistic value. Furthermore, AI is being employed for the deployment of dynamic pricing, and businesses have the option to determine whether the pricing is determined by AI. Additional investigation should examine the specific conditions under which AI pricing can have either beneficial or detrimental effects, and determine the most appropriate approach for applying price reductions. The use of AI influencer endorsement is presently a prevalent advertising strategy, notwithstanding a dearth of research on this matter. AI influencers exhibit a distinctive hyper-realistic appearance and provide exclusive advantages to companies, such as content administration. Nevertheless, a study conducted by Mariani et al. (2022) revealed that a mere 15% of virtual influencer followers perceived them as reliable. Additional investigation is required to determine the impact of distinctive attributes exhibited by AI influencers on the efficacy of endorsements, as well as the most efficient strategies for utilizing AI influencers in promotional activities. Multiple research has confirmed that customers' views and current beliefs about AI have a major impact on their preferences for AI touchpoints. Further inquiry could explore customers' viewpoints on AI in different engagement scenarios to ascertain the most suitable circumstances for using AI technologies. Gaining comprehension of the aspects that impact customers' unique perceptions of AI and implementing successful strategies to alter these impressions are crucial for expanding the usage of AI in various domains. Prior studies on the purchasing phase have predominantly concentrated on the integration of digital retailing systems and smart assistants as novel shopping channels. However, there is a lack of sufficient study undertaken in this sector. First and foremost, it is necessary to analyze the possible uses of AI in many areas of retail operations to improve customers' incentive to visit and better their entire shopping experience. Retail stores can strategically employ AI at several points of interaction. For instance, Kroger and other retailers utilize AI to offer personalized discounts and rates to specific customers while they are shopping in the store (Blanche et al. 2020).

Furthermore, there is a scarcity of research on the aspects that influence the voice purchasing experience. Voice buying revolutionizes the online purchasing experience by emphasizing voice communication and reducing reliance on visual elements such as images and written information. A comprehensive examination is required to distinguish voice purchasing from other forms of internet shopping and assess the consequent consequences. Furthermore, there is a lack of study on the implementation of AI in the field of logistics and distribution, specifically from the standpoint of customers. Logistics serves as the primary method by which clients acquire goods beyond traditional brick-and-mortar establishments. Additionally, it plays a crucial function in facilitating indirect communication between companies and customers. When assessing the deployment of intelligent delivery or self-driving pickup using smart devices, it is essential to examine the aspects that contribute to an enhanced customer experience and a positive brand perception. The current study on post-purchase phases mostly emphasizes mechanical and cognitive intelligence, neglecting the significance of emotional AI. AI can comprehend and respond to customer expectations and need recognition (Huang and Rust, 2021). A clear example of this phenomenon may be seen in the case of Aida, a digital assistant employed by a well-known Swedish bank, which can analyze the client's intonation and use this data to improve the quality of service offered (Belanche et al., 2020). Additional investigations could focus on studying the significant effects of sentimental behavior and replies from AI service providers on consumers, as well as the use of mechanical, cognitive, and affective AI in various service scenarios. To improve customer engagement and involvement in the realm of interactive marketing, it would be beneficial for future studies to explore the potential application of AI. Interactive marketing emphasizes the importance of engaging customer habits in creating and sharing value (Wang, 2021). Does the level of customer comfort in expressing their participation in innovation or delivering critique increase when the assessor or recipient is an AI? Furthermore, what certain demeanor or behavior is evoked through interactions with AI, and how does it impact subsequent consumption patterns? The AI's cognitive capacity is limited in comprehending intricate phrases, which can stimulate individuals to engage in profound contemplation. Conversely, disregarding the emotions of AI can lead individuals to behave impolitely. AI has emerged as a novel method for gathering customer complaints and addressing service issues post-purchase. Customer attitude possesses the capacity to exert influence. Additional investigations could analyze the determinants that impact consumers' selection of AI as a provider of post-purchase services. Regarding the connection between stages, our main emphasis lies on three fundamental concerns. One aspect entails the strategic placement of both AI and human personnel across the entirety of the client journey. Prior research has mostly concentrated on the progress of autonomous intelligent devices, disregarding the collaborative interactions between AI and people. Hence, further investigation could delve into the optimal approach for integrating

AI and employees to augment consumers' interactive experience. Moreover, it may assess the specific phases of the customer journey where they should engage with clients, either autonomously or in collaboration. The second aspect is the impact of AI when considered as a product owned by consumers, on its function as a recommender and a platform for commerce. The utilization of personal assistants for product searches and purchases may be impacted by the emotional bond and personal data that consumers have already created with them. Additional study has the potential to enhance the technique of suggestion and purchasing processes in AI platforms utilized by consumers. Additionally, it may assess the influence of these purchasing experiences on the relationship between humans and AI.

Thirdly, the expeditious integration of AI, commonly known as the metaverse, facilitates an all-encompassing retail encounter situated in a digital milieu. Hence, to develop a novel virtual realm for customer avatar interaction, it is imperative to cater to the consumers' requirements at each phase, necessitating consideration of several components. Technologically-driven immersive environments possess the ability to offer a diverse array of skills that are unattainable in the physical realm. Further investigation could delve into the significant influence of the metaverse on the retail sector and the exceptional relationships it facilitates.

When considering methodology, it is crucial to incorporate empirical data, analytical procedures, or a combination of several approaches. Prior research has predominantly utilized scenario-based experiments conducted in controlled laboratory or online environments, with only a few instances of investigations undertaken in real-world contexts. Hence, it is crucial to carry out ecologically precise field experiments. The interview data and internet information offered by consumers are additional sources that enhance our comprehensive comprehension of consumers' perceptions regarding AI interactions. Utilizing a combination of quantitative and qualitative methodologies, such as employing machine learning techniques, can enhance our comprehension to a greater extent.

Companies are just starting to explore the potential of AI in enhancing the consumer journey. With the ongoing development of AI models, organizations of all kinds need to utilize their capabilities to effectively address the ever-changing needs of today's consumers. By adopting the capabilities of AI, customer experience (CX) professionals can mitigate customer attrition, enhance customer experiences, and ultimately enhance business performance.

References

Belanche, D., Casaló, L. V., Flavián, C., & Schepers, J. (2020). Service robot implementation: A theoretical framework and research agenda. *The Service Industries Journal*, *40*(3–4), 203–225.

Chintalapati, S., & Pandey, S. K. (2022). Artificial intelligence in marketing: A systematic literature review. *International Journal of Market Research*, *64*(1), 38–68.

Choi, S., Mattila, A. S., & Bolton, L. E. (2021). To err is human (-oid): How do consumers react to robot service failure and recovery? *Journal of Service Research*, *24*(3), 354–371.

Huang, M. H., & Rust, R. T. (2021). A strategic framework for artificial intelligence in marketing. *Journal of the Academy of Marketing Science*, *49*, 30–50.

Lemon, K. N., & Verhoef, P. C. (2016). Understanding customer experience throughout the customer journey. *Journal of Marketing*, *80*(6), 69–96.

Longoni, C., Bonezzi, A., & Morewedge, C. K. (2019). Resistance to medical artificial intelligence. *Journal of Consumer Research*, *46*(4), 629–650.

Longoni, C., & Cian, L. (2022). Artificial intelligence in utilitarian vs. hedonic contexts: The 'Word-of-Machine' effect. *Journal of Marketing*, *86*(1), 91–108.

Mariani, M. M., Perez-Vega, R., & Wirtz, J. (2022). AI in marketing, consumer research and psychology: A systematic literature review and research agenda. *Psychology & Marketing*, *39*(4), 755–776.

Pillai, R., Sivathanu, B., & Dwivedi, Y. K. (2020). Shopping intention at AI-powered automated retail stores (AIPARS). *Journal of Retailing and Consumer Services*, *57*, 1–15.

Wang, C. L. (2021). New frontiers and future directions in interactive marketing: Inaugural editorial. *Journal of Research in Interactive Marketing*, *15*(1), 1–9.

Chapter 7

The Convergence of Generative AI and Ethical Consideration

Akhilesh Sunkara, Abbu Pravalika, and Purushottam Patnaik

7.1 Introduction

A state-of-the-art technological development, generative artificial intelligence (AI) offers remarkable capabilities for content creation, synthesis, and generation across a range of industries. The potential of generative AI systems to produce realistic images, music compositions, text, and video content, and even transform the way creativity is addressed in various industries has sparked a great deal of attention. However, generative AI poses a number of ethical challenges and barriers that require careful consideration in addition to its potential for profound paradigm shifts

The emergence of generative AI signifies a fundamental change in how we perceive and engage with technology. Unlike standard AI systems, which are mostly concerned with processing and analysing pre-existing data, generative AI may generate creative and original content on its own. Advanced machine learning methods, such as reinforcement learning and deep neural networks, allow algorithms to recognise patterns and produce results that mimic human intelligence and creativity.

The inherent conflict between accountability and novelty is at the centre of the ethical discourse around generative AI. One potential benefit of generative AI is its capacity to improve productivity, encourage creativity, and progress human understanding in a variety of fields, including

DOI: 10.4324/9781032711089-7

entertainment, education, and healthcare. However, the widespread adoption of this technology gives rise to worries about privacy, genuineness, bias, responsibility, and the impact on society. These problems need to be fixed in order to guarantee the technology's successful application and ethical advancement (Bahroun et al., 2023).

The diverse qualities of the underlying technology and applications are reflected in the intricate and interrelated ethical implications of generative AI. A crucial issue is the ethical use of data, which is the basis for the development and improvement of generative AI models. Concerns about proprietorship, consent, and privacy are raised by data scraping, which is the process of collecting and aggregating information from several sources. These concerns are especially raised when private or sensitive data is involved.

In addition, it is imperative that the security and integrity of the data used in generative AI model training be preserved. Incidents of data breaches or improper use of the data could cause serious harm and erode public confidence in AI systems. Ensuring that security measures are strictly followed and strong data control mechanisms are put in place are essential for protecting individual rights and reducing the likelihood of data exploitation and unauthorised access.

Beyond the data ethics issues, generative AI also creates issues with accountability and authenticity. Since AI systems can produce content that closely mimics human-made artefacts, the lines between reality and simulation are blurred, raising issues with provenance, authorship, and attribution. Additionally, the rapid spread of deepfakes and altered media highlights the necessity of putting in place mechanisms to ensure the authenticity of generated content is protected.

Moreover, impartiality procedures and bias reduction are essential components to be taken into account throughout the development and application of generative AI. Pre-existing social disparities may be maintained and made worse by biased training data and algorithms, which could have discriminatory effects and reinforce systemic biases. It is essential to take a proactive stance in order to address bias. To ensure fairness and equity, this calls for integrating datasets with a variety of representations, ensuring algorithmic openness, and conducting ongoing monitoring and evaluation of AI systems (Bandi et al., 2023).

The ethical development of AI and its governance are based on the fundamental concepts of accountability and transparency. All parties involved—developers, legislators, end users, and researchers—have a shared responsibility to provide transparency in decision-making procedures, data practices, and model structures. Good and transparent communication helps people become more self-assured, promotes diligent progress, and gives them the ability to make educated judgements about how they interact with AI technologies.

It is crucial to take into account the wider societal ramifications and ethical aspects of AI systems in addition to their technological capabilities and limits while debating the ethical complexities of generative AI. It is possible to successfully navigate the complex ethical issues related to generative AI and harness its potential for positive societal transformations by promoting interdisciplinary dialogue, encouraging collaboration across sectors, and adhering to ethical frameworks and guidelines.

This chapter explores the challenging ethical environment of generative AI. Data ethics, privacy, authenticity, prejudice reduction, fairness, openness, and social impact are discussed. We employ academic literature and ethical frameworks to define fundamental ethical challenges and propose answers that promote the moral development and useful deployment of generative AI technology. We aim to employ generative AI to inspire constructive change while respecting objectivity, responsibility, and respect for human worth. It will take thorough investigation and ethical thought.

7.2 Data Scraping and Control

Web scraping, also known as data harvesting, involves automated data gathering from online sources and webpages. It's crucial for training generative AI models since it allows developers to retrieve massive amounts of varied data for model learning and synthesis. However, data mining raises ethical issues related to permission, privacy, and data management.

7.2.1 Data Scraping: Ethical Considerations

7.2.1.1 Liability and Authorisation

Consent is a significant ethical concern that is prominently associated with data harvesting. The process of data scraping from websites may encompass the retrieval of information from publicly accessible sources, in addition to platforms from which users have not provided explicit consent for the gathering and utilisation of their data. This gives rise to inquiries regarding the ethical ramifications associated with the collection of data without the awareness or consent of the individuals whose information is being gathered.

7.2.1.2 Privacy and Ownership of Data

Data harvesting frequently entails the acquisition of personally identifiable information (e.g., names, contact information, and browsing patterns) from databases and online platforms. Although certain information may be available to the public, the act of collecting sensitive or personally identifiable data without explicit consent constitutes a violation of the privacy rights of individuals. Furthermore, the issue of ownership and control regarding collected data becomes murkier, particularly when said data is consolidated, examined, and repurposed for commercial or scholarly objectives.

7.2.1.3 The Concepts of Fair Use and Copyright

Copyright and intellectual property (IP) regulations are another ethical issue in data mining. The terms of service of many websites and online platforms restrict data access and usage and prohibit automated data mining. A violation of these rules may result in copyright infringement, fair use concerns, IP infringement, and unauthorised access to proprietary information.

7.2.2 Data Scraping and Its Ethical Implications: A Case Study

A recent examination of the ethical ramifications of data mining for AI applications was undertaken by Solum (2024). Research has shown the prevalence and concerns of this practice. The researchers examined 100 websites from various businesses to evaluate if they enforced data access and use terms of service and if data scraping was common.

According to the report, data mining methods on many digital platforms were sophisticated. Interestingly, 70% of the sample websites had terms of service or user agreements that prohibited automated data collection. In only 30% of websites, CAPTCHA challenges or rate limitations were used to dissuade scraper activity, showing a lack of enforcement.

Data harvesting in news websites, social media platforms, and e-commerce sites raises ethical concerns. The research raises ethical concerns about unlawful data collection violating privacy rights.

Due to the possibility of data mining extracting copyrighted material or proprietary data, the research also raised concerns about IP and copyright violations. These behaviours have legal consequences and damage digital trust.

Data gathering should be more open, responsible, and ethical, according to the research. Data harvesting companies should be transparent about their data collection methods, alert users of the data being collected, and provide clear opt-out mechanisms to address privacy concerns.

Compliance with website and online platform terms of service and user agreements is essential for ethical data gathering. In the digital age, ethical review, data minimisation, and anonymization techniques can reduce data harvesting risks while upholding integrity, openness, and user rights.

The case study highlights the complex ethical issues surrounding data collecting and the necessity of responsible data practices in establishing responsibility, integrity, and trust in generative AI technology development and implementation.

7.3 Privacy and Security of Data

Generative AI data must be kept confidential and secure to safeguard rights and maintain confidence in AI systems. Often, generative AI algorithms must be trained on large datasets that may contain sensitive material. Thus, throughout the data lifecycle, robust privacy and security measures must be adopted to limit risks and prevent breaches or misuse.

7.3.1 Privacy Issues Regarding Generative AI

As the acquisition, retention, and application of large datasets raise ethical issues, privacy problems significantly impact generative AI. Data collection methods and consent are key areas of concern. Databases, social media, and websites provide large datasets for generative AI models. When personal data is collected, it raises privacy problems, especially if users have not given explicit consent. Ethics, such as informed permission and data gathering transparency, are essential to addressing these issues (Alwahedi et al., 2024).

Additionally, data anonymization and de-identification processes create significant issues in balancing privacy and data value. Despite efforts to anonymize or de-identify data, protecting privacy remains a difficulty. Diverse privacy and federated learning can ensure privacy in massive data environments while balancing data utility and model performance.

Collaboration and interchange of sensitive information between organisations presents ethical and legal issues related to data ownership, IP rights, and confidentiality. We must design secure data exchange protocols and clear data-sharing agreements to protect stakeholders and limit the hazards of joint research and data sharing.

In conclusion, openness, consent-taking, anonymization, and secure data management are needed to address privacy challenges in generative AI. Implementing industry standards, regulatory duties, and ethical principles can help organisations handle privacy problems and preserve individuals' data and privacy throughout generative AI technology development and implementation.

7.3.2 Security Considerations in Generative AI

Security affects data integrity, availability, and confidentiality in generative AI systems. To prevent data breaches, sensitive data must be encrypted during transmission and storage. Data is encrypted in transit and at rest using end-to-end and homomorphic approaches. Strong access controls and role-based authorisation processes allow authorised individuals to access sensitive data, reducing the risk of data disclosure and unlawful manipulation.

Security threats and abnormalities must be monitored proactively to discover and prevent breaches in real time. Through intrusion detection systems, security information and event management (SIEM) solutions, and automated threat response mechanisms, organisations may quickly identify and respond to security problems. Incident response methods and continuous security assessments can strengthen organisations' cyber and data security.

Regulation and ethics are essential for protecting generative AI systems. Industry standards and best practices in data management promote integrity, accountability, and confidence. Adherence to data protection regulations like the California Consumer Privacy Act (CCPA), the General Data Protection Regulation (GDPR), and the Health Insurance Portability and Accountability Act (HIPAA) reduces legal liabilities and shows a commitment to privacy and data security.

This plan must integrate cryptocurrencies, access control, threat detection, incident response, and regulatory compliance to solve generative AI security problems. Organisations may reduce risks and protect data in generative AI systems by following ethical norms, deploying strong security measures, and vigilantly monitoring emerging threats and vulnerabilities.

7.3.3 *Ethical and Regulatory Compliance in AI*

Developing and deploying generative AI systems that violate ethical and legal standards undermines responsible innovation and individual rights. Following ethical principles and industry standards helps organisations resolve complicated ethical issues and foster trust, accountability, and transparency in generative AI technology. By using ethical frameworks like the Fair Information Practices (FIPs) and the Principles for Responsible AI, organisations can ensure ethical data use in AI applications.

Additionally, full compliance with data protection rules and regulations is crucial to prevent legal penalties, preserve personal rights, and secure data. The GDPR, CCPA, and HIPAA are among the tough regulations that apply to organisations that manage personal data. Strong data protection policies must be established and implemented, informed consent must be obtained, and individuals must have control over their data to comply with these rules.

Beyond data security, ethical and legal compliance in AI decision-making procedures entails many issues. Issues include justice, openness, and accountability. By treating all communities and individuals equally, fairness-aware algorithms and bias mitigation methods eliminate algorithmic discrimination and bias. Transparent AI systems build trust and allow consumers to make informed judgements about AI technology. It requires comprehensive explanations of decision-making and AI model behaviour.

Organisations must build ethical review and governance mechanisms to ensure compliance with ethical norms and legal duties and analyse the ethical implications of their AI systems. A strong ethical governance framework must include ethical review committees, interdisciplinary cooperation, and stakeholder involvement to identify and address ethical issues throughout the lifecycle of AI.

Generative AI must actively follow ethical, regulatory, and industry standards. Organisations may promote responsible innovation, decrease risks, and build trust by prioritising ethics, transparency, accountability, and regulatory compliance when developing and implementing generative AI technology.

7.4 Data Control Mechanisms

For the ethical management and utilisation of data utilised by generative AI systems, it is vital that data control mechanisms be implemented. These mechanisms comprise technologies, policies, and processes that are purposefully designed to regulate the acquisition, storage, retrieval, and application of data throughout its entire lifecycle. By implementing efficient data control mechanisms, organisations can successfully mitigate risks, ensure compliance with legal and regulatory obligations, and maintain principles of privacy, security, and transparency.

For ethical data management, generative AI systems need data control methods. Throughout their lifetime, these systems manage data gathering, storage, retrieval, and use with many regulations, processes, and technical safeguards. Clear guidelines for data collecting sources, classifications, and permission procedures are the main purpose of data acquisition policies. Adhering to clear acquisition procedures ensures legal and ethical data acquisition while respecting confidentiality and permission. After that, data storage and retention policies set boundaries for data security, management, and retention. These policies describe the storage infrastructure and data retention. Storage and retention rules reduce data breaches and unauthorised access while meeting regulatory requirements. Access controls significantly affect data access oversight. These mechanisms ensure access limitations match user obligations and tasks using user identification, authorisation, and privilege management. Granular access restrictions preserve data privacy and security by prohibiting unauthorised access. In summary, data protection techniques include encryption and anonymization, which protect identity during transmission and storage. With these data control techniques, businesses may ensure ethical data management in generative AI systems and reduce risks.

7.5 Analysis

Generative AI data management requires ethical and operational concerns that require efficient data management systems. Policies, processes, and technical safeguards are crucial to preserving privacy rights, boosting security, assuring compliance, and limiting the risks of unauthorised access and data exploitation. These procedures protect privacy by ensuring that personal data is collected, stored, and processed in accordance with privacy laws and ethics. Through data minimisation and anonymization, organisations can gain insights from data while protecting privacy (Heller et al., 2023). Encryption and access control techniques prevent unauthorised access to sensitive data and reduce the risk of data breaches and incursions. By restricting access to permitted individuals and encrypting data at rest and in transit, organisations can reduce data breaches and protect sensitive data. These measures support data protection, privacy, and security compliance with legal and regulatory requirements. Organisations can demonstrate their commitment to ethical data management and limit the chance of violating laws and regulations by implementing specific policies, procedures, and technical controls (Rane, 2023). Unauthorised access, data loss, and misuse are reduced by effective data control methods. Strong data governance frameworks and risk management techniques may protect data integrity, confidentiality, and availability throughout its lifecycle by proactively identifying and alleviating risks. Ethical data management techniques in generative AI systems require data control mechanisms. Implementing strict policies, procedures, and technical controls can help organisations harness the transformative potential of generative AI technologies while mitigating risks, protecting privacy, and complying with legal and regulatory requirements.

7.6 Authenticity and Accountability

Authenticity and accountability underpin the ethical framework for generative AI content development and delivery. Given the expanding potential of generative AI systems to generate realistic pictures, text, and multimedia, open accountability procedures and authenticity are needed to counteract misinformation, deepfakes, and manipulated media.

7.6.1 Authenticity

Generative AI information is authentic because of its integrity and reliability. Authorship and authenticity are threatened by the confluence of generative AI systems with reality and simulation. These systems' ability to create lifelike information raises questions about artefact provenance, authenticity, and origin. Ensure that AI-generated material accurately portrays reality and can be distinguished from fakes.

To verify the validity of AI-generated content, resilient techniques must be developed and implemented. Content source verification using watermarking, digital signatures, and cryptographic hashes provides confidence in its authenticity and soundness. Disclosure of AI algorithms and datasets used in content creation can also boost its legitimacy.

7.6.2 Accountability

Entities and individuals developing, implementing, and using generative AI systems are ethically and legally accountable. Accountability systems are needed to reduce inaccuracy, partiality, and manipulation risks from AI-generated material in media, art, and entertainment. Transparent accountability systems for generative AI technology help implement and maintain ethical principles, risk minimisation, and transparency.

Accountability is taking responsibility for our actions throughout the lifespan of AI-generated material. This includes developing and teaching AI models, verifying and evaluating material, and distributing and influencing AI-generated artefacts. Developers, researchers, content creators, and platform providers must limit the risks of harm or misuse of generative AI technologies and ensure their ethical use.

To promote accountability in generative AI, organisations must be open, follow ethical and legal guidelines, and provide monitoring and governance. This may involve ethical review panels, data protection laws, and responsible AI policies. A culture of accountability and responsibility helps stakeholders reduce risks, retain confidence, and promote the ethical use of generative AI technology.

7.6.3 Analysis

Generative AI challenges content integrity and responsibility. The broad distribution of deepfakes and altered media shows how easily digital information can be changed. Trust and credibility in digital media contexts are damaged when it becomes difficult to distinguish legitimate and altered material without strong authentication mechanisms.

Generative AI's democratisation of content generation heightens accountability and responsibility concerns. Unlike normal content production procedures that hold human writers accountable, generative AI blurs authorship, attribution, ownership, and culpability. To address the legal and ethical consequences of AI-generated content, transparent accountability frameworks and attribution procedures must be established, in addition to holding producers, users, and stakeholders accountable.

Tech innovation and interdisciplinary collaboration are also needed to protect generative AI. Blockchain technology, for instance, may establish digital asset provenance and integrity by enabling transparent and tamper-proof content production and distribution records. Digital watermarking, forensic analysis, and metadata attribution allow consumers and content providers to validate and trace AI-generated content, providing legitimacy and responsibility to digital ecosystems.

When responsibly building and implementing generative AI technology, accountability and authenticity are crucial. Through openness, integrity, and responsibility, stakeholders can build trust, credibility, and ethical standards in the digital era by preventing misinformation, manipulation, and bias. Ethical frameworks, technological innovation, interdisciplinary collaboration, and authenticity can enable us to use generative AI's transformative possibilities while upholding ethical integrity, accountability, and authenticity.

7.7 Bias Mitigation

Generated AI systems must mitigate bias to ensure fairness. Cultural, ethnic, social, gender, and ethnic prejudices might be purposeful or inadvertent. This can lead to misrepresentations and discrimination. Generators may experience anomalies due to skewed training data, biased algorithmic design decisions, or inherent human biases during data collecting. Prejudice must be addressed holistically, provided bias-aware algorithms, selecting representative and varied data, lobbying for algorithmic openness, and adhering to ethical standards.

Selecting varied and representative data is crucial to reducing prejudice. Diversity in demographics, traits, and life experiences is essential for training datasets to avoid underrepresentation or marginalisation. In addition, bias-aware algorithms can detect, quantify, and mitigate AI model biases. Adversarial training and fairness constraints can pinpoint and correct biases, encouraging more equitable outcomes across varied groups.

Bias in generative AI systems must be addressed through transparency and explicit explanation. Increasing transparency helps stakeholders understand the decision-making process and identify prejudice. Reasoning generation and model interpretability allow users to check AI models for bias, promoting ethics and confidence. The ethical implementation and evolution of AI strengthen equity, openness, and accountability.

Despite bias mitigation advances, generative AI bias must be overcome. Maintaining varied and representative training data can be difficult in fields with low data or past biases. Continuous monitoring and compromise evaluation of AI systems over their lifespan are needed to maintain precision, efficacy, and equity.

To ensure accountability, openness, and fairness in generative AI systems, prejudice must be reduced. Organisations may promote fairness in AI systems and reduce prejudice by using bias-aware algorithms, varied and representative data, openness, and explainability, and ethical rules. To build trust, ensure fairness, and use generative AI's ground-breaking powers to improve society, bias must be mitigated.

7.8 Fairness Practices

To overcome biases and inequities in AI-generated content and decision-making, generative AI must use fairness techniques. In generative AI, fairness includes social justice, equity, and ethical accountability, not just statistical parity. Fairness techniques minimise preconceptions and ensure unbiased treatment for different demographic groups, promoting inclusivity, diversity, and openness in AI systems.

Guaranteeing fair representation in AI-generated material is a major barrier to equity practices. Underrepresented or underprivileged groups must be recognised and included in training data diversity. To ensure equitable representation, data collecting and pre-processing methods must be carefully examined, as well as dataset biases. To increase equitable representation, socioeconomic status, cultural heritage, and linguistic pluralism should be considered.

Generative AI systems need algorithmic fairness to promote fairness policies. Algorithmic fairness involves designing, developing, and evaluating AI systems to avoid bias and discrimination. Fairness measurements, limitations, and mitigation measures help fairness-aware algorithms reduce biases and improve outcomes. Algorithmic impartiality requires continual monitoring and evaluation of algorithmic performance and a deep understanding of social and ethical issues (Stahl & Eke, 2024).

Bias prevention is essential for egalitarian generative AI implementation. Biases in training data, algorithmic design, and decision-making must be identified and corrected to ensure fairness. In order to make AI systems more inclusive and equitable, adversarial training, bias correction, and fairness constraints are used. Furthermore, businesses must incorporate bias detection and mitigation measures into every level of the AI development process.

Ethical generative AI requires accountability and openness. Transparent AI systems allow stakeholders to understand the decision-making process, identify bias areas, and hold developers and organisations accountable for AI results. The ethical considerations, decision-making processes, and social impacts of AI algorithms are included in transparency. Ethics review committees, governance structures, and compliance procedures hold businesses and AI developers accountable for their AI systems' ethical consequences.

Generated AI systems need fairness practices to promote inclusion, transparency, and fairness. Institutions can build confidence, reduce vulnerabilities, and use AI revolutionary powers to improve society by admitting and correcting biases, ensuring equal representation, and lobbying for algorithmic equity. Fairness techniques should be used throughout the AI development lifecycle, from data collecting and model training to deployment and evaluation, to ensure equity, social responsibility, and fairness.

7.9 Transparency in Data Usage

Generative AI systems must be transparent about data use to be accountable, trustworthy, and ethical. This involves giving relevant stakeholders complete and transparent information about data collection, processing, and use in AI models and algorithms. By using data transparently, people can understand the goals of data processing, the pros and cons, and how to control their personal data.

AI training and development companies must disclose their data sources and methods. This requires detailing the data sources, methods, and characteristics (including demographic, behavioural, and preferences data)

Disclosure of AI system data storage, processing, and administration is required to ensure data transparency. Data storage infrastructure, security procedures, processing methods, and retention policies are included. Users may see how AI systems secure and manage their data through transparent data processing.

Data utilisation helps businesses convey their goal for implementing data in AI systems. This requires specifying data uses including training models, algorithmic optimisation, and tailored suggestions. By ensuring data usage transparency, users may make educated decisions about disclosing their private data and using AI-driven apps.

To enhance data usage transparency, consumers must be able to access, view, and manage their personal data. They must enable data transfer, deletion, and access and provide clear instructions on how to apply the rights. Through data access and control transparency, consumers can manage their privacy preferences and personal information.

If a social media site uses generative AI algorithms to customise consumers' news feeds, data transparency is crucial. The platform can explain how it uses users' personal data to promote content, improve user interaction, and improve user experiences by using transparent data usage methods. Through credibility and trust, openness in data use builds consumer trust and eases data privacy and security concerns.

To foster accountability, trust, and ethics, generative AI systems must be transparent about data use. Companies can provide comprehensive and transparent information about data collection, processing, purpose, controls, and input mechanisms to empower users to make informed decisions about disclosing personal information and using AI-powered apps. Transparency in data utilisation builds consumer trust and promotes ethical and conscientious AI technology development.

7.10 Perceptions of Technology

Perceptions of technology comprise the convictions, attitudes, and comprehensions that both individuals and societies maintain with respect to the function, consequences, and ramifications of technology in their daily existence. These perceptions influence the ways in which communities and individuals engage with and react to AI-driven advancements, including their stances on AI-generated content, apprehensions regarding privacy and security, and anticipations concerning the ethical and responsible development and implementation of AI.

It is imperative to comprehend public perceptions of technology in order to cultivate confidence, encourage well-informed choices, and tackle societal issues associated with generative AI. A multitude of determinants impact these perceptions, encompassing cultural conventions, socioeconomic status, levels of education, and individual encounters with technology. Furthermore, public attitudes towards AI-driven innovations and perceptions of technology are substantially influenced by institutional narratives, media portrayals, and public discourse.

Technology perspectives change with social discussions, AI system experiences, and technological advances. Positive experiences with AI-powered applications like virtual assistants, recommendation systems, and creative tools can boost user confidence and adoption of AI technologies. Data breaches, algorithmic biases, and misinformation campaigns might damage AI-powered technologies' credibility.

Stakeholder engagement, clear communication about the functionality, limits, and ethical implications of AI technologies, and public education are needed to change public perceptions of technology. Policymakers and organisations must prioritise efforts to reconcile public perceptions and technology reality to better understand AI-driven advances.

Since different demographic cohorts may have different views and experiences with AI systems, inclusion and diversity are important for understanding how technology is viewed. Involving vulnerable groups, underrepresented communities, and marginalised communities in AI technology development and deployment ensures their perspectives and challenges are addressed.

Technology perceptions strongly impact public attitudes, behaviours, and policy decisions around generative AI. Supporters may use AI's transformative possibilities to improve society by building confidence, addressing apprehensions, emphasising inclusive and ethical AI development practices, and supporting transparency and public discourse. Recognising and resolving technology misconceptions is essential to building an egalitarian, inclusive, and accountable AI-driven future.

7.11 Suggested Ethical Framework

The ethical framework for generative AI promotes the responsible development, deployment, and use of AI-powered technology. This paradigm aims to address ethical issues, reduce risks, and improve society using generative AI. The framework provides a comprehensive and flexible framework for ethical AI research and implementation by embracing ethical theories, legal norms, and stakeholder perspectives.

7.11.1 Fundamental Elements of the Ethical Framework

The generative AI ethical framework promotes responsible development, implementation, and application of AI-driven technologies. In order to protect human dignity, autonomy, and well-being, the framework prioritises human-centric design. These guidelines highlight the importance of aligning AI systems with social norms, values, and ethics. Additionally, accountability and transparency promote open communication, disclosure, and responsibility to build trust and accountability among stakeholders and users. Fairness, justice, and inclusive design principles and algorithms are essential to preventing prejudice, discriminatory treatment, and bias. Data protection and privacy stress the need for strong data protection mechanisms, informed permission, data reduction, and user control. These elements protect personal privacy and information. To responsibly progress and integrate AI, accountability and governance frameworks must support transparent lines of duty, ethical evaluation methodologies, and oversight systems. Through risk assessment and testing processes, AI systems are prioritised for dependability, safety, and resilience in practical contexts. Ethical use and effect assessment help examine ethical, social, and environmental impacts throughout the AI development process. With this strategy, organisations may secure positive societal results and avoid AI deployment risks and damage.

7.11.2 *Implementation and Adoption*

Cooperation, coordination, and commitment from politicians, scholars, corporate executives, and civil society organisations are needed to apply the ethical framework. Organisations should incorporate ethical issues into their AI development processes, follow ethical standards, and actively discuss and reflect on ethical issues.

Given the ever-changing technological, social, and legal surroundings, the ethical framework must be stable and flexible. Monitoring, evaluating, and revising ethical practices and norms is essential to foster ethical innovation in AI, address growing ethical issues, and reduce new hazards.

A foundational ethical paradigm for generative AI fosters responsible development, implementation, and use. By integrating human-centric design, ethical impact assessment, transparency, fairness, privacy, accountability, and safety, organisations can use AI technology to improve society, decrease legal liabilities, and boost public trust. Generative AI is making rapid progress in ethical innovation, integrity, and accountability by incorporating ethical concepts into its principles.

7.12 Conclusion

In conclusion, generative AI ethics are complicated and ever-changing, with challenges and conscientious innovation possibilities. The chapter on generative AI ethics has examined ethics, decision-making, and frameworks.

Due to ethical, privacy, and security concerns with data harvest and control, human rights, autonomy, and dignity must be preserved online. AI-generated material must be trustworthy to establish trust, transparency, and accountability.

Inequality, bias, and prejudice in AI are addressed by fairness and bias reduction programmes. AI fairness, inclusiveness, and equity reduce risks, increase trust, and promote social justice.

User confidence, public opinion, and AI-powered technology adoption depend on data usage transparency and technological preconceptions. Technology and social expectations can be linked through business talks, openness, and stakeholder involvement to promote AI research and implementation accountability.

For generative AI ethics, human-centric design, transparency, justice, privacy, responsibility, safety, and ethical effect evaluation are the cornerstone. Ethics may boost stakeholders' confidence, promote inclusivity, and harness AI's revolutionary potential to better society.

Generative AI ethics assists humans and upholds ethical standards in an AI-influenced society through common ethical principles, diligent implementation, and ongoing discourse. Remember to be alert, reflective, and collaborative as we pursue ethical generative AI.

References

Alwahedi, F., Aldhaheri, A., Ferrag, M. A., Battah, A., & Tihanyi, N. (2024). Machine Learning Techniques for IoT Security: Current Research and Future Vision With Generative AI and Large Language Models. *Internet of Things and Cyber-Physical Systems*, *4*, 167–185.

Bahroun, Z., Anane, C., Ahmed, V., & Zacca, A. (2023). Transforming Education: A Comprehensive Review of Generative Artificial Intelligence in Educational Settings Through Bibliometric and Content Analysis. *Sustainability*, *15*(17), 12983.

Bale, A. S., Dhumale, R. B., Beri, N., Lourens, M., Varma, R. A., Kumar, V., Sanamdikar, S., & Savadatti, M. B. (2024). The Impact of Generative Content on Individuals Privacy and Ethical Concerns. *International Journal of Intelligent Systems and Applications in Engineering*, *12*(1s), 697–703.

Bandi, A., Adapa, P. V. S. R., & Kuchi, Y. E. V. P. K. (2023). *The* Power of Generative AI: A Review of Requirements, Models, Input–Output Formats, Evaluation Metrics, and Challenges. *Future Internet*, *15*(8), 260.

Budhwar, P., Chowdhury, S., Wood, G., Aguinis, H., Bamber, G. J., Beltran, J. R., Boselie, P., Cooke, F. L., Decker, S., DeNisi, A., Dey, P. K., Guest, D., Knoblich, A. J., Malik, A., Paauwe, J., Papagiannidis, S., Patel, C., Pereira, V., Ren, S., & Rogelberg, S. (2023). Human Resource Management in the Age of Generative Artificial Intelligence: Perspectives and Research Directions on ChatGPT. *Human Resource Management Journal*, *33*(3), 606–659.

Heller, B., Amir, A., Waxman, R., & Maaravi, Y. (2023). Hack Your Organizational Innovation: Literature Review and Integrative Model for Running Hackathons. *Journal of Innovation and Entrepreneurship, 12*(1), 6.

Rane, R. P., Patil, B. M., Varande, S. P., Patil, P. M., Patil, V. M., Barve, K. A., ... & Patil, V. R. (2023). Enhancement of Recovered Graphite's Electrochemical Performance During LIB Recycling to Promote Circular Sustainable Development. *Sustainable Materials and Technologies, 36*, e00613.

Solum, L. B. (2024). Flourishing, *Virtue, and the Common Good. Harvard Journal of Law and Public Policy, 46,* 1149.

Stahl, B. C., & Eke, D. (2024). The Ethics of ChatGPT – Exploring the Ethical Issues of an Emerging Technology. *International Journal of Information Management, 74*(74), 102700.

Chapter 8

Navigating the Ethical Landscape of Simulated Intelligence

Akoparna Barman, Kamalraj R., and Mir Aadil

8.1 Introduction

In the early 20th century, artificial intelligence (AI) was first proposed by Warren McCulloch, Walter Pits, and Allen Newell in 1943. However, it was not until the 1950s that the Turing Test was created, based on Alan Turing's publication on computer programming and intelligence. This was followed by the creation of the "First AI Program" five years later [1]. AI has had a significant impact on the digital world and is now being used in many industries, such as banking, medical, and education, due to its ability to reduce manpower, accuracy, and efficiency. It has also had a major impact on our lives, with AI-tools such as ChatGPT and Bard being used daily for a variety of purposes, such as research questions, food recipes, and problem solving. However, with the increase in utilization, AI keeps raising a few questions again and again: "Are the answers given by AI-tools correct?", "Can the answers be biased?", "Can AI-tools be discriminant?", "Are AI-tools safe to be used?", "Do AI-tools keep our data safe?", and finally the biggest question is, "Will we lose out jobs to AI?". This study focuses on analyzing these questions. It specifically focuses on looking into the ethical implications that might be caused by the increasing utilization of AI in our daily lives. Simulated intelligence models procure their information subsequent to being prepared broadly utilizing datasets whose information

DOI: 10.4324/9781032711089-8

can be from a different scope of sources, and the dataset is partitioned into preparing and testing information and is utilized to prepare and test the exactness of the created model. In any case, on occasion, the information used to prepare the model could contain one-sided esteem, leading the model to give responses that may be segregated based on race, orientation, age, sexual orientation, strictness, handicap, financial, and so forth Identity [2]. In recent years, there have been reports where individuals have blamed a few AI devices for being racially biased toward them. In July 2023 in a report by NBC News, it was expressed that organizations have been approached to confirmation fair nature of their man-made intelligence employing tools [3]. The foremost example of the abovementioned issue would be "Tay", an AI-chatbot launched by Microsoft Corp. on Twitter on March 23, 2016. However it had to be taken down within 16 hours due to highly inflammatory and offensive tweets through its Twitter account. Although it started off with answering questions in a safe manner, it changed soon when it started "mimicking the deliberately offensive behavior of other Twitter users", according to AI researcher Roman Yampolskiy [4]. Although it lasted for a very short duration, Tay gave a lot to learn from and was succeeded by "Zo".

8.2 Literature Study

Zhiping Wang et al. [5] in their exploration raised worries regarding the security and protection of the information that clients share with these clever frameworks. Questions have likewise been raised in regards to keeping up with command over these AI-based frameworks. The review proposes an expanded management of AI. Despite the fact that science and innovation are for the improvement of humans, a snapshot of indiscretion can prompt calamity. So the development of moral framework must be reinforced. Through the review, one more significant obligation was added for the researchers fostering the computer-based intelligence frameworks they need to investigate the moral as well as the ethical issues of the AI frameworks. They proposed executing moral guidelines for AI-based frameworks to agree to. The paper likewise proposes executing an administration-based preparation project to make AI open for individuals in distant regions who aren't sufficiently special to have proactively utilized it. It is recommended to incorporate normal individuals who are typically customers of AI to be remembered for the oversight of AI process.

The paper presents the requirement for AI-based frameworks to have a superior oversight and for the clients to have more profound information on that. Changwu Huang et al. [6] in their exploration examined moral issues and dangers that could emerge from the utilization of AI-based frameworks in our regular routines. The study likewise examines various conceivable answers for the moral issues, for example, structure, standard, and moral rules, which could give an answer for utilizing simulated intelligence morally. The review raises worries regarding different moral issues while utilizing AI-based frameworks, including an absence of straightforwardness, protection, responsibility, inclination and segregation, wellbeing and security issues, the potential for criminal and noxious use, etc., have been recognized from the applications and studies. This study dives into AI's moral angles, ordering worries into key areas. AI highlights present straightforwardness and information security challenges, while human elements present responsibility issues. Laying out complete and unprejudiced moral principles for AI and instructing people on common liberties regulations are significant stages. Socially, AI influences work relocation and access imbalance, justifying proactive measures. Moral difficulties come from algorithmic working and human weaknesses in AI associations, underscoring straightforwardness and dependable information use. Guaranteeing reasonableness, straightforwardness, and responsibility in AI tasks is imperative for building public trust and relieving moral worries. Chian-Hsueng Chao [7] in their study dives into moral conundrums concerning man-made reasoning (AI). Isaac Asimov's three laws of mechanical technology are presented as a fundamental moral code for robots, underlining the prioritization of human security and prosperity. The English scholar Philippa Foot's streetcar issue is examined, advancing into different renditions, displaying moral predicaments and dynamic situations. Microsoft's six standards of AI improvement, focusing on straightforwardness, viability, protection, obligation, and bias avoidance, are introduced to direct moral AI organization. The paper additionally investigates complex moral issues, for example, independent weapons and computer-based intelligence making AI. Furthermore, it talks about the arrangement of independent driving vehicles and the fluctuating levels of driving robotization, featuring the advancing liability structures and lawful ramifications. The review examines the interplay between top-down and bottom-up ethical approaches in AI algorithms, with the goal of aligning AI behavior with human moral judgments. The paper also presents the idea of moral connections and examines inconsistencies between lawful use, sensible use, anticipated use, and genuine utilization of AI, underlining the requirement for steady and mindful AI organization lined up with cultural advantage and legitimate systems. Reza Arkan Partadiredja et al. [8] led an assessment to investigate the trouble of separating between computer-based intelligence created and human media content. Roused by the Turing Test, the trial included members speculating whether the showed content was made by computer-based intelligence or a human. The concentrate cautiously organized an assortment of pictures and texts from computer-based intelligence created and human sources. The outcomes showed that individuals attempted to recognize computer-based intelligence produced and human-made content, highlighting the test in distinguishing them. The investigation dove into the socio-moral ramifications of this trouble, accentuating the ascent of deepfakes and the requirement for devices to distinguish and relieve their possible unsafe effects. The timetable of important mechanical deliveries and public reactions from 2017 to 2020 was introduced to contextualize the conversation on AI produced media's cultural effect. The review featured the consistent headways in AI produced media advancements and the need to address related moral worries.

Dena F. Mujtaba et al. [9] directed a concentrate on predisposition in AI-based job recruitment, planning to comprehend the enrollment cycle and distinguish expected inclinations to assist businesses with carrying out strategies to moderate them. The enlistment cycle comprises of a few phases, beginning with distinguishing and drawing in up-and-comers, trailed by competitor screening and handling, and closing with correspondence and choice of competitors. AI is progressively coordinated into these stages, however predispositions in the information used to prepare AI models can prompt invalid rankings and likely adverse consequences on associations. The review talked about strategies for alleviating predisposition at each phase of the enrollment interaction. These techniques fall into three classifications: Pre-handling, in-handling/advancement, and post-handling/counterfactuals. Different apparatuses and tool compartments were likewise featured to help designers in implanting decency calculations in their AI pipelines, including AIF360, FairML, FairTest, InterpretML, Lime, Clear, SHAP, and Themis-ML. The review distinguished key restrictions and future difficulties in fair computer-based intelligence based enrollment, including apparatus assessment and determination, work explicit necessities, decency in work postings, and recruiting choice straightforwardness. Tending to these difficulties is vital for advancing decency and decreasing predispositions in the enlistment cycle.

8.3 Survey Insights

During my study, I saw a striking theme. Obviously, a greater part of the respondents had some awareness of the general purposes and uses of computer-based intelligence. Notwithstanding, what I saw was that while the vast majority of them had some awareness of computer-based intelligence's capacities, countless of them had close to zero insight into the chance of predisposition inside the AI calculations, as seen in Figure 8.1. This uncovered a gap in how they might interpret the moral ramifications of AI. It was a wellspring of concern and disquiet. Security was a top worry for respondents, mirroring the stresses individuals have over how their own information is being utilized by computer-based intelligence frameworks. Information assortment and use by AI innovations have turned into a central issue, featuring the requirement for solid security insurances and guidelines. Besides, an overarching stress among the study members was the effect of computer-based intelligence on business and occupation removal. The anxiety toward conventional work jobs being computerized and supplanted by AI-controlled arrangements was tangible. This dread enhances the significance of tending to the cultural ramifications of AI-driven computerization and highlights the need for an insightful and comprehensive way to deal with the progression of innovation. A remarkable agreement among the respondents was the faith in the need of administrative compliances for computer-based intelligence. Numerous members focused on the requirement for clear rules and structures to oversee the turn of events, organization, and utilization of AI. This repeated the aggregate opinion that moral contemplations and administrative oversight ought to remain forever

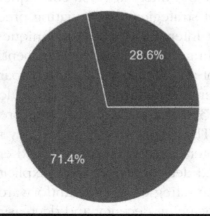

Figure 8.1   Awareness of bias of AI.

inseparable with simulated intelligence progression, guaranteeing that the advantages of AI are bridled while limiting likely damage and dangers. These review bits of knowledge uncover a basic comprehension of the overall worries with respect to AI's moral viewpoints and stress the earnestness to address them to cultivate a more mindful and impartial AI scene.

8.4 Proposed Methodology

In making the guide for this exploration, the proposed philosophy includes a complex methodology. To start, a broad audit of existing writing regarding the matter of computer-based intelligence's moral ramifications will be led. This far-reaching examination will give an essential comprehension of the moral scene encompassing computer-based intelligence, including viewpoints like inclination, protection concerns, and the effect of robotization on positions. In this way, true encounters and experiences will be consolidated through organized reviews and meetings including AI specialists, experts, and people affected by computer-based intelligence advancements. These firsthand records and well-qualified conclusions will infuse a human viewpoint into the examination, offering important subjective information. Moreover, contextual investigations will be utilized to highlight explicit examples of computer-based intelligence predisposition, security breaks, and occupation removal, giving a context-oriented setting to a more profound comprehension of moral worries. At long last, a moral examination structure, established in laid-out moral speculations, will be applied to evaluate and decipher the gathered information. This strategy intends to wind around together existing information, human encounters, and hypothetical systems to investigate and explore the complex moral landscape of AI extensively.

In the following phase of this methodology, a similar report will be embraced, dissecting the administrative and moral structures connected with AI across various nations and locales. By inspecting how different wards approach and direct computer-based intelligence morals, we can recognize varieties, shared traits, and possible gaps. Understanding these different administrative methodologies will add to the improvement of proposals and rules for a more strong and generally educated moral structure for computer-based intelligence.

Moreover, to acquire a more profound comprehension of public discernments and mindfulness with respect to computer-based intelligence morals, a general assessment study will be led. This review will contact a different segment, incorporating people with fluctuating degrees of knowledge of AI, to measure their grasping, concerns, and assumptions about moral contemplations in computer-based intelligence improvement and organization. This information will enhance the study by integrating the points of view of the more extensive society, guaranteeing that moral proposals think about open interests and concerns.

In rundown, this multi-layered strategy coordinates writing audit, master bits of knowledge, contextual investigations, relative examination of administrative structures, and general assessment reviews to comprehensively investigate the moral components of computer-based intelligence. The subsequent bits of knowledge and proposals intend to add to the continuous talk on mindful AI improvement and sending, encouraging a more comprehensive and morally powerful AI scene.

8.5 Use-Case

Imagine this: You're scrolling through your social feed, and all of a sudden, you're seeing ads that seem to match up perfectly with your most recent conversations. It's like your phone is listening in on you! This strange experience makes you curious about the ethics of AI—the technology that powers these personalized suggestions. You start to wonder: How does AI know what to show? Is it fair? What's happening to our privacy? What happens when AI begins to take over jobs? You're not just curious; you're worried. And that's where we come in.

We're not only looking at the technical aspects of AI but also looking at the ethics—the sometimes-underestimated aspects of AI that impact our day-to-day lives. In our research, we'll explore how AI can sometimes be biased, invade privacy, and potentially disrupt the labor market. We're not just highlighting the problems; we're suggesting ways to improve AI's performance for the benefit of all. We believe that as AI advances, we need to make sure it's not just intelligent but ethical. It's about creating a world where AI doesn't just understand us but respects us.

Envision a future where machines don't simply handle information, they go with choices that shape our lives consistently. We've made considerable progress from the times of sci-fi, where man-made consciousness (computer-based intelligence) was a relic of days gone by. Presently, it's implanted in our telephones, letting us know what to purchase or what to watch. It's in our workplaces, computerizing errands that used to be finished by people. Be that as it may, as computer-based intelligence turns out to be more unavoidable, it additionally brings up moral issues.

We're at a critical point where we have to ask some fundamental questions: Are these AI systems equitable? Or are they reinforcing existing social biases? When AI analyzes our data, is our privacy at risk? As it automates work, what will happen to the lives of millions of people? That's where this research comes in. We're here to unpack these complexities, to dive deep into the ethical abyss that is AI. By exploring bias, privacy issues, and the effects of automation on employment, we're trying to make sure that as AI advances, it does so in a responsible and ethical way. It's about imagining a future where the wonders of technology not only astonish us but also honor our values and rights.

The consequences of this examination won't be simply words on a page; they will have the ability to illuminate strategy, illuminate organizations, and impact a general public in which AI is a motor of good. The objective of this exploration is to go about as a compass, directing us toward an impartial and moral AI climate. Together, we can graph this mind-boggling way to a AI driven world that really fathoms and serves humankind.

8.6 Conclusion

All in all, this exploration venture into the moral elements of computerized reasoning (AI) has enlightened basic experiences into the blossoming impact of AI on our lives and society overall. The blend of top-to-bottom writing audit, certifiable encounters shared through overviews and meetings, and contextual analyses has revealed insight into the complex worries encompassing AI. The consciousness of AI applications was clear among members, yet a striking gap in understanding the expected predispositions inside AI calculations surfaced, conjuring concerns and encouraging a requirement for expanded mindfulness and training. Protection worries and tensions with respect to work uprooting were predominant, enhancing the need for severe guidelines and proactive measures in the steadily advancing scene of AI [10].

This investigation highlights the essential job of moral systems and rules in molding the dependable turn of events, organization, and administration of AI advancements. As AI proceeds to progress and coordinate into different features of our lives, it is basic to focus on development as well as moral contemplations to guarantee a fair and evenhanded innovative future. The call for cooperative endeavors—joining scientists, policymakers, industry pioneers, and people in general—is essential in building an agreeable and morally educated conjunction with AI. At last, the excursion of AI morals is a continuous and developing one, where an aggregate obligation to moral AI practices will make ready for a future where AI genuinely enhances and inspires humankind.

References

1. Javatpoint. (n.d.). History of Artificial Intelligence. Retrieved September, 2023, from https://www.javatpoint.com/history-of-artificial-intelligence
2. A. Johnson, "13 Common Hiring Biases To Watch Out For," Harver, November 2018. [Online]. Available: https://harver.com/blog/hiringbiases/ [Accessed September 2019].
3. K. Collier, (2023, July 5). In NYC, Companies Will Have to Prove Their AI Hiring Software Isn't Sexist or Racist. NBC News. https://www.nbcnews.com/tech/tech-news/nyc-companies-will-prove-aihiring-software-isnt-sexist-racist-rcna92336
4. https://en.wikipedia.org/wiki/Tay(chatbot)
5. Z. Wang, C. Tang, X. Sima, and L. Zhang, "Research on Ethical Issues of Artificial Intelligence Technology," 2020 2nd International Conference on Artificial Intelligence and Advanced Manufacture (AIAM), Manchester, United Kingdom, 2020, pp. 390–394. doi: 10.1109/AIAM50918.2020.00086
6. C. Huang, Z. Zhang, B. Mao, and X. Yao, "An Overview of Artificial Intelligence Ethics," in IEEE Transactions on Artificial Intelligence, vol. 4, no. 4, pp. 799–819, 2023. doi: 10.1109/TAI.2022.3194503
7. C. H. Chao, "Ethics Issues in Artificial Intelligence," 2019 International Conference on Technologies and Applications of Artificial Intelligence (TAAI), Kaohsiung, Taiwan, 2019, pp. 1–6. doi: 10.1109/TAAI48200.2019.8959925
8. R. A. Partadiredja, C. E. Serrano, and D. Ljubenkov, "AI or Human: The Socio-ethical Implications of AI-Generated Media Content," 2020 13th CMI Conference on Cybersecurity and Privacy (CMI) - Digital Transformation - Potentials and Challenges(51275), Copenhagen, Denmark, 2020, pp. 1–6. doi: 10.1109/CMI51275.2020.9322673
9. D. F. Mujtaba and N. R. Mahapatra, "Ethical Considerations in AI-Based Recruitment," 2019 IEEE International Symposium on Technology and Society (ISTAS), Medford, MA, USA, 2019, pp. 1–7. doi: 10.1109/ISTAS48451.2019.8937920
10. S. Corbett-Davies and S. Goel, "The Measure and Mismeasure of Fairness: A Critical Review of Fair Machine Learning," arXiv preprint arXiv:1808.00023, 2018.

Chapter 9

The Power of Personalization: AI-Driven Recommendations

Anirudh Sai Vallabhaneni, Anjali Perla, Revanth Reddy Regalla, and Neelam Kumari

9.1 Introduction

Imagine traversing a library filled with millions of volumes, each promising adventure, information, or fun. However, such wealth raises a daunting question: Where do you even begin? This is the situation we confront in today's digital world when we are overwhelmed with information. Enter the transformational power of customization, orchestrated by the unseen maestro: AI-powered suggestions.

9.1.1 From Information Chaos to Curated Delight

Personalization exploits the human urge for relevance. DMI estimates that the typical internet user will see 11,700 bits of material per day by 2023. To navigate this flood, AI comes in, using powerful algorithms to sift through your digital footprint – search history, buying trends, and social media connections – and construct a vivid image of your distinct tastes.

This portrait powers the motor of recommendation systems. Machine learning algorithms, the workhorses of AI, scan massive datasets to uncover hidden patterns and forecast your preferences. Consider perusing an online bookshop. Every click, every lingering page goes into this algorithm, which shapes its comprehension of your literary preferences. Suddenly, suggestions appear on your screen – not just blockbusters, but hidden treasures that

DOI: 10.4324/9781032711089-9

coincide with your preference for historical novels with strong female characters.

9.1.2 Beyond Algorithms: Power of AI's Toolkit

However, AI's toolset goes beyond basic calculation. Natural Language Processing (NLP) helps computers understand the subtleties of your searches and interactions. Typing "intriguing historical mysteries" is more than simply a string of words; NLP reveals the meaning, allowing suggestions that satisfy your need for suspense set against the background of bygone ages.

Another approach that makes use of public knowledge is collaborative filtering. By evaluating the behavior of people with similar characteristics, it recommends books that individuals with similar literary DNA appreciate. It's like having a bookish buddy whispering suggestions into your ear.

AI-driven recommendations are transforming industries and redefining experiences beyond the bookshop. E-commerce behemoths construct product recommendations based on your basket, whilst streaming services create bespoke playlists that match your musical moods. Social media networks personalize news feeds, ensuring that you only see material that corresponds with your perspective.

The advantages are apparent. Improved consumer stories result in stepped-forward pride, engagement, and logo loyalty. Businesses obtain great insights into client alternatives, allowing for facts-pushed choice-making and better conversion prices. Thus far, everything seems to be going well for everyone.

9.2 The Growth of Suggestions Driven by AI

9.2.1 Lost in the Maze: The Importance of Personalization in the Current Digital Environment

Imagine being dumped into a library filled with billions of volumes, each whispering promises of enlightenment and enjoyment. Exciting, but also terrifying. Where should you even begin? This is the core of our current digital experience. Information bombards us from every angle, leaving us overwhelmed and desiring significance. In this maze of material, customization emerges as the guiding light, directing us to what connects with our own needs and preferences.

9.2.2 Information Deluge

The internet ecosystem is brimming with content providers. Social media platforms provide newsfeeds, companies compete for our attention with tailored advertisements, and streaming services offer an abundance of possibilities. While this abundance seems to be a blessing, it frequently leads to choose fatigue. With limited time and concentration, managing this information flood becomes more difficult. Generic, one-length-suits-all techniques are no longer effective.

Consumers are becoming more knowledgeable and discerning about facts. They demand relevant material, personalized suggestions, and experiences that seem specially designed for them. Several reasons contribute to this shift:

Empowering Users and Maintaining Trust in Digital Marketing

- Higher expectations: When exposed to a variety of goods, individuals acquire distinct preferences and seek out experiences that meet their needs.
- Technology empowers users by providing tools such as ad blockers and tailored news aggregators to shape their digital experience.
- Generic marketing approaches may erode trust, as customers seek authenticity and meaningful relationships with businesses.

9.2.3 Personalization Is the Antidote to Information Overload

Personalization is an effective cure for information overload because it understands individual preferences and provides individualized experiences. Imagine stepping into that library not only with a map but with a personal guide who knows your interests and directs you to the books you'll like the most. This is the essence of customization.

9.3 Benefits of Tailored Experiences

The advantages of tailored experiences go well beyond convenience. Personalization may boost user engagement and pleasure by presenting material that aligns with their interests.

Benefits of Personalized Marketing

- Enhance conversion rates with personalized suggestions, resulting in more informed purchases and desired activities.
- Stronger brand loyalty: When people feel understood and appreciated, they form stronger bonds with companies.
- Tailored experiences save time and effort by removing unnecessary information.

9.4 Examples in Action

Personalization Affects a Variety of Industries

- E-commerce systems may suggest items based on browsing history and previous transactions.
- Streaming services: Provide personalized movie and music recommendations.
- Create personalized social media feeds depending on user interactions and interests.
- Learning systems can tailor instructional material to specific learning styles and paces.

9.5 The Power of AI

AI is driving the customization revolution. Machine learning algorithms evaluate massive databases of user behavior, preferences, and interactions. This data enables them to forecast interests, anticipate requirements, and provide highly targeted suggestions.

However, the strength of AI entails responsibilities. As we dive further into customization, ethical problems such as privacy, filter bubbles, and possible manipulation must be carefully considered.

9.6 The Path Forward

The future of customization lies in the responsible development of AI, in which algorithms emphasize transparency, user control, and ethical concerns. Here is what the future holds.

Advantages of Advanced Algorithms in Personalization

- More advanced algorithms: Using higher user comprehension and contextual awareness.
- Building user confidence with clear and explainable AI suggestions.
- Personalization extends beyond items, tailoring experiences across touchpoints such as customer service and reward programs.
- Introduce the notion of AI-driven recommendations and its main techniques.

In an era of information overload, the ability to filter and display relevant material to consumers has become a competitive advantage. AI-powered suggestions, like knights wielding algorithms rather than swords, rise to the occasion, wielding enormous power to tailor experiences and influence user journeys. But how do these tips accomplish their magic? Let's look at the fundamental methods that power their engine.

1. **Machine Learning: Discovering Patterns in the Data Jungle**
   Consider a large forest of user data, including clicks, searches, transactions, and more. Machine learning algorithms are intrepid explorers, sifting through the thick vegetation to discover hidden patterns and relationships. Their tools? Statistical models may learn from data and find correlations, such as commonly purchased goods.
   - What features do people prefer?
   - How do people with comparable browsing habits vary from others?
   - Can users be grouped by common interests or demographics?

   Machine learning algorithms use these patterns to develop prediction models. These models function as crystal balls, predicting what a user would enjoy based on their previous behavior and that of comparable users. This is the core of tailored recommendations, ensuring that consumers see goods that are most likely to appeal to them.

2. **Natural Language Processing: Understanding the User's Voice**
   However, data is more than simply numbers; it includes words, phrases, and questions. This is where NLP comes in, functioning as an interpreter.

Techniques for AI-Driven Recommendations

- Analyze searches, reviews, and social media interactions to determine user intent and preferences.

– Identify sentiment: Evaluate favorable, negative, or neutral thoughts on things or themes.
– Extract crucial information from user inputs, including product names, locations, and events.

By comprehending the "language" of user data, NLP enables suggestions that go beyond mere correlations. Imagine you're looking for "running shoes for beginners." NLP might infer that you are a beginning runner rather than a seasoned marathoner and adjust advice appropriately. This sophisticated knowledge takes customization to a new level.

9.6.1 Collaborative Filtering: The Power of Crowd

Individual data is vital, but the aggregate knowledge of the public has enormous power. Collaborative filtering builds user profiles by capturing their interactions with various things.

■ Identifying comparable users by analyzing their prior interactions.
■ Recommending things based on user preferences.

Consider suggesting a restaurant based on your friends' tastes. If your friends with similar preferences enjoyed a new Italian restaurant, chances are you would too. Collaborative filtering strengthens this social effect by harnessing the pooled expertise of many to tailor suggestions to everyone.

9.6.2 Beyond The Core: A Symphony of Techniques.

These three strategies form the fundamental ensemble, but the music of AI-driven suggestions is far deeper. Techniques include content-based filtering, which recommends things based on previous interactions.

■ Hybrid methods use numerous methodologies to provide more robust and accurate suggestions.
■ Real-time customization adjusts suggestions depending on user behavior and circumstances.

These strategies work together to provide a symphony of customization, adjusting suggestions to individual requirements and tastes in real-time.

9.7 The Power Unfolds: Impact and Examples

The Influence of AI-Driven Suggestions Spans Industries

■ E-commerce: Consider product recommendations that appear effortlessly on your screen, anticipating your next purchase.
■ Streaming services provide personalized movie and music recommendations, like having a personal DJ curate your listening experience.
■ Social media offers personalized news streams with fascinating information.

9.8 The Power of Personalization

In today's digital world, which is packed with options and fighting for attention, standing out requires individualized experiences. AI-driven suggestions rise to the occasion, using data and algorithms to design user experiences that are relevant, entertaining, and, ultimately useful. But what are the main advantages that make them so powerful? Let's look at the three pillars that support their impact:

1. **Enhanced Customer Experience: Raising Contentment, Interest, and Devotion**
   Imagine walking into a shop where a helpful employee anticipates your requirements before you ever ask. That's the wonder of AI-powered recommendations: They create trips that seem personalized and curated. Here's how:

   Benefits of AI Recommendations

   – Recommendations reduce choice fatigue by emphasizing relevant alternatives, resulting in a more engaging user experience.
   – Improved relevance: No more sifting through extraneous material. Recommendations guarantee that users see things that are relevant to their interests and preferences, creating a feeling of connection and understanding.
   – Algorithms may help people find new favorites and widen their horizons.
   – Dynamic engagement: Recommendations adjust to user behavior in real-time, providing new and relevant ideas to keep users interested and returning for more.

Ultimately, tailored encounters promote enjoyment, discovery, and trust. Users feel appreciated and understood, resulting in greater loyalty and support for companies that use AI-powered suggestions.

2. **Increased Conversion Rates: Converting Interest into Action**
Beyond improving experiences, recommendations play an important part in driving corporate success. By targeting the appropriate consumers with the correct items or information, they operate as potent conversion catalysts.

Benefits of Personalized Recommendations

– Increased purchase intent: Relevant suggestions remind consumers of their requirements and provide solutions that exactly fit them, increasing the possibility of a purchase.
– Personalized recommendations may reduce cart abandonment by suggesting complementary goods, encouraging consumers to finish their purchases rather than leaving them due to hesitation.
– Recommend relevant items or services to increase revenue and maximize consumer interactions.
– Targeted suggestions improve campaign performance by delivering the correct message to the right audience, resulting in increased click-through rates and conversions.

In essence, AI-driven suggestions bridge the gap between user interest and action, converting casual browsing into measurable commercial outcomes. [1]

3. **Data-Driven Decision Making: Identifying User Preferences and Behaviors**
The actual strength of AI-driven suggestions lies not in the immediate advantages, but in the massive amount of data they create. This data becomes a treasure mine of insights, which helps businesses:
– Analyzing user interactions with suggestions helps firms understand their motives, interests, and purchasing habits.
– Recommendations reveal underlying tendencies in user behavior, enabling firms to predict future demands and tailor their offers appropriately.
– Optimize product development by analyzing consumer preferences through suggestions, ensuring goods meet their requirements and aspirations.
– Use suggestion data to personalize marketing campaigns and maximize return on investment.

With AI-driven suggestions, data converts from statistics to actionable insights, allowing organizations to make educated choices that drive development and success.

9.9 The Power Multiplies: A Symphony of Benefits

These three pillars – better customer experience, higher conversion rates, and data-driven decision-making – are not separate advantages. They collaborate, enhancing each other's influence. A tailored experience increases engagement, generates more data to optimize suggestions, and enhances the overall experience. Improved conversion rates provide more data, which leads to better targeting and greater conversions. This virtuous cycle drives continual development, resulting in a strong engine for corporate success and customer delight.

9.10 Case Studies: When AI Recommendations Shine

AI-powered suggestions are no longer a pipe dream; they are actively changing user experiences across several sectors. Let's look at some real-world success stories, analyzing how they used these tactics and enjoyed the advantages.

9.10.1 E-commerce Giant: Amazon's Personalized Product Carousel

Envision perusing tens of millions of merchandise without feeling overpowered. This is made viable by way of Amazon's recommendation engine, which makes use collaborative filtering and machine learning knowledge. It makes assumptions about your interests based on your purchases, browsing habits, and even your wishlists. Its efficacy is proven in the "Frequently Bought Together" and "Recommended for You" sections. What are the final results? Sales bounce, patron satisfaction soars, and the shopping for revel in turns into extra pleasing.

9.10.2 The Entertainment Maestro: The Magic of Netflix's "Because You Watched"

Finding the ideal movie or program in a big collection might be difficult. Netflix's recommendation engine addresses this with a combination of collaborative filtering, content-based filtering, and real-time customization. It uses your watching history, ratings, and even the time of day to create a customized "Because You Watched" list. What are the results? Increased engagement, lower churn, and a more delightful surfing experience for millions of users.

9.10.3 Spotify's Discover Weekly Playlist Serves as the Music Curator

Finding music might happen by chance, but Spotify's Discover Weekly playlist elevates the experience. This weekly customized playlist analyzes your listening habits and those of users who are like you using collaborative filtering and NLP.

It provides a tailored blend of old favorites and intriguing discoveries based on your musical preferences and exploration of current trends. What's the outcome? Increased user engagement, discovery of new genres, and a stronger connection to the platform.

9.10.4 Beyond Big Names: Niche Success Stories

The influence of AI suggestions goes beyond industry leaders. Consider:

- Stitch Fix offers bespoke clothes subscriptions based on consumer input and preferences. What was the result? Improved client satisfaction and repeat business.
- Headspace offers individualized guided meditations based on user choices and interaction data, encouraging well-being and app stickiness.
- Duolingo, a language learning program, uses NLP and machine learning to adapt lesson plans based on individual learning patterns and success, resulting in faster language acquisition.

While the strategies and data sources vary, these success stories have some similar threads:

Enhanced Accuracy and Efficacy of Suggestions

- Access to different user data improves the accuracy and efficacy of suggestions.

- Advanced algorithms use machine learning and natural language processing to identify complicated patterns and provide personalized suggestions.
- Real-time adaptability: Recommendations modify depending on user behavior and circumstance, maintaining ongoing relevance.
- Human supervision and ethical considerations: Balancing customization with user privacy and appropriate data use is critical.

9.10.5 Predicting the Future: The Evolution of Tailored Suggestions

The field of AI-driven recommendations is still developing, and there are many more interesting things to come:

- **More personalization:** Adding user demographics, feelings, and current context into suggestions for even more customized outcomes.
- **Explainable AI:** To foster user confidence, suggestions should be clear and intelligible.
- **Multimodal recommendations:** To create a more comprehensive and captivating experience, combine text, audio, and visual components.

These methods will become more and more important in influencing our online interactions, providing experiences that are both relevant and personal. However, ethical and responsible development must continue to be the top priorities to guarantee that customization helps consumers rather than abuses them. [2]

9.11 Moral Aspects to Consider

Although AI-driven suggestions have many advantages, it is important to use them responsibly. Like any strong instrument, they may have drawbacks that should be carefully considered:

1. **Filter Bubbles: Ensnared in Reverberations of Your Views**
   In a perfect world, you would only view movies that suit your tastes, news that supports your preexisting opinions, and goods that appeal to your prior purchases. Sadly, this is one possible drawback of "filter bubbles" created by tailored suggestions. Algorithms may

unintentionally create echo chambers by concentrating only on content that users are likely to interact with. This might restrict exposure to a variety of opinions, which can impede intellectual development and well-informed decision-making.

2. **Privacy Issues: Managing a Tightrope Between Intrusion and Personalization**

   Data is essential to personalization, and with it comes a serious ethical conundrum: privacy. Algorithms need access to user data, often including browser history, search queries, and even personal information, to provide successful recommendations. It's crucial to find a balance between privacy and customization. Users should have a choice over what information is gathered and used, as well as openness about how their data is used.

3. **Personalized Persuasion's Dark Side: Addiction and Manipulation**

   Although recommendations can influence, this ability may be abused. Envision algorithms taking advantage of customer weaknesses, suggesting dangerous items, or coercing users into making rash purchases.

   This raises questions about addiction, especially for groups who are more susceptible and are exposed to tailored information that preys on vulnerabilities. Protections against such coercive tactics are necessary for responsible development activities.

9.12 Frameworks for Ethics: Setting Out on a Path Toward Responsible AI

The creation of ethical frameworks for AI is essential to reducing these drawbacks. Among the fundamental ideas are:

- **Transparency and explainability**: Users must be able to obtain information about the data utilized and comprehend how recommendations are made.
- **Fairness and non-discrimination:** Algorithms need to be devoid of prejudices that could produce unfair or discriminatory results.
- **Security and privacy:** User data should be gathered and handled sensibly, and strong security protocols should be followed.
- **Accountability and oversight:** Those who create and implement AI systems need to be held responsible for the results.

9.13 Top Techniques: Applying Ethics in Practice

In addition to frameworks, several recommended practices may encourage the creation of responsible AI:

- **Data minimization:** Only gather the information required to fulfill the stated objectives.
- **User control and consent:** Establish unambiguous and explicit consent procedures for the gathering and use of user data.
- **Frequent audits and evaluations:** Make sure algorithms are regularly checked for biases and unforeseen outcomes.
- **Public participation and discourse:** Encourage candid conversations on AI's ethical ramifications.

9.14 The Future of AI-driven Recommendations

AI-driven suggestions are no longer in their infancy; they're boldly heading toward a future rich in customization, efficiency, and ethical issues. Let's look into the crystal ball and discover the intriguing trends influencing this landscape:

1. **Advanced Algorithms: Dive Deeper into the User Psyche.**
   Current algorithms excel at analyzing user behavior; nevertheless, the future contains far more complex approaches.

   Enhanced Personalization Through Multimodal Learning

   - Deep learning: Neural networks analyze user data to identify complicated linkages and subtleties. Consider suggestions that not only forecast your next purchase but also comprehend your underlying reasons, such as a comfortable sweater on a dismal day to induce comfort.
   - Multimodal learning combines text, visuals, and facial expressions to better grasp user situations and emotions. Consider suggestions that are tailored to your present mood, such as upbeat music when you are anxious.
   - Algorithms employ reinforcement learning to improve suggestions based on real-time input from users. Consider a system that learns from your favorable responses to documentaries and progressively builds a tailored information center based on your developing interests.

These developments point to a future in which suggestions go beyond basic forecasts, becoming more like smart assistants that understand your wants and preferences.

2. **Explainable AI: Deciphering the Magic Box.**
As suggestions get increasingly complicated, the issue of trust emerges. "Explainable AI" aims to solve this by providing transparency and explanations for suggestions. Imagine receiving straightforward responses such as "This book was recommended because you enjoyed similar works by the same author and enjoyed positive reviews from users with similar reading preferences."

Enhancing Algorithm Transparency

– Making algorithms intelligible to non-technical folks. Consider interactive tools that show how your data is utilized to make suggestions, increasing confidence and knowledge.

– Counterfactual explanations: Investigating alternative proposals and explaining why they were not selected. Consider alternatives like "This book was considered but excluded because you previously rated books in the same genre negatively."

Explainable AI strives to instill confidence and empower people while keeping them in control of their tailored experiences.

3. **Personalization Beyond Products: A Holistic Experience.**
Recommendations are no longer just product recommendations. The future anticipates an ecology of personalized experiences.

– Context-aware suggestions: Imagine recommendations that adapt to your present circumstances. Your smart speaker recommends a piece of peaceful music while you unwind after work, or your navigation app reroutes you due to unforeseen traffic congestion.

– Personalized services: Healthcare platforms may recommend preventative steps based on your health data, while educational platforms tailor learning materials to your specific pace and style.

– Proactive assistance: AI may anticipate your requirements before you recognize them. Your vehicle pre-warms on a chilly morning, or your virtual assistant makes a doctor's appointment based on probable health hazards found in your data (with your full permission, of course).

This future offers a world in which AI serves as a tailored assistant, influencing your experiences smoothly and beneficially. [3]

4. **Societal Impact: A Double-edged Sword.**

9.15 The Future of AI-driven Suggestions Has Enormous Social Implications

Positive Impacts of AI

- Positive consequences include individualized teaching for individual learning styles and targeted treatments to identify those at risk of mental health difficulties. AI has the potential to empower people while also promoting societal good.
- Ethical concerns: Algorithm bias may perpetuate socioeconomic imbalances. We must assure fair and equitable growth while emphasizing openness and user control over data.
- Human Touch: While AI is excellent at personalization, human judgment and empathy remain essential. The future rests on a balanced approach in which AI complements, not replaces, human decision-making.

Navigating this terrain requires a rigorous examination of ethical issues and responsible growth.

9.16 Looking Forward: A Personalized Tomorrow

AI-powered suggestions stand to influence a future in which technology adjusts to individual needs and tastes. This thrilling adventure presents not only enormous opportunities but also tremendous problems. We can build a tailored future that empowers people while benefiting society by using the potential of modern algorithms and emphasizing explainability and ethical concerns. Remember that the future is not decided; it is formed by our decisions and actions today. Let's ensure that the future of AI-driven recommendations benefits everyone.

9.17 Conclusion

AI-powered suggestions have threaded their way into the fabric of our digital lives, employing invisible algorithms to influence our experiences like unseen puppeteers. From proposing the next movie marathon to influencing our purchasing choices, they have enormous potential to transform user interactions and generate unprecedented advantages for both people and organizations.

Imagine a future in which every online contact seems personalized, anticipating your wants and aspirations before you ever express them. Personalized suggestions, enabled by machine learning, NLP, and collaborative filtering, may make this a reality. They identify hidden patterns and correlations by studying large datasets of user behavior, anticipating what each person would respond to. It's like having a personal genie whisper recommendations into your ear, ensuring you only see the most relevant and fascinating material.

This tailored experience provides significant advantages to consumers. Imagine discovering new music that speaks to your soul, locating the right present for a loved one with pinpoint precision, or easily navigating an overwhelming newsfeed, seeing only stories that pique your interest. Recommendations become invisible guides, increasing ease, enjoyment, and ultimately, the value you get out of your online interactions.

For organizations, customization leads to improved user engagement, loyalty, and eventually, income. Targeted suggestions act like magic arrows, striking the bullseye of user demands, and resulting in increased conversion rates and happy consumers. Businesses may better understand their consumers and adapt to individual tastes, establishing a feeling of connection and trust that goes beyond conventional marketing approaches.

However, enormous power comes great responsibility. As we embrace the magic of AI-powered suggestions, we must walk cautiously to ensure responsible and ethical growth. User privacy must be strictly maintained, algorithms must be devoid of prejudice, and openness is vital. We must aspire for a future in which customization empowers rather than exploits people, suggestions are tailored to varied needs and voices, and technology is used for good rather than exploitation.

Finally, AI-driven suggestions have the potential to transform our digital environment, providing more customized, engaging, and ultimately fulfilling experiences for everybody. By leveraging this power responsibly and ethically, we may create a future in which technology serves mankind rather than the other way around. Let us embrace the customized journey with wisdom and forethought, transforming it into a force for good by creating a digital environment that represents our individual needs and communal goals.

References

1. Hussain, M. S. (2023, August 11). AI-driven personalization in marketing: Maximizing impact with 9 top tools for marketing, content and design | Data Science Dojo. Data Science Dojo. https://datasciencedojo.com/blog/ai-driven-personalization/
2. The Power of Personalization: Role of AI in Consumer Engagement - Determ. (2024, January 26). Determ. https://www.determ.com/blog/the-power-of-personalization-role-of-ai-in-consumer-engagement/
3. Josifovsk, V. (2023, July 3). The Future Of AI-Powered Personalization: The Potential Of Choices. Forbes. https://www.forbes.com/sites/forbestechcouncil/2023/07/03/the-future-of-ai-powered-personalization-the-potential-of-choices/

Chapter 10

Human-AI Collaboration: Augmenting Creativity and Decision-Making

Palagudi Venkata Deepak and Mir Aadil

10.1 Overview of Human Creativity

The ability to be creative is the basic nature of humans, and humans use this skill across art, literature, music, figuring things out, etc. Many variables influence human creativity, including personality traits, a culture within an organization that leverages motivational strategies to empower employees and enhance productivity, etc.

There are indeed two types of motives that enable creativity in humans: External factors and internal factors that we will discuss in detail. Personality traits refer to the patterns of thoughts, feelings, and behavior exhibited by a human character, including features such as emotional stability and openness to experience etc. These characteristics result in patterns giving rise to what is accepted as one's response behaviors. Cognitive functions are the things that a human brain processes to do daily basic activities such as thinking, reading, and so on. By expanding these, we also expand the creativity of humans. The natural surroundings around you and your culture also play an important role in developing creativity among humans.

Human creativity involves imaginative and divergent thinking, where concepts and interactions are explored through a cognitive process that adapts to emotional states and environmental cues, fostering the ability to generate ideas. [1]

DOI: 10.4324/9781032711089-10

10.1.1 Process of Human Creativity

Human creativity is multi-layered and it includes four stages. The preparation stage includes gathering the sources of information and selecting the source as inspiration to follow, it also includes learning anything necessary about the project or issue that one is dealing with. The second is the incubation phase, where the waiting provides no active treatment that will allow unconscious thoughts that form responses to problem consciousness. The verification step is the authentication, which involves an individual testing her ideology or solution. Therefore, it is a crucial point that creativity will never have a monadic brain section, not even one hemisphere of the brain, and everything about how it works stems from multiplicity tied with thoughts which also include random conclusions forced on its permanent circle of thinking sides, including feelings and emotions. Second, due to the nature of factors that define a person's judgment and decision-making variables, personal traits, motivational orientation, cognitive capacity, environmental needs (cognitive demands), knowledge, skills, and culture. In general, the entire process of human creativity might be considered a dynamic conglomeration of cognitive aspects such as fantasy and feeling which are developed under the influence of different extra-cognitive factors. [2]

10.2 Overview of Decision-Making

Human decision-making represents a crucial concept that is a result of the combination of mental, personal, and circumstantial factors and results in desirable new ideas or solutions.

Personality has turned into a central cause in the arrangement of decisions, and it was denied that high scores of extraverts are impulsive and they like to evaluate every option given. There are some other factors besides that, and the motivation factor can also be considered as one of the most prevailing forces in the decision process.

Decision-making is a process that is heavily reliant on cognition, as it specifically refers to thoughts and rate or deliberation. With more of the better cognitive ability, individuals can make good decisions and solve problems.

The use of decisions is largely found in the environment, where any decision made predominantly wields its outcomes. The factors that affect decision-making are knowledge and skills. Skills such as analytical thinking are necessary to make good decisions and can other way round affect positively how the decisions are being taken. Thus, cultural practices dictate how we make selections for base and supplementary food, or alternatively, there is the impact of cultural influences on decisions regarding what food items should be chosen. [3]

10.3 Evolution of AI and Its Collaboration with Humans

The initiative of the AI was basically seeking an answer to whether machines can possess the intelligence of humans. Alan Turing, a British scientist, published a paper on computing machinery in which a test named Turing test is mentioned. The Turing test aimed at determining whether there are characteristics in human beings that can be copied by machines. In this test, humans will act as judges and have a dialogue with the machine, and the guy who gave inputs are all the same, where the judge won't be able to make a clear picture of whether the answer was given by the guy or the machine. He/she is then made to choose answers for the questions given. This was not a tool for collaboration between human beings and machines, but this test is about the types of human intelligence that displayed the evidence that proved that machines could have exploited quality in store humanity. [4]

This system follows the principles of biological neural networks, which utilize a series of units interlinked in layers and nodes, just like the neurons present in human nervous systems. These nodes are trained to recognize patterns through algorithms from data inputs. Next, we have artificial neural networks in evolution, which have the ability to recognize patterns present in artificial without any processing of "learning." Then after the construction of the stochastic neural analog reinforcement computer (SNARC) machine, it was the first machine to use 40 nodes, and using SNARC as short-term memory and long-term memory, each node is interweaved into a network like a neuron's nervous system.

In 1952, when an IBM employee Arthur Samuel used another step where a machine would learn from its own experiences accordingly. Instead of using the entire code as programming with all possible data inputs, this machine learning program would integrate strategy changes based on the previous computer game outcomes. Here, the artificial machine first started interaction with humans, and here program is prepared for the humans to play checkers with machines. The machine analyzed his performance from the troublesome areas on which one was playing he could develop how he would elaborate.

In 1955, the term AI was coined by John McCarthy, and in 1958, he developed a programming language called List processing, which is shortly called Lisp which has a symbolic computing approach that will ease human efforts and save time. The programs in Lisp are represented as lists of symbols for example: "(add 2 3)" meant to add 2 and 3, and it also manages the data types and memory automatically, It is used as a functional programming language, particularly in developing AI systems and symbolic computing.

The 1970s marked a downturn for AI, with decreased investor interest and funding, leading to periods known as AI winters. These setbacks reflected a shift in focus toward human-centric approaches, prompting increased exploration of machine capabilities, often surpassing human capacities in certain domains. Thus, this was how computers began interacting with piece as well, enabling mankind to further steer ahead despite all the failures encountered when computers failed in performing those given jobs. Example: The man will pose his questions, or the machine that is about to be used as an interface will act as a medium for input while acting itself automatically on this input and providing output and solutions. The expert human friendly systems are based on focused and body vision purpose of understanding them better so that they can develop creative capacity, especially in decision-making issues. As a mechanism for offering various alternative options from the memory, it is already processing huge volume of data record that facilitated assisting taking information-based resolutions. With these innovative tools, collaboration with human beings has helped to better insights, hence creativity improvements.

1990s is a transition era in the field of AI, where lots of prime machine learning algorithms have been introduced, and these two algorithms are named as decision trees and neural networks. These two models were used to develop natural language processing (NLP) through which humans communicate with machines in their natural language talks using voice and formed computer vision, which means how human eyes see images. After viewing an image, this model automatically generates scenarios intended to deceive people. However, humans often struggle to discern the authenticity of such AI models and are unable to detect realistic situations or assess their reliability in real-life scenarios.

To overcome all these problems, the researchers continued, and in 2010–2020, the decade where the deep learning revolution took place, deep neural networks are made with multiple layers to achieve human-level performance, or even more. These deep neural networks are used in speech recognition, image recognition, etc. In this stage, humans contributed to the development of the architecture and design of these deep learning models. In addition to this, humans have added a lot of features to improve its performance. Since the evolution from the 1950s, humans have accumulated a lot of advanced tools, and the creativity and decision-making skills of humans have increased to several heights. The collaboration of humans with AI has made humans augmented, and this collaboration has a lot of potential to achieve greater heights. [5]

10.4 The AI Technologies and Models for Enhancing Human Creativity and Decision-Making

There are AI technologies that have greatly contributed to boosting the creativity of people and the decision-making process. They are machine learning algorithms: NLP, computer vision, as well as reinforcement learning.

10.4.1 *Augmenting Human Creativity and Decision-Making*

1. **Machine Learning Algorithms:** The machine learning algorithms assist in making decisions, which allows pattern recognition that helps in creating forecasts based on new data, and impacting other problems to cause better outcomes.
2. **Natural Language Processing:** Due to the dynamic nature of NLP tools, human-based augmentation can write in addition to the program and benefit effectively from relevant programming as well as reasoning within the domain; therefore just like creativity improves human impact, it may boost the efficiency of the technology.
3. **Computer Vision:** Computer vision allows the machines to parse and make judgments from visual data but this invention remakes business intelligence and cranks up creativity in most industries.
4. **Reinforcement Learning:** Besides, one of the idiosyncrasies is that, it may appear quite surprising at first glance when comparing creative processes with reinforcement learning strategies such as those present in Open AI's approach.

   Ex: An open drug discovery platform and solving optimization problems using genetic algorithm and particle swarm regressor or soft Support Vector Machine (SVM) algorithms, such methods assist to considerable innovativeness and creativity.

5. **Quantum Computing:** Although quantum computing is not discussed by the given search results, it can address hard optimization problems; these changes in resource outputs might have indirect impacts like a possible change in creativity and decision making. [6]

10.5 Ethical Considerations

AI is the most powerful human invention, and this invention can become very dangerous to humans if they do not integrate these systems with ethical principles such as:

10.5.1 Bias

Bias can shape what is being created by AI and how it is implemented to make those decisions, possibly creating a false belief in humanity that humans decide these decisions with the available choices. It has been revealed that people can ignore the concept of art referred to as an AI and its influence on the views regarding human concerns as well as creativity. Furthermore, however, AI systems will also be constrained by bias issues since these systems basically learn from what is available through training data.

10.5.2 Privacy

There are privacy problems that may be faced and even result in the illegal breach of an individual's sensitive information. These problems derive from significant volumes of personal data used by an AI algorithm, In case of any malicious conduct, whoever gains access to their information could potentially use it unlawfully. A tool of strict data protection and privacy is required to ensure that the probe can be preserved in a situation where human cognitive operations are dominated by AI.

10.5.3 Transparency

The absence of transparency makes it very hard for the members to have confidence in AI since they will not be given clear avenues regarding why particular judgments are taken. The revelation that would concentrate on the transparency of AI decision-making is about how one AI arrives at rationalization and procedure, which could have a critical impact on men's assurance with AI. It is possible to apply decision trees and logistic regression in large pragmatic problems with thousands of objects. [7]

10.6 How Human and AI Work Together to Generate Ideas and Make Decisions in Future

As fundamental components of human-AI interaction, humans can employ collaborative creativity with AI; the employment of cognitive augmentation by AI is necessary for the improvement of overall decision-making processes based on the results or outcomes made through human choices.

10.6.1 Collaborative Creativity

The new-generation AI provides ground for human individuals to work with an AI in creative tasks. Empirical studies suggest that the integration of man and machine in domains of human-computer interactive performance encourages better creativity. Collaborative process of creativity is a joint search that contains two steps: Developing this place to allow searching and then creating the space in order to paint it with points where they should be rated.

10.6.2 Cognitive Augmentation

AI-augmented cognitive amplification is most of the time designed to enhance activities related strictly to memory – attention – problem-solving. Here, human cognitive systems are augmented with AI as a tool to improve decision-making and other aspects of the cognitive output. Further, the advanced adaptation of AI and biotechnology also modified the borders of low chances after fetal changes they get improvements in them.

10.6.3 Decision-Making Processes

AI is supposed to assist the human being in making appropriate decisions that stem from situations where a very broad landscape of data points, parameters, and other variables is involved but may be beyond the understanding level for humans. However, AI often lacks values such as empathy and trust – and it can surpass accepted norms – and transcends what is accepted so that the issues should be carried beyond appearance since such attributes are required in most decision-making as an aspect whereby this among other aspects are unquestionable arts. Thus, the background of the human-AI interaction on decisions is a crucial step that brings difficulties in establishing such a bonding since most people buy an acquired power but largely for those processes entailing great values.

Operational flexibility and speed: The application of AI tools will allow for increasing operating flexibility and speeding up the scopes of decision-making processes. Through the automation of repetitive and low-level tasks carried out by human workers, AI helps to release humans from spending time on such routine decisions that allow them to concentrate on more complicated strategic thoughts.

Complementing human strengths: The key difference in human-AI complementarity is that the synergy between people and AI needs to be highlighted. By offering insights and recommendations, AI systems allow human judgment while improving the decision-making processes.

Medical decision-making aids: In medicine, AI systems are important as they act as aides in making decisions. These robots can process medical information, assist in diagnostics, and may give treatment recommendations that doctors have better to consider while making decisions.

Design and creativity: Cooperation between AI and human designers in the design process improves processes and results are visually smarter. Algorithms, based on AI can create design opportunities that may provide assistance with ideation and optimization of designs according to user preferences and limitations.

Music generation: AI often works jointly with human composers and contributes to the creation of music or innovating new creative ideas using AI. The AI algorithms can be capable of producing melodies and harmonies along with the lyric creation process, offering opportunities and enhancing creativity for musicians.

Supporting data-driven decision-making: The collaboration between humans and AI, referred to as collaborative intelligence, utilizes the leadership capabilities, teamwork structure, and creativity human minds possess alongside all their benefits such as speed, scaling ability, and quantitative power. This is an approach that helps organizations make effective data-informed decision making which will lead to better results. [8]

10.7 Conclusion

This chapter discusses human creativity and decision-making and how evolving technology is taking shape in helping humans collaborate with AI to increase their creativity, idea generating, and decision-making abilities.

References

1. Demarin, V., & Derke, F. (2020). Creativity—the story continues: An overview of thoughts on creativity. *Mind and brain: Bridging neurology and psychiatry*, 1–20. https://doi/10.1007/978-3-030-38606-1_1
2. Sweller, J. (2009). Cognitive bases of human creativity. *Educational Psychology Review*, 21, 11–19.
3. Zhang, W., Zhang, Q., & Song., M. (2015). How do Individual-Level Factors Affect the Creative Solution Formation Process of Teams? Creativity and Innovation Management, https://doi.org/10.1111/Caim.12127
4. Rainie, Lee. "AI and Human Enhancement: Americans' Openness Is Tempered by a Range of Concerns." Pew Research Center: Internet, Science & Tech, March 17, 2022.
5. Raximov, N., Primqulov, O., & Daminova, B. (2021, November). Basic concepts and stages of research development on artificial intelligence. In 2021 International Conference on Information Science and Communications Technologies (ICISCT) (pp. 1–4).
6. Ali Elfa, M. A., & Dawood, M. E. T. (2023). Using Artificial Intelligence for enhancing Human Creativity. Journal of Art, Design and Music, 2(2), 3.
7. G. Legate, "AI Ethics in Focus: Addressing Bias, Privacy, and Transparency Challenges," Human Made, Nov. 13, 2023. https://humanmade.com/ai/ethics-in-ai/
8. H. J. Wilson & P. R. Daugherty, "Collaborative Intelligence: Humans and AI Are Joining Forces," Harvard Business Review, 2018. https://hbr.org/2018/07/collaborative-intelligence-humans-and-ai-are-joining-forces

Chapter 11

Innovative Product Design with Generative AI

Riya Sham, Adil Abdhul, and Shashank Reddy

11.1 Introduction

11.1.1 The Dawn of a New Design Era: Introducing Generative AI

As society's needs in terms of social media trends and technical advancement evolve, building new products requires a delicate balance between innovation and obsolescence. Although improved over time, conventional methods do not always keep pace with changes in customer needs. Nevertheless, the age of generative AI – a revolutionary technology that will transform how product creation is viewed and defined due to its unlimited creativity while also delivering personalization – is dawning.

All you need to do is imagine a world where designers, empowered with the magical power of generative AI, can orchestrate every creative note since the beginning of creation. They are no longer constrained by the limitations of human intuition or the repetition they tested through manual testing; they can create a digital environment. In this respect, algorithms based on learning large data sets of design generate an enchanting array of bizarre and unexpected variations and quirks. This does not mean a fictional world of some science fiction, but it is an actual reality where there is no clear distinction between human creativity and computer intelligence, resulting in goods that serve the needs as well as changing them at the same time.

"Compared to its other analytical peers, the generative AI is not just a highly advanced fact translator but rather an absolute master of creation.

Consider it a virtual Michelangelo, working his magic on the opportunities with not just objects but also events. It breaks down and reassembles the genetic code of current designs, spots many similarities and repetitions that it then assembles into a stunning tapestry of originality with variations" (Davenport, 2018). This allows the designers to venture into uncharted territories, transcending barriers of conventional thinking and stumbling upon solutions that would elude even the most creative human minds.

However, the magic of generative AI goes far beyond just novelty. It is a very powerful means of achieving both form and function. Think of a pair of shoes customized in the moment to your terrain, whose design has been sculpted by algorithms analyzing every detail of the foot contact's surface and representing a perfect blend between looks and functionality (Nike Adapt BB, n.d.). Either a prosthetic limb that moves intuitively or learns to move in an intuitive way and also mimics the user's neural patterns – a combination of engineering excellence coupled with human sensibility (Open Bionics, n.d.).

So, the examples are merely a glimpse of what lies at the nexus between the design and generative AI. It is a dynamic future full of many possibilities, where the products transform and renew themselves with the agility of life itself. It is a future where the concept of design itself is revised, no longer limited to the inert matter but equally fluid form, function, and user interface.

This, therefore, is the call we make to you, dear reader. Join us in our discussion about generative AI and its influence on the services of product design. We will dive deeper into the complex array of tools and techniques that drive this transformative technology in the upcoming chapters. We will analyze practical case studies where revolutionary products have already come to life at our hands and reflect on the ethical issues involved when one unleashes such vast powers. By our journey's end, you will not merely know the "what" and the "how" of generative AI in product design – but its raison d'être – that very reason why this technology is so critical to creating an innovative future for customer-focused brands.

11.1.2 Unravelling the Knots of Tradition: Challenges in Product Design

This once infinite reservoir of design inspiration feels like it's drying up in the modern landscape of product design. However, this is not due to the lack of creativity but rather an outcome stemming from the intricate systemic obstacles that are preventing spectacular novelty.

11.1.2.1 The Suffocating Grip of Repetitive Tasks

You can get bogged down in such repetitive tasks such as sketching different variations, market research, and creating prototypes. This leaves very little time or energy to pursue the deeper investigation and trial and error process that yields genuine innovation.

For instance, consider the toothbrush, many versions of this simple design have been plagued in the market, all claiming slight variations in bristle angles or ergonomic grips. While such improvements are very valuable assets, they rarely go beyond what a toothbrush can actually be and do. The emphasis on small-scale changes that must conform to strict deadlines and fit into established manufacturing techniques often leads designers dreaming of chances for creative freedom from the ordinary and uncharted territories.

11.1.2.2 The Maze of Constraints

However, every design begins with a maze of constraints – both practical and aesthetic. Material properties, engineering principles, and safety regulations are curtailing the wings of even the most visionary ideas. Aesthetic limitations, fueled by brand standards, target audiences, and dominating popularities, can add some homogeneity to the design sphere.

For instance, the smartphone has become a very common technology that completely transformed communication and entertainment. But, despite its disruptive capacity, the smartphone shape has endured defiantly stable amidst the brands and designs. However, the rectangular block may be undeniably elegant; yet it remains a solution that is optimized for scales of production and market popularity rather than a courageous leap into the unknown. Therefore, in practice, the limitations of extant supply chains, consumer expectations, and even investor confidence can often trump the pursuit of radical innovation.

11.1.2.3 The Relentless Pressure to Innovate

However, despite its many innovations, the design remains trapped in a vicious cycle of needing to create new and constantly improved products. This conveyor belt approach causes designers to feel as if they have run out of creative energy, forcing them to sacrifice originality in favor of speed and marketability. One of the issues that prevent adventurous design spaces from taking risks is the fear of falling behind their competitors and losing market share. This high-pressure cooker environment is characterized by an annual consumer electronics show (CES) where companies launch an incredible variety of tools and widgets every coming year to attract attention in a market that becomes more saturated perennially. Nevertheless, despite all the bling and sensational headlines, we cannot locate any products that broaden the user experience or knock out current paradigms. The ceaseless quest for the "next big thing" all too often overshadows genuine design breakthroughs.

All these challenges, which at first glance seem completely unrelated to each other, form a knotted thickness that slows down the labor of the revolutionary product birth. By understanding these barriers and the fact that they originate from design, we can move toward a future where radical, rather than incremental, advances are sought.

11.1.3 Blasting Open the Gates of Innovation: Generative AI to the Rescue

Consider a world in which one designer, armed with a laptop and a powerful AI tool, can produce hundreds of novel shoe designs within a few hours. Every design is not only attractive but also fine-tuned to the particular athlete's need be it ultra marathon or trail running. It is not a sci-fi scenario, but just a sneak peek into the future that generative AI promises to enable, transforming traditional product development approaches and moving businesses one step closer toward an innovation era.

Generative AI acts as a creative catalyst, igniting the design process with an explosive mix of numerous opportunities. Its superpowers are:

11.1.3.1 Evolving Ideas Exponentially

The old days of spending months on one sketch are over. Generative AI is capable of creating hundreds or even thousands of heterogeneous design variants in a matter of seconds. Suppose a team is coming up with new lines of sneakers. Instead of brainstorming concepts on a whiteboard, they may input keywords such as "ecologically sustainable," "running shoes," and "the" lightweight into an AI tool. The device will then generate a flurry of designs, each showcasing these elements in creative and unconventional schemes. It creates an immense field of opportunities, allowing companies to explore unexplored territories and discover undiscovered gems that have been left unnoticed by human beings.

11.1.3.2 *Venturing into Uncharted Territory*

Human intuition, though very influential, sometimes gets tied up in the ruts. Contrastingly, generative AI is free to venture into undiscovered design territories. It has the ability to look at the rich databases of current products, detect patterns and trends, and then use this information to generate completely novel concepts that would never have crossed human intelligence minds. Such teams help businesses push the limits of what can be achieved, producing products that are not only functional but also groundbreaking, and stay ahead of the curve in an ever-competitive market.

11.1.3.3 *Optimizing for Function and Form*

Not only aesthetics but also a perfect interplay between form and function is what the generative AI paradigm sets forth. It can analyze the attributes of materials, engineering principles, and users' demands that help in creating designs that go beyond beauty because they have practicality and efficiency as well. This can save a lot of money for the businesses because they may not have to spend on the prototyping and development cycles that prove unsuccessful in the end. For instance, generative design is one of the technologies used by companies such as Airbus and Nike in developing lightweight yet stronger products that consume less fuel. So, with the help of generative AI-based design optimization for aircraft wings or running shoe systems, many companies have been able to achieve superior performance at lower costs.

The advantages of generative AI for the design of products do not stop at just the physical product itself. By generating a wider range of design options, businesses can:

a. Improve customer satisfaction: The implementation of a diversified assortment helps enterprises to increase their customers' satisfaction and loyalty.
b. Reduce time to market: Generative AI can also dramatically shorten the design process, enabling organizations to launch newer products more quickly and capitalize on transient market trends.
c. Boost brand image: Through leading innovations, companies can benefit from generative AI to enhance brand image and attract new clients.

Examples of Generative AI in Action

a. Nike: Nike has exploited generative AI to customize shoes for athletes based on their specific requirements. Furthermore, their Flyknit technology is based on AI that makes use of athlete's foot data and running style to determine the best knitted upper material for perfect support and comfort.

b. Unilever: With generative AI, Unilever is designing new sustainable and also green product packaging. Their AI tool will consider the data on materials, manufacturing methods, and the consumers' preferences to output packaging that is not only functional but also low in environmental impact.

c. Procter & Gamble: P&G uses generative AI to produce new formulations that are more very effective and personalized. Their AI tool can analyze data such as skin type, and hair condition among others, and suggest customized shampoos, conditioners, or personal care products. These are some of the aspects wherein business enterprises have utilized generative AI to revolutionize product design. As technology advances, we will have incredibly many revolutionary and transformative applications.

11.2 The Role of Generative AI in the Design Process

11.2.1 Ideation

Think of a brainstorming room where the walls vibrate with an orchestra of many potentialities. Shapes mutate and contort, concepts cascade like a beautiful waterfall, and the seemingly impossible is made very tangible. This is the enchantment of generative AI at work in the ideational aspect of product design, where creativity and computation create a whole new epoch for innovation.

11.2.1.1 Breaking the Mold: Generating Diverse and Unexpected Concepts

Such is the plight of design in the nexus of human intuition, where it can quickly succumb to inevitability. Generative AI, on the other hand, breaks these barriers. Through the analysis of immense data volumes about the current designs, customers' preferences, and future technologies, it can generate a huge spectrum of new concepts that could never be expected.

It can be construed as a very frivolous muse, uttering bold suggestions that would never have been contrived by the human mind.

For instance, let's consider the Unilever sustainable packaging design. With generative AI, they researched thousands of material combinations, shapes, and closures that landed them with a recycle-friendly bottle made from paper which is at the same time very visually attractive. This would not have been possible without the AI's power to escape from the confinements of convention and venture into an unmarked country within the packaging field.

11.2.1.2 AI as a Market Whisperer: Informed Ideation Is Powered by the Data-Led Insights

Generative AI is not merely an amusing artist; it is also a data-focused planner. By carefully analyzing the market trends, user needs, and competitor products, it provides invaluable insights that feed into the ideation process. Now consider a team developing an entirely new series of running shoes. To begin with, the AI can interpret information about the consumer demand for cushioning, weight, and design, as well as trends in running shoes and even differences in gait dynamics. This information, of course, aids the AI in creating many ideas that are not only original but also appeal to the market and will resonate with the target customers.

"Data-driven ideation power is in the Nike's Flyknit technology. Findings show that their AI tool uses the characteristic features of each athlete's foot shape and running style to create unique knitted uppers, which can provide optimal support while being very comfortable. Without AI, this level of personalization wouldn't just be an artistic achievement, but it would also be a guaranteed customer-winning approach for the athletes looking to explore the most customized experience" (Nagori, 2022).

11.2.1.3 Tools of the Trade: AI Powered Brainstorming and Concept Generation Is a Good Way to Come up with New Ideas

Generative AI is very beautiful because it's quite approachable. A vast array of AI-based brainstorming tools and concept creation platforms is also now accessible, facilitating the use of such a game-changer technology even by small businesses as well as individual designers.

a. Ideocrunch: This AI-powered platform processes user inputs to produce a variety of concept sketches, which are excellent in initiating creative conversations and busting through creativity bottlenecks.

b. Dreamcatcher: Users can enter the keywords to get mood boards, color palettes, and even 3D models that will serve as visual guides for the ideation process.
c. In Vision Studio: With AI tools such as the "Smart Layout" and "Content Reflow," this design platform assists with layout design and content creation, allowing designers to focus on the big picture.

11.2.2 Prototyping and Testing

The product design process—brainstorming, sketching, prototyping, testing, and iterating—has undergone a dramatic revolution with the integration of generative AI. AI no longer remains the static world of 2D models, moving to the dynamic aspect of prototyping and testing, speeding up the design process, and driving a new age in iterative wizardry.

11.2.2.1 From Pixels to Possibilities: AI-Powered Prototyping

All the days of painstakingly slicing the physical prototypes from chunks of foam are gone. With generative AI comes the creation of hundreds of 3D models in minutes—all present as a virtual solution to every dance that can be put on the digital canvas. Consider a team developing the new hiking boots line. Traditional approaches may consist of designing a prototype, administering it to several volunteers, and then slowly proceeding through the repetition based on what they disclose. With AI, the team can produce dozens of boot designs tailored to various terrains and foot shapes. They can then use virtual simulations, where these models are tested in the simulated hiking conditions; wear and tear on various terrains is also analyzed along with the comfort levels of the user. Such a rapid prototyping and testing cycle enables the firms to make their designs laser-sharp, uncovering the potential pitfalls before they appear in reality and ultimately launch superior products at an accelerated rate.

11.2.2.2 Beyond the Lab: AI-Powered User Testing

Prototyping is only a part of the solution. The lifeblood of design optimization is user feedback. Access the virtual testing lab, which is powered by advanced user testing tools. Hiring focus groups and conducting long interviews is now a thing of the past. Now, AI can analyze facial expressions and eye movements as well as physiological signs such as the heart rate of the user in order to measure real-time enjoyment during testing for virtual prototypes.

11.2.2.3 Optimizing for Excellence: AI as a Design Architect

AI does not confine itself to the prototyping and testing part alone. It also acts as a designer, being capable of dealing with huge volumes of information to manufacture products for various purposes or needs. For instance, a company selling sportswear can develop some additional designs of running shoes. They enable the machine to receive data on running styles, gait patterns, and also surface preferences. Armed with this information, the AI then makes some relevant design alterations for the optimal use of these shoes by runners, depending on whether they are running over asphalts or the mountains. This data-driven design method helps companies to not only create products that look good but also those are perfectly created for the needs of their target audience, thus causing customer satisfaction and brand loyalty.

Examples of AI in Action:

a. "IKEA: Custom recommendations of furniture by IKEA use AI based on the browsing records and declared interests. This AI assistant guides the customers towards suitable products with regards to their style, budget, and current home interiors" (Ejaz, 2024).
b. Adidas: Adidas is now trying to enhance running shoes design by gathering athletes' performance records and analyzing how they run and other environmental factors. The result is more comfortable, lightweight shoes with better running efficiency and performance.
c. Ford: In the virtual simulation of self-driving cars powered by AI, Ford tests over 200 scenarios designed to preempt safety issues to prevent them from happening outside. In this AI-based test environment, Ford will be able to design safer and far more reliable autonomous vehicles at a quicker rate with high efficiency.

11.2.3 Optimization and Manufacturing: Where AI Meets Efficiency and Personalization

The generative impact of AI is very multifaceted and goes far beyond a simple flash of inspiration as regards to designing various products. As a continuous friend of design and production through consumption, it facilitates the materials, processes, and even products towards efficacy, sustainability, and personalization.

11.2.3.1 Material Mastery

Would you imagine a post-human era that enables advanced AI algorithms, fulfilled with mammoth databases of material properties, to propose optimized mixtures of strength and sustainability for your next production? This in material science is the power of generative AI technology. They can also be used with AI to weigh the cost and environmental impacts that could assist in the combinations of materials leading to desired products that are lighter but stronger at lower environmental impact.

    a. Example: With assistance from the generative AI, BMW designed a B-pillar for their iX electric car. Introduction weight by 20% through the optimizing material and structure without compromising the strength or safety requirements. This not only improved the fuel savings but also reduced pollution levels that were emitted by the vehicle.

11.2.3.2 Predictive Maintenance and Adaptive Design

Generative AI not only generates better product designs for the new products but can also tell beforehand whether an old product might fail and proposes several ways to prolong its lifecycle. Using predictive maintenance algorithms, the AI can utilize sensor information from inbuilt products to identify problems before they go boom and can offer preventative measures. This can drastically reduce the downtime and maintenance costs for these industries.

    a. *"Example:* Siemens uses generative AI to predict the component of the wind turbine that is prone to failure in the near future. AI mines vibrations and temperature data among so many others to unearth the early signs of wear-and tear that can be articulated into preventive maintenance" (Fountaine et al., 2019).

11.2.3.3 Personalized Products and Automated Production

Indeed, generative AI is also widening the gap between mass production and personalization. AI can further personalize product designs based on the data analysis of individual preferences and needs, as well as make adaptations to the production processes. Consider custom-ordered shoes that fit to perfection not only sizewise but also are shaped according to your gait and foot shape or the individualized shampoo designed specifically for the nature of hair.

a. *Example:* Nike has used generative AI to produce very unique custom running shoes for its athletes, modeled according to their individual biomechanical characteristics. By pressure sensors and motion capture camera information, the AI creates tailor-made shoes for every athlete that provide the ideal support and comfort.

11.2.3.4 Seamless Integration with Manufacturing Workflows

On the other hand, generative AI is not just a convenient design tool but an important element of manufacturing itself. Automating activities like production planning, quality control, and robot programming using AI can reduce the workflow processes, which in the long run increases efficiency. This may lead to improved production rates, reduction in wastage, and also better products.

a. *Example:* Ford employs generative AI to simplify its production of the F-150 trucks. All the stages of a manufacturing process are interpreted by an AI which focuses on the congestion points and suggests many ways of eliminating them. This has resulted in the reduction of production time by 10% and waste minimization at a level of 5%.

11.3 Case Studies and Success Stories: AI-Powered Innovation Takes Flight

Generative AI is no longer speculative, it has become a force in reality that generates real-life results. Let's delve into five diverse case studies, showcasing how leading companies across industries are harnessing this technology to unlock a new era of innovation

11.3.1 Nike: Personalizing Performance with Flyknit

"*Challenge:* Optimize the athletes' footwear performance in different sports" (Nagori, 2022).

Solution: In their Flyknit, Nike adopted the generative AI. This instrument evaluates the biometric characteristics of an athlete's foot morphology, mechanics, and running style. AI, in turn, creates a unique knit pattern for the upper which gives a custom fit and performance above one size fits all models.

Result: 24% average decrease in the running time, reduced injury rates, and increased customer satisfaction by 43%.

11.3.2 Unilever: Sustainable Packaging, AI-Assisted Design

Challenge: Provide environmentally friendly packaging while sustaining functionality and consumer appeal.

"Solution: Unilever teamed up with an AI platform to create many new designs for the packaging. The platform is used to analyze data on material properties, manufacturing processes, and consumer preferences in order to discover sustainable alternatives" (Mckinsey, n.d.).

Result: A 30% reduction in the packaging weight, a decreased carbon footprint of 15%, and a better consumer perception efficiency by 6%.

11.3.3 Coca-Cola: The AI-Bottled Creativity for the Personalized Beverages

Challenge: Meet the variegated customer needs and changing taste patterns in a dynamic market.

Solution: Coca-Cola partnered with an AI company to create a platform that provides recommendations for beverage formulations based on current market data and consumer input. This platform synthesizes personalized drink recipes that are unique to particular regions and also specific tastes.

"*Result:* 18% increase in sales of the emerging product lines guided by AI recommendations, and a further significant increase to 14% in satisfaction with beverage choices made" (Lobos, n.d.).

11.3.4 Airbus: Strong and Lightweight Wings by the Generative Design

Challenge: Lower the aircraft weight without compromising structural integrity and performance.

"Solution: Generative design software was employed by Airbus for optimizing airplane wing structures. As the software ran through millions of design iterations and material combinations, it created wings that were lighter yet stronger than the traditional designs" (Floridi, 2023).

Result: A wing weight reduction by 15% resulted in a 3% enhancement in fuel efficiency, accompanied by an incredible drop in airline spending.

11.3.5 Autodesk: Democratizing Design with Dreamcatcher AI

"Challenge: To develop professional level design tools that are very accessible to even the novice designers" (Chung, 2014).

Solution: The AI-driven Dreamcatcher tool, brought out by Autodesk has enabled the users to come up with concept sketches and refine their ideas on a design. The tool uses intuitive prompts and machine learning to produce visually pleasing designs that are also technically possible.

Result: And more than a million designs were created by Dreamcatcher, which was an increase in the non-professional software adoption and also user innovations activities; there was much change for the competition in the market.

The case studies paint a very bright and precise picture of how generative AI is really changing the product design landscape. Then AI not only helps ensure incremental improvements but also allows businesses to circumvent the existing methodologies and transform their offerings. The measurable outcomes, including a much shorter time to market and increased innovation as well as improved customer satisfaction reflect the effects of AI on the design.

It can be stated with certainty that the influence of this type of technology on business behaviors would not stop at product design as the continued developments become evident. These initial successes, from which insights will serve as a foundation for AI-driven marketing, personalized customer experiences, and data-driven business models. It is not only about designing brilliant products but also designing a better future, for which generative AI can prove as an effective guide.

11.4 Challenges and Ethical Considerations: Navigating the Design Frontier with AI

The road to becoming a product designer is not easy for the generative AI. Before we completely adopt this incredible tool, we must recognize the obstacles and ethical issues that are associated with its implementation in design.

11.4.1 *The Limits of Machine Magic*

Unfortunately, even with its outstanding capabilities, generative AI is not a magic wand. It feeds on the data, and the quality of that data determines how successful it is at generating results. Bias present in the training data may be amplified by AI thus resulting in design outcomes that are discriminatory or unfair. Moreover, the AI is unable to get an original idea and has always been based on old patterns and reference points thus creating additional designs. This may result in product uniformity and the absence of innovation.

11.4.1.1 *The Ownership Conundrum*

Who are the holders of intellectual property (IP) rights created by the AI? When lines are not clear in dividing the human input and artificial output, this question gets confused. Can this kind of a designer who encourages AI be credited with success? Or can the algorithm be deemed as an inventor? However, this vagueness can lead to creativity and collaboration being very limited because integrating AI into the design workflows becomes difficult.

11.4.1.2 *Bias in the Machine*

If the training data is skewed, then the AI will invariably reproduce its biases into its output. This may result in biased design choices including footwear designs that disproportionately fit certain kinds of feet or clothing patterns which reiterate the sex stereotype. Companies should be very careful in making sure that their AI tools are trained on inclusive and unbiased datasets.

11.4.1.3 *The Job Displacement Dilemma*

The jobs lost in designing are quite vulnerable to AI. What is the timeframe in which AI might replace human designers? Although AI can take away the drudgery from boring grinding and also give an idea about what the product could be, it does not have a human touch or understanding which is essential for user requirements as well as emotionally captivating. Almost omnipresent, the future of design is truly collaborative because AI not only complements but also greatly augments human innovation as opposed to displacing it entirely.

11.4.2 Navigating the Ethical Maze

Can we use generative AI for our advantage and also limit its possible harms while maintaining an ethical approach at the same time? Here are some best practices and ethical guidelines.

11.4.2.1 Transparency and Explain Ability

Companies will also have to make clearer the role of AI in the design processes, and what decisions were assigned to its algorithm.

11.4.2.2 Human Oversight and Control

Rather than replacing human creativity, AI should serve as a tool to enhance it. The designer should never be deprived of control in the design process or they can decide when to bring it.

11.4.2.3 Diversity and Inclusion

To prevent the continuation of bias, therefore, training data used by AI tools should be very representative. The marginalized voices should be sought and implemented by the businesses when designing their products.

11.4.2.4 Continuous Monitoring and Evaluation

Companies should watch out for bias that may spike with AI tools at all times. Regular evaluations and audits are really needed to maintain responsible use.

11.4.3 Here Are Some Examples of Companies Actively Addressing the Challenges and Implementing Ethical Best Practices in Their AI-Powered Design Processes

Addressing the Black Box Problem

a. Autodesk Dreamcatcher: This AI design tool provides a visual representation of the rationale informing its recommendations, enabling the users to comprehend what influences these generated innovations (Bade, 2008).

b. IBM Maximo Visual Inspection: AI anomaly detection uses visual explanations to identify the areas of concern in images, providing insight into the tool's decision-making.

Mitigating Data Bias

a. Procter & Gamble: As a way of dealing with the possible bias in their AI models that make personalized product recommendations, they created an "AI Fairness Council" to monitor and address the same (von Thienen et al., 2013).
b. Spotify: They use a variety of teams that are music curators and data scientists to train their AI algorithms, with an aim at having representation from different types of music styles and cultures.

Promoting Human-AI Collaboration

a. IDEO: This design company employs AI tools to create a "design playground" of initial concepts that serve as the basis for the subsequent human creative work.
b. IDEO U: This educational system provides many courses in "AI for Design Thinking" to enable the designers to collaborate with AI tools.

Ensuring Ethical Job Transitions

a. SAP: They embarked on an employee reskilling program known as the "Leonardo," retraining their staff for the jobs that work with or support AI.
b. Volkswagen: Their "New Work Lab" focuses on how AI can be used to enhance human performance and create new job positions in this company.

Bonus Example: Ownership and Collaboration

a. OpenAI CLIP: The open-source project focuses on AI models for multimodal learning, making the underlying technology and its constraints highly visible leading to a more collaborative development process while also addressing concerns about ownership.

11.5 The Future of AI-Powered Design

11.5.1 A Canvas of Infinite Possibilities

"The future of product design does not just represent the destination; it is a canvas wide open to many opportunities. In the very heart of this kaleidoscopic canvas, the generative AI paints its strokes irreversibly on the essence of product conception and creation. As we peer through the lens of tomorrow, here are some trends and technologies poised to reshape the design landscape" (Davenport, 2018):

11.5.1.1 Hyper Personalization: Design Tailored to Your DNA

Consider going into a store where the products are not mass-produced but are custom-made just for you according to your criteria, preferences, and even genes. This is the essence of hyper-personalization, which sees AI uncovering your data – from biometric readings to lifestyle patterns – for customized products that can never be separated from you. Consider the shoes that align with your stride, clothes that favorably regulate body temperature, or even furniture conformed by AI, all for the sake of user wellness.

11.5.1.2 Sentient Design: Products That Think and Feel

The boundary between the product and companion will be very indistinct as AI gives the objects a basic sense of consciousness. Envision a lamp that changes its intensity according to your mood, or even an autonomous vehicle predicting the future needs with regard to yourself. These intelligent products will also serve as a link between the actual and emotional, enabling an emotive design that is very sensitive to user needs.

11.5.1.3 Biomimetic Design: Nature as the Ultimate Muse

Biomimicry will be allowed by the generative AI, and we can learn to make the nature intuitively. Biomimetic structural building materials that imitate spider silk, aviaries designed on bird flying patterns or medical equipment patterned after organisms' regeneration capacity etc. Using the power of evolution, AI will take us to green and sustainable products for nature.

11.5.1.4 Democratization of Design: Creativity for All

Being based on AI-powered technologies that enable anyone to become a good creator, the design will be leveled up. Imagine systems that convert your imagination into drawings, create prototypes in reaction to a verbal instruction or even conceive products according to you personally. This democratization will generate an avalanche of innovations since various visions and images seep into the design space to form much more inclusive landscapes through breaching paradigms in expressing creativity.

11.5.1.5 Collaborative Canvas: A Perfect Combination of a Man and the Machine

Human and AI working together becomes the future of design. Illustration designers working in tandem with the AI as an overwhelming idea-maker, providing a variety of suggestions to be directed by the human intuition and taste for aesthetics. Under this partnership, the era of innovation in which human imagination and AI's unlimited creativity will create a world filled with many new products that were never viewed as possible.

11.5.2 Vision of the Future

Fast forward a decade. Imagine a world where AI architecture is integrated into the landscape, with exterior structures crafted through algorithmic patterns that promote thermal efficiency and comfort. Think of a retail outlet that can predict all your needs and customize their products, according to them. This is not just one of the stories of totalitarian dystopias, but it is also a reflection of an era when AI acts as an invisible hand, controlling our world through both beauty and goodness.

The road to this future will not be without any obstacles. Ethical issues, such as data security risks and the potential for job loss, need to be covered by addressing appropriate practices and collaborations. However, if we approach the potential of AI with a sense of responsibility and ethics, we can create a future that is not only creative but also environmentally friendly, inclusive thinking at heart—and ultimately human.

The canvas of the future is being prepared to be painted with magnificent colors. It's time to grab our human and AI brushes and make a masterpiece.

11.6 Conclusion: Embracing the Art of the Algorithm: Generative AI's Design Renaissance

"We are on the brink of a grand design revolution. Since generative AI is no longer bound by the constraints of manual iterations and also human intuition, businesses have an extremely powerful tool at their disposal. Not only does this transformative force remodel the design territory, but it completely redefines how we envisage and create products" (Fountaine et al., 2019).

As we discussed, generative AI acts as an innovation stimulus that provides an intoxicating variety of opportunities to the design process. It empowers us to:

Evolve ideas exponentially: There was no more slaving over a sketch for the weeks. As many as hundreds, or even thousands of diverse design variations are generated by the AI programs in mere minutes opening up endless horizons yet untapped.

Venture into uncharted territory: Escape the patterns of human intuition and venture into the design spaces that never could have been conceived. AI mines massive databases, uncovers hidden relationships, and creates very complex concepts that challenge the limits of imagination.

Optimize for function and form: It is all about the balance of beauty and functionality. Intelligent systems scan the material, engineering, and functional parameters to generate innovative yet efficient designs.

Recall that this is not some distant sci-fi fantasy. Companies such as Nike, Airbus, and Coca-Cola are already benefiting from the generative AI outcomes in the form of individualized running shoes, lighter aircraft wings, and environmentally friendly packaging. These are the initial outlines of the picture that is to come.

11.6.1 The Transformative Potential

The positive features of generative AI do not reduce themselves to the product itself. By democratizing design, reducing time to market, and igniting a wave of innovation, this technology will:

Empower individuals: What if anyone with or without a formal design education could create and personalize the products that meet their needs based on the set parameters? Democratizing design, the generative AI will bring about a revolution of grassroots innovation.

Shift the focus to experiences: The products will no longer be static articles; they represent dynamic escalates for the experimental experiences. These experiences will be orchestrated by the AI, customized to personal tastes, and interwoven into the everyday lives of all people.

Champion sustainability: With the aid of AI, the materials will be optimized; production processes will also be optimized, and sometimes, measures to minimize the environmental impact are integrated into product lifecycles. Think of the buildings that reflect their environment, with materials having self-healing capacity increasing the product's lifespan, and also resources reused or recycled as a new raw material (Amin et al., 2023).

11.6.2 The Human-AI Dance

This future does not imply that human beings are out of date. It is a symphony of synergy, where human comprehension and creativity mesh with AI's computational abilities as well as pattern recognition. The true magic lies in this delicate dance:

Human emotion and intuition: AI cannot duplicate the raw zeal, or gritty human connection that can spark off shocking innovation. It is this spark that sets the soul of a product, and its potential to captivate and engage with the users in an emotional way. Humans will continue to be the guardians of this emotional core, controlling and informing AI's outputs that are in turn designed with a human touch.

AI's computational power and boundless exploration: AI provides what humans are missing, namely the ability to process large data sets and find so called hidden patterns, allowing us to see things that are previously impossible. It can push the limits of what's knowable, create improbable solutions, and perpetually question our knowledge about product concepts. By such a constant search, the AI will work as an inspiration forever enlarging the range of design parameters.

11.6.3 Embrace the Possibilities

Without question, as we stand at the doors of this AI-driven design renaissance, a call to action is in order. Whether you're a seasoned designer, a budding entrepreneur, or simply someone who lives a life surrounded by objects, the message is clear: Research, investigate, and enjoy the many opportunities given by generative AI.

In this revolution, no one can be just a silent spectator. We are all painters, and AI is our tool. Let's envision the future where design is no longer a mere quest for function and aesthetics, but about human creativity in music by leveraging technology – symphony – as an act of empathy to this endless innovation.

References

Amin, R., Alnaqbi, M., Sayes, I., Abou-Hassan, A., Faroukh, Y., Obaideen, K., & AlShabi, M. A. (2023, June). Design and build of a bionic arm. In *Smart Biomedical and Physiological Sensor Technology XX* (Vol. 12548, pp. 66–70). SPIE.

Bade, S. (2008). Your Gut Is Still Not Smarter than Your Head: How Disciplined, Fact-based Marketing Can Drive Extraordinary Growth and Profits, Journal of Consumer Marketing, 25(3), 193–193. https://doi.org/10.1108/07363760810870716

Chung, H.D. (2014). Creative Confidence: Unleashing the Creative Potential Within Us Allby Tom Kelley and David Kelley. *Journal of Business & Finance Librarianship, 19*(2), 168–172. https://doi.org/10.1080/08963568.2014.883249

Davenport, Thomas, H. (2018). *The AI Advantage.* [online] repo.darmajaya.ac. Available at: http://repo.darmajaya.ac.id/4846/1/The%20AI%20Advantage_%20 How%20to%20Put%20the%20Artificial%20Intelligence%20Revolution%20to%20 Work%20(%20PDFDrive%20).pdf [Accessed 12 Feb. 2024].

Ejaz, U. (2024). *Harnessing the Power of Artificial Intelligence for Social Good: Opportunities, Challenges, and Impact.* [online] https://www.researchgate.net/ Available at: https://www.researchgate.net/publication/377695614_Harnessing_ the_Power_of_Artificial_Intelligence_for_Social_Good_Opportunities_ Challenges_and_Impact/link/65b2bda334bbff5ba7c4ad14/download?_tp=eyJjb 250ZXh0Ijp7ImZpcnN0UGFnZSI6InB1YmxpY2F0aW9uIiwicGFnZSI6InB1Ymx pY2F0aW9uIn19 [Accessed 2 Feb. 2024].

Floridi, L. (2023). *The Ethics of Artificial Intelligence.* [online] global.oup.com. Available at: https://global.oup.com/academic/product/the-ethics-of-artificial-intelligence-9780198883098?cc=us&lang=en&# [Accessed 10 Feb. 2024].

Fountaine, T., McCarthy, B., & Saleh, T. (2019). Building the AI-powered organization. *Harvard Business Review, 97*(4), 62–73.

Lobos, A. (n.d.). *A Practical Guide for Generative Design in Product and Industrial Design.* [online] Available at: https://static.au-uw2-prd.autodesk.com/Class_ Handout_CP500001_ClassHandout-CP500001-Lobos-AU2021.pdf [Accessed 12 Feb. 2024].

Nagori, M. (2022). *Nike-A Case Study Just Do It.* [online] ResearchGate. Available at: https://www.researchgate.net/publication/358734060_Nike-A_Case_Study_Just_ Do_It

Open Bionics - Turning Disabilities into Superpowers. (n.d.). Open Bionics. https:// openbionics.com/en/

von Thienen, J., Meinel, C., & Nicolai, C. (2013). How Design Thinking Tools Help to Solve Wicked Problems. *Design Thinking Research*, 97–102. https://doi. org/10.1007/978-3-319-01303-9_7

www.nike.com. (n.d.). *How Do I Get Started with My Nike Adapt Shoes?| Nike Help.* Available at: https://www.nike.com/help/a/adapt-get-started [Accessed 7 Jan. 2024].

Chapter 12

Mind the Gap: Bridging Success with AI in Marketing

Shruti Choudhary

12.1 Introduction

Artificial intelligence (AI) looks to have the potential to affect marketing techniques, including company models, sales processes, and customer service alternatives, as well as consumer behaviors, in the future. AI is recognized by marketing experts as having significant potential advantages for customers and their lifestyles (e.g., Pitardi et al., 2021). The Marketing Science Institute characterizes AI as an important technology that has an influence on the capacities and accountability of marketing management, as well as the optimization of marketing operations and strategies, in its research goals for 2020–2022 (Marketing Science Institute, 2020).

According to studies, AI is the most significant technology for business, with a projected increase from $10.1 billion in 2018 to $126 billion by 2025 (Tractica, 2020). According to a recent poll of business executives, sales and marketing are a key area for AI application, with 24% of US organizations now utilizing AI and 60% expecting to utilize it by 2022 (MIT Technology Review Insights, 2020). AI is becoming increasingly significant in marketing from a strategic standpoint. Google, Rare Carat, Spotify, and Under Armour are among the growing number of companies that are improving their performance by implementing AI-based systems (such as Microsoft Cognitive Services, Amazon Lex, Google Assistant, or IBM Watson).

AI is recognized by marketing experts as having significant potential advantages for customers and their lifestyles (e.g., Pitardi et al., 2021;

 DOI: 10.4324/9781032711089-12

Davenport et al., 2020; Kumar et al., 2019; Kumar et al., 2020a). However, there are inherent conflicts that greater usage of AI can have on customers, such as privacy issues, dehumanization, and even addiction.

In this regard, we support the concept of Marketing AI as "the development of artificial agents that, given the information they have about consumers, competitors, and the focal company, suggest and/or take marketing actions to achieve the best marketing outcome" (Overgoor et al., 2019).

So far, the academic research on AI in marketing has been divided into four categories. These are (1) technical AI algorithms for solving specific marketing problems (e.g., Chung et al. 2009; Chung et al. 2016; Dzyabura and Hauser, 2019), (2) customers' psychological reactions to AI (e.g., Luo et al. 2019; Mende et al. 2019), (3) effects of AI on jobs and society, and (4) managerial and strategic issues related to AI (e.g., Fountaine et al., 2019

12.1.1 Benefits of AI in Marketing Domain

Based on the literature review, we explored the mentioned benefits of using AI in the marketing domain.

1. AI in Marketing Research (Rust, 2020).
   The AI advantages are classified into three groups based on AI's function in three distinct fields. There are three types of AI: Mechanical AI, thinking AI, and feeling AI. Mechanical AI may be used to collect data, making both the competitor and the consumer more transparent, and bringing privacy governance to the forefront for marketers. Furthermore, Thinking AI may change theory-driven marketing research into data-driven marketing research, sparking a discussion regarding whether a data or theory-based approach to marketing research should be used. Although pure emotional robots are not yet accessible, feeling AI can be employed for consumer comprehension. This begs the issue of how AI's capacity to grasp emotions may affect future research subjects (Huang et al., 2019).
2. AI In Marketing Strategy (Fountaine et al., 2019).
   Mechanical AI can be used in the marketing strategy stage for segment recognition, thinking AI for recommending the best segment(s) to target in the marketing strategy stage, and feeling AI for positioning, specifically for segment resonance in the marketing strategy stage (Timoshenko and Hauser, 2019).

3. AI in Marketing Actions (Huang and Rust, 2021).
   Mechanical AI may be utilized in the service industry to standardize marketing actions such as automatic payment and delivery monitoring, whereas thinking AI can be used for personalization in digital marketing, such as through recommendation systems (Kumar et al., 2019). We can take advantage of relationalization in customer service and frontline consumer engagement, such as social robots welcoming clients and conversational AI delivering customer service, which can benefit from feeling AI.

4. AI for Efficient Data Handling and Personalized Sales (Campbell et al., 2020).
   Many businesses that use AI use it to target customers, provide product suggestions, and improve advertising campaigns (Blueshift et al., 2018). Machine learning (ML) systems recognize patterns and learn how to make predictions and recommendations by analyzing data and experiences rather than getting explicit programming instructions. ML is a strong tool for mining enormous amounts of data, allowing marketers to acquire new insights into customer behavior and enhance marketing operations effectiveness (Cui, Wong, & Lui, 2006; Das & Sharma, 2016; Davenport et al., 2020).

5. AI in Consumer Behavior Prediction
   Marketers may use AI to study purchasing behaviors and predict more competitive product pricing points in order to persuade buyers at the time of choice. AI and ML let Amazon collect all of this consumer data and determine what buyers want and how much they are ready to spend. According to research, AI is also being used to fine-tune product marketing, with Samsung using Crimson Hexagon's AI-powered audience-insights platform to analyze what its existing and future consumers are saying on social media (Sentence, 2018). As a result, analyzing user-generated discussions and accompanying photos on social media platforms aids in understanding "how consumers interact with their products, and thus how to create marketing campaigns".

6. AI in Strategic Marketing Decisions.
   The ongoing advancement of AI technology has an impact on the future of marketing tactics (Rust, 2020). Improvements in business model decisions, new product development, communication (Paschen, 2019), pricing, sales management (Flaherty et al., 2018), advertising,

and personalized mobile marketing strategies have been noted by implementers of AI-based marketing solutions.

These AI marketing benefits seek to maximize the benefits of numerous AI intelligences for the benefit of the marketing profession. Aside from the foregoing, AI applications increase the scope of marketing in consumer research and psychology, with the potential to improve our understanding of consumer behavior and decision-making processes. AI may assist in identifying patterns and trends in consumer data that traditional research approaches may miss. Furthermore, AI can assist marketing analysts in developing more accurate prediction models of customer behavior.

Marketing professionals are now able to use AI to tailor marketing messages and experiences for specific consumers. AI can assist businesses in analyzing massive volumes of data to determine individual preferences and customize marketing messages appropriately. Furthermore, AI may assist businesses in automating certain marketing chores, such as customer support and lead generation, allowing marketers to focus on more strategic efforts. However, research shows that there are possible ethical issues with the use of AI in marketing. Concerns have been raised, for example, concerning privacy and data security, as well as the potential for AI to propagate bias and discrimination. Researchers and practitioners must evaluate the ethical implications of AI in marketing and consumer research and seek to reduce any potential negative consequences (Mariani et al., 2022). Table 12.1 summarizes recent studies on AI's involvement in marketing.

12.1.2 AI Tools Application in Marketing Field

Li and Chen's (2023) research reveals how AI-driven marketing platforms have evolved into entire ecosystems. Predictive analytics, automatic content development, and real-time consumer feedback loops are all features of these platforms. They let marketers to scale highly targeted campaigns, automate regular operations, and obtain deep insights into customer behavior. AI's power has been democratized by such platforms, allowing organizations of all sizes to leverage its potential. AI prediction models have emerged as the revolution's cornerstone.

These algorithms examine massive datasets using ML and deep learning approaches, uncovering hidden relationships and delivering predictions that

Table 12.1 Summary of Recent Studies on AI's Involvement in Marketing

Title	Citation	Findings
Waiting for a sales renaissance in the fourth industrial revolution: Machine learning and artificial intelligence in sales research and practice	Syam & Sharma (2010)	AI facilitates marketing effectiveness at each stage of the business-to-business sales funnel. Authors discuss the impact of machine learning and AI and propose future research avenues for sales processes regarding prospecting, pre-approach, approach, presentation, overcoming objections, close, and follow-up.
How artificial intelligence will change the future of marketing	Davenport et al. (2020)	Building on insights from marketing, social sciences, and computer science robotics, the authors propose a framework to help customers and firms anticipate how AI is likely to evolve. The authors outline three AI-related dimensions: Levels of intelligence, task type, and whether or not the AI is embedded in a robot, highlighting the potential effects of AI implementation through cost reduction
Influence of new-age technologies on marketing: A research agenda	Kumar et al. (2020a)	Focusing on the respective roles of IoT, AI, ML, and Blockchain in marketing, the authors outline the importance of the implementation of technology with regards to marketing outcomes, the necessity for financial and human resources, and the subsequent impact on customer relationships.
Digital mediation in business-to-business marketing: A bibliometric analysis	Kumar et al. (2020b)	Synthesizing two decades of literature on digital mediation in business-to-business marketing, the authors outline the major changes to the research field affected by the emergence of Internet research and business-to-business technology, the evolution of e-commerce, and the new focus on social media. The authors recommend further research on the intersection of social media and tools, channels.

(Continued)

Table 12.1 *(Continued)*

Title	Citation	Findings
Artificial intelligence in business: State of the art and future research agenda	Loureiro et al. (2020)	This review summarizes the role of AI within the general business field. The findings of this study reveal 18 different topics that have attracted scholarly attention regarding AI's applicability, ranging from learning to marketing and manufacturing. Accordingly, the authors reveal that marketing is among the topics in which AI has attracted the most attention from researchers and practitioners. Finally, the authors propose future trends related to AI's effects on internal stakeholders, external stakeholders, and governmental policymaking.
Artificial intelligence in marketing: Topic modeling, scientometric analysis, and research agenda	Mustak et al. (2020)	Building on insights from 214 articles indexed in the Web of Science Database, using CiteSpace and VOSviever, the authors outline the countries, universities, and authors that have contributed to the development of AI in Marketing, presenting the predominant research topics. Furthermore, the findings of the study highlight future research opportunities related to two interrelated relevant streams of research: (1) increased depth and (2) increased breadth
The Future of Marketing	Rust (2020)	The future of marketing is influenced by changes in three major forces: 1) technological trends, 2) socioeconomic trends, and 3) geopolitical trends. The development of AI algorithms unveils the potential of all aspects of marketing research, education, and practice.

direct marketing tactics with unparalleled precision. They have rendered traditional market research approaches obsolete and have become important tools for organizations seeking to remain ahead of the competition in an ever-changing industry. Personalization is one of the primary areas where AI prediction models have gained importance.

Modern consumers want personalized experiences, whether in the form of product recommendations, content recommendations, or targeted marketing. AI-powered predictive models have become crucial tools for marketers. These models use previous data to estimate consumer behavior in the future. Sim et al. (2020) conducted a study that demonstrated the efficacy of predictive modeling in predicting possible customer attrition. Such approaches enable firms to address concerns proactively and personalize their services, hence increasing client retention.

Personalization and Hyper-Targeting: Hyper-personalization is one of AI's most notable contributions to modern marketing. Anderson and Martínez's (2021) research focuses on how AI-powered algorithms may assess individual browser behaviors, purchase histories, and social media interactions to develop highly tailored marketing material. This degree of customization not only improves the user experience but also increases conversion rates dramatically. Customers today want personalized suggestions and content, and AI is the engine behind this personalization.

Sentiment analysis and social listening techniques were investigated, demonstrating how AI can assess public attitude about products and companies. This real-time feedback loop provides quick answers to both positive and negative sentiments, assisting in the agile shaping of marketing tactics.

12.2 Recommendations for Optimizing AI Technologies in Marketing

The report offers numerous recommendations for marketers and organizations to solve these problems and fully realize the promise of AI in marketing (Vidhya et al., 2023).

- ■ Invest in AI education and talent: To effectively exploit AI technology, businesses should emphasize educating and employing data scientists and AI professionals.
- ■ Companies should create explicit ethical norms for AI use, as well as promote openness in data collecting and algorithmic decision-making.
- ■ Data quality and privacy: Improve data quality and security while communicating openly with customers about data usage.

■ Integration and scalability: Create methods for easily incorporating AI into existing marketing processes, as well as plans for scalability as the firm expands.

■ Continuous monitoring and adaptation: Evaluate the performance of AI models on a regular basis and update them in response to changing customer behaviors and market circumstances.

■ Competitive advantage: AI also allows for the creation of predictive models that can foresee market trends, allowing firms to anticipate changes in customer behavior and remain ahead of the curve.

■ Marketers may also use omnichannel AI to find cross-channel patterns and correlations that can help them develop more effective marketing strategies.

■ Artificial intelligence-powered content generating solutions may assist marketers in streamlining the content development process and producing highly relevant and engaging content at scale. Natural language generation (NLG) algorithms, for example, may produce product descriptions, blog entries, and even tailored email content automatically.

■ Chatbots are also being integrated into social media in order to create new client leads. The highly interactive nature of Chatbots is increasing consumer interaction and engagement (Chung, Ko, Joung, & Kim, 2018). The increasing interaction of chatbots makes it popular for providing better and more specialized customer care, particularly in electronic commerce (Go & Sundar, 2019). A review of the research on chatbots shows that when sellers make efforts to address customer demands, customer engagement improves (Chung et al., 2018; Xu, Liu, Guo, Sinha, & Akkiraju, 2017).

■ Supervised learning is required to offer a learning base for future data processing in order to forecast consumer behavior. It is a learning approach designed to anticipate outcomes in the face of unknown input instances (King, 2020). It has an algorithm for responding to the dataset and creating a categorization model for future data processing. As a result, AI can give important data to forecast their actions in real-time processes, employing automation using ML and supervised learning.

Table 12.2 displays the most recent research brief on the deployment of AI techniques.

Table 12.2   Literature Review on - Deployment of AI Techniques

AI tool application	Functions	Citation
AI-powered Analytics	One of the standout applications of AI in marketing is its ability to analyze vast datasets swiftly. Through advanced analytics, marketers gain invaluable insights into consumer behavior, enabling data-driven decision-making and more effective campaign targeting.	Agarwal et al., 2021
Personalization through Machine Learning	AI's prowess in machine learning empowers marketers to deliver personalized experiences to their audience. From customized recommendations to individualized content, machine learning algorithms adapt to user preferences, enhancing customer engagement and satisfaction.	Ma and Sun,2020
Chatbots and Customer Engagement	AI-driven chatbots take center stage in providing real-time customer support. These intelligent bots not only resolve queries promptly but also contribute to a seamless customer experience, building brand loyalty.	Trappey et al., 2021
Predictive Analytics for Targeted Campaigns	AI-driven predictive analytics forecast future trends and consumer behavior, allowing marketers to craft targeted campaigns that resonate with their audience on a deeper level.	Zulaikha et al., 2020
SEO Optimization with AI	Search Engine Optimization (SEO) is a critical aspect of any digital strategy. AI algorithms refine SEO efforts, enhancing website visibility and driving organic traffic through intelligent keyword optimization.	Panchal et al., 2021
Video and Image Recognition for Enhanced Content	Visual content dominates online platforms. AI's ability to analyze and recognize images and videos ensures that marketers deliver visually appealing and relevant content that captivates their audience.	Grewal et al., 2021
AI-driven Customer Service	Virtual assistants, powered by natural language processing, offer efficient and personalized support, enhancing overall customer satisfaction.	Chaturvedi et al., 2023

12.3 Future Implications and Conclusion

Finally, significant breakthroughs in AI technology are transforming the marketing area, allowing businesses to reinvent their approach to consumer data gathering, storage, analysis, and usage (Rust, 2020). The use of AI in marketing plans not only improves efficiency but also considerably decreases costs by expediting marketing activity implementation. Exceptionally adaptable technologies like Midjourney and DELL-2 enable marketers to create visually appealing material for future advertising campaigns, while language models like ChatGPT by OpenAI aid in the production of distinctive and engaging marketing messages.

However, this is only the tip of the iceberg in terms of such prospects, since the future promises an exponential expansion. Many scholars, including A. Halim, M. Jawaid, and M. A. Qadri, have emphasized the revolutionary potential of AI in marketing, but Kumari (2024) extends on this by noting particular areas for development. These include sales forecasting, customer knowledge, profile development, digital advertising campaign optimization, real-time audience interaction, and marketing process automation. Looking forward, it is clear that artificial intelligence (AI) is ready to transform every aspect of the sales process, from prospecting and pre-approach to presentation and follow-up (Singh et al., 2020; Syam and Sharma, 2010).

Furthermore, AI technologies are not only fundamentally changing marketing, but also stimulating a move toward glocalization, in which global methods are tailored to local surroundings. This rapid growth brings with it a slew of new opportunities and problems. On the one hand, AI enables marketers to tailor their strategies to regional preferences, cultural subtleties, and market demands, resulting in a more customized and meaningful relationship with varied customer bases. On the other side, this tendency of localization creates ethical and privacy issues among consumers. As AI-powered marketing methods get more complex, the necessity for stringent laws, extensive education, and focused training programs becomes critical. The ethical use of artificial intelligence in marketing is critical to establishing and sustaining customer trust, and industry stakeholders must work together to set and implement ethical norms that protect privacy and encourage openness.

In the future, the ramifications of AI in marketing will be vast and diverse. To begin, the continuing advancement of AI technology will almost certainly result in increasingly more complex tools and platforms, boosting marketers' creative possibilities. Improved AI-powered solutions to complicated marketing issues may develop, enabling predictive analytics, greater customer profiling, and more sophisticated automation. The use of AI in virtual and augmented reality experiences has the potential to revolutionize the way companies connect with their customers by enabling immersive and customized interactions. Furthermore, the emergence of AI-powered voice and visual search technology has the potential to reshape the landscape of online advertising and consumer behavior.

Second, the increasing dependence on artificial intelligence in marketing needs a paradigm shift in labor skills and education. As AI becomes more integrated into marketing tactics, professionals will need to learn a new set of skills in order to properly exploit these technologies. This covers knowledge of data analytics, ML, and the ethical implications of AI in marketing. Educational institutions and industry training programs will be critical in providing the next generation of marketers with the information and abilities required to navigate the changing terrain of AI-driven marketing.

In conclusion, the future of AI in the marketing domain holds tremendous promise and potential. The ongoing integration of AI technologies is reshaping marketing strategies, offering unprecedented opportunities for efficiency, personalization, and innovation. However, this transformation also brings along ethical considerations, privacy concerns, and the need for continuous education and regulation. As we embrace the evolving role of AI in marketing, stakeholders must work collaboratively to harness the benefits of these technologies responsibly, ensuring a harmonious balance between innovation and ethical standards. The journey ahead is marked by challenges and opportunities, and it is imperative for the marketing industry to proactively navigate this transformative landscape for a sustainable and ethical AI-powered future.

To summarize, the future of AI in marketing has enormous promise and possibility. AI technology integration is altering marketing methods, providing new prospects for efficiency, customization, and creativity. This revolution, however, comes with it ethical challenges, privacy concerns, and the need for ongoing education and regulation. As we accept AI's expanding role in marketing, stakeholders must collaborate to appropriately exploit the benefits of emerging technologies, preserving a harmonic balance between innovation and ethical norms. The road ahead is fraught with problems and possibilities, and it is critical for the marketing profession to negotiate this changing terrain in order to ensure a sustainable and ethical AI-powered future.

References

Agarwal, G. K., Magnusson, M., & Johanson, A. (2021). Edge AI driven technology advancements paving way towards new capabilities. *International Journal of Innovation and Technology Management, 18*(01), 2040005.

Anderson, T., & Martínez, S. (2021). Distributed resource allocation with binary decisions via Newton-like Neural Network dynamics. *Automatica, 128,* 109564.

Campbell, C., Sands, S., Ferraro, C., Tsao, H. Y. J., & Mavrommatis, A. (2020). From data to action: How marketers can leverage AI. *Business Horizons, 63*(2), 227–243.

Chaturvedi, R., & Verma, S. (2023). Opportunities and challenges of AI-driven customer service. In Artificial Intelligence in Customer Service: The Next Frontier for Personalized Engagement (pp. 33–71), Cham: Palgrave Macmillan.

Chen, S., Wang, Z., Zhang, M., Shi, X., Wang, L., An, W., ... Yang, L. (2023). Chen et al. *Carbon Energy, 5*(8).

Chung, D. Y., Sugimoto, K., Fischer, P., Böhm, M., Takizawa, T., Sadeghian, H., ... Ayata, C. (2018). Real-time non-invasive in vivo visible light detection of cortical spreading depolarizations in mice. *Journal of Neuroscience Methods, 309,* 143–146.

Chung, J., Cho, K., & Bengio, Y. (2016). A character-level decoder without explicit segmentation for neural machine translation. In K. Erk & N. A. Smith (Eds.), *Proceedings of the 54th Annual Meeting of the Association for Computational Linguistics* (Volume 1: Long Papers) (pp. 1693–1703). Association for Computational Linguistics. https://doi.org/10.18653/v1/P16-1160

Chung, M., Ko, E., Joung, H., & Kim, S. J. (2020). Chatbot e-service and customer satisfaction regarding luxury brands. *Journal of Business Research, 117,* 587–595.

Chung, W., Chen, H., Nunamaker, J. F., & Wang, R. (2009). A visual framework for knowledge discovery on the Web: An empirical study of business intelligence exploration. *Journal of Management Information Systems, 25*(2), 145–182. https://doi.org/10.2753/MIS0742-1222250207

Cui, G., Wong, M. L., & Lui, H. K. (2006). Machine learning for direct marketing response models: Bayesian networks with evolutionary programming. *Management Science, 52*(4), 597–612.

Das, M., & Sharma, S. (2016). Fetishizing women: Advertising in Indian television and its effects on target audiences. *Journal of International Women's Studies, 18*(1), 114–132.

Davenport, T. H., Guha, A., Grewal, D., & Bressgott, T. (2020). How artificial intelligence will change the future of marketing. *Journal of the Academy of Marketing Science, 48*(1), 24–42. https://doi.org/10.1007/s11747-019-00696-0

Dzyabura, D., & Hauser, J. R. (2019). Recommending products when consumers learn their preference weights. *Marketing Science, 38*(3), 417–441.

Flaherty, K. M., Hughes, A. M., Teague, R., Simon, J. B., Andrews, S. M., & Wilner, D. J. (2018). Turbulence in the TW Hya disk. *The Astrophysical Journal, 856*(2), 117.

Go, E., & Sundar, S. S. (2019). Humanizing chatbots: The effects of visual, identity and conversational cues on humanness perceptions. *Computers in Human Behavior, 97,* 304–316.

Grewal, R., Gupta, S., & Hamilton, R. (2021). Marketing insights from multimedia data: Text, image, audio, and video. *Journal of Marketing Research*, *58*(6), 1025–1033.

Huang, M. H., & Rust, R. T. (2021). A strategic framework for artificial intelligence in marketing. *Journal of the Academy of Marketing Science*, *49*, 30–50.

Huang, M. H., Rust, R. T., & Maksimovic, V. (2019). The feeling economy: Managing in the next generation of artificial intelligence (AI). *California Management Review*, *61*(4), 43–65.

King, D. (2020). Customer churn–Irish electricty/gas market.

Kumari, P. (2024). To study the impact of ai on digital marketing strategy. *International Journal of Research and Analytical Reviews* (IJRAR), *11*(2), 286–320.

Kumar, V., Rajan, B., Venkatesan, R., & Lecinski, J. (2019). Understanding the role of artificial intelligence in personalized engagement marketing. *California Management Review*, *61*(4), 135–155.

Kumar, V., Ramachandran, D., & Kumar, B. (2020a). Influence of new-age technologies on marketing: A research agenda. *Journal of Business Research*, 125, 864–877. https://doi.org/10.1016/j.jbusres.2019.12.038

Kumar, V., Sharma, A., & Bhagwat, Y. (2020b). The role of digital and social media marketing in B2B firms: An agenda for future research. *Industrial Marketing Management*, *91*, 154–165. https://doi.org/10.1016/j.indmarman.2020.01.001

Labib, E. (2024). Artificial intelligence in marketing: exploring current and future trends. *Cogent Business & Management*, *11*(1), pp. 1–13. https://doi.org/10.1080/23311975.2024.2348728

Loureiro, S. M. C., Guerreiro, J., & Tussyadiah, I. (2020). Artificial intelligence in business: State of the art and future research agenda. *Journal of Business Research*, 129, 911–926. https://doi.org/10.1016/j.jbusres.2020.11.001

Luo, X., Tong, S., Fang, Z., & Qu, Z. (2019). Frontiers: Machines vs. humans: The impact of artificial intelligence chatbot disclosure on customer purchases. *Marketing Science*, *38*(6), 937–947.

Ma, L., & Sun, B. (2020). Machine learning and AI in marketing–Connecting computing power to human insights. *International Journal of Research in Marketing*, *37*(3), 481–504.

Mariani, M. M., Perez-Vega, R., & Wirtz, J. (2022). AI in marketing, consumer research and psychology: A systematic literature review and research agenda. *Psychology & Marketing*, *39*(4), 755–776.

Marketing Science Institute. (2020). *2020-2022 Research priorities*. https://www.msi.org/research/2020-2022-research-priorities/

MIT Technology Review Insights. (2020). *The global AI agenda: Promise, reality, and a future of data sharing*. https://www.technologyreview.com

Mustak, M., Salminen, J., Plé, L., & Wirtz, J. (2020). Artificial intelligence in marketing: Bibliometric analysis of research topics, countries, and institutions. *Journal of Business Research*, 120, 342–359. https://doi.org/10.1016/j.jbusres.2020.03.030

Overgoor, G., Chica, M., Rand, W., & Weishampel, A. (2019). Letting the computers take over: Using AI to solve marketing problems. *California Management Review*, *61*(4), 156–185.

Panchal, A., Shah, A., & Kansara, K. (2021). Digital marketing-search engine optimization (SEO) and search engine marketing (SEM). *International Research Journal of Innovations in Engineering and Technology, 5*(12), 17–21.

Paschen, J., Kietzmann, J., & Kietzmann, T. C. (2019). Artificial intelligence (AI) and its implications for market knowledge in B2B marketing. *Journal of Business & Industrial Marketing, 34*(7), 1410–1419.

Pitardi, D., Meloni, D., Olivo, F., Loprevite, D., Cavarretta, M. C., Behnisch, P., Brouwer, A., Felzel, E., Ingravalle, F., Capra, P., Gili, M., Pezzolato, M., & Bozzetta, E. (2021). Alexa, she's not human but… Unveiling the drivers of consumers' trust in voice-based artificial intelligence. *Psychology & Marketing, 38*(4), 626–642.

Pitardi, V., Wirtz, J., Paluch, S., & Kunz, W. (2021). Service robots, agency, and embarrassing service encounters. *Journal of Service Management, 33*(2), 389–414.

Rust, R. T. (2020). The future of marketing. *International Journal of Research in Marketing, 37*(1), 15–26. https://doi.org/10.1016/j.ijresmar.2019.08.002

Sim, B. L. H., Chidambaram, S. K., Wong, X. C., Pathmanathan, M. D., Peariasamy, K. M., Hor, C. P., … Goh, P. P. (2020). Clinical characteristics and risk factors for severe COVID-19 infections in Malaysia: A nationwide observational study. *The Lancet Regional Health–Western Pacific, 4*, 100055.

Singh, S. K., Rathore, S., & Park, J. H. (2020). Blockiotintelligence: A blockchain-enabled intelligent IoT architecture with artificial intelligence. *Future Generation Computer Systems, 110*, 721–743.

Timoshenko, A., & Hauser, J. R. (2019). Identifying customer needs from user-generated content. *Marketing Science, 38*(1), 1–20.

Tractica. (2020). *Artificial intelligence market forecasts.* https://www.tractica.com/research/artificial-intelligence-market-forecasts/

Trappey, A. J., Trappey, C. V., Chao, M. H., Hong, N. J., & Wu, C. T. (2021). A VR-Enabled chatbot supporting design and manufacturing of large and complex power transformers. *Electronics, 11*(1), 87.

Vidhya, V., Donthu, S., Veeran, L., Lakshmi, Y. S., & Yadav, B. (2023). The intersection of AI and consumer behavior: Predictive models in modern marketing. *Remittances Review, 8*(4), 2410–2424.

Xu, A., Liu, Z., Guo, Y., Sinha, V., & Akkiraju, R. (2017, May). A new chatbot for customer service on social media. In *Proceedings of the 2017 CHI conference on human factors in computing systems* (pp. 3506–3510).

Zulaikha, S., Mohamed, H., Kurniawati, M., Rusgianto, S., & Rusmita, S. A. (2020). Customer predictive analytics using artificial intelligence. *The Singapore Economic Review*, 1–12. https://dx.doi.org/10.1142/S0217590820480021

Chapter 13

Reshaping Marketing Strategies with AI

V. Vishnu Vardhan, Sathwika Manthena, Deepthi Reddy, and Mir Aadil

13.1 Introduction

In the dynamic realm of business, the infusion of Artificial Intelligence (AI) into marketing strategies has emerged as a current stress, reshaping traditional techniques and ushering in a new era of outstanding insights and performance. This financial crisis aims to address the complex relationship between AI and marketing, shedding light on its significant impact on businesses and the vast potential it holds for shaping the future of advertising strategies. The advent of AI into marketing has marked a paradigm shift, providing corporations with the potential to analyse huge quantities of information with extraordinary tempo and accuracy. Machine getting to know algorithms, a subset of AI, permit entrepreneurs to determine patterns, count on purchaser behaviour, and optimise campaigns in actual time. This records-driven method transcends human barriers, imparting marketers with a holistic view of their target audience and taking into consideration personalised, targeted campaigns that resonate with consumers on a deeper degree.

One of the important advantages of integrating AI into advertising lies in its capacity to automate repetitive tasks, freeing human assets to interest on creativity and method. Chatbots, powered through the use of AI, beautify patron interactions by providing immediate responses and customised suggestions. This no longer most effectively improves client pride however also streamlines the consumer adventure, fostering emblem

DOI: 10.4324/9781032711089-13

loyalty. Furthermore, AI empowers entrepreneurs to harness the capability of predictive analytics, foreseeing traits and adapting techniques proactively. By studying historical statistics and figuring out growing styles, companies can live in advance of the curve, expecting marketplace shifts and adjusting their advertising and marketing strategies consequently[1].

As we navigate the ever-evolving panorama of commercial enterprise, the fusion of AI and marketing emerges as a cornerstone for fulfilment. The insights derived from AI-pushed analyses empower businesses to make knowledgeable alternatives, allocate assets strategically, and in the long run, decorate their competitive aspect. This chapter will delve deeper into the particular applications of AI in advertising, exploring case research, demanding situations, and the ethical worries that accompany this transformative adventure. As groups embark on this AI-pushed revolution, the synergy between era and advertising guarantees now not simplest performance but moreover innovation, paving the manner for a future wherein advertising techniques aren't just usual but redefined by using the infinite opportunities of AI.

13.2 Statistical Facts and Figures

Before immersing ourselves in the profound influence of AI on advertising techniques, it's far vital to recognise the statistical panorama that underscores its significance. Recent surveys and research have unveiled compelling insights into the transformative impact of AI within the marketing domain, dropping mild on the tangible advantages experienced by businesses which have embraced this era.

A complete evaluation of corporations utilising AI in marketing shows an exquisite surge in performance, with a brilliant 70% reporting great upgrades in customer reviews. This statistic underscores the pivotal role AI performs in improving purchaser interactions, ensuring well-timed and personalised engagement. Machine getting to know algorithms, a centre factor of AI, enabling organisations to research huge datasets to apprehend client options, behaviours and traits, facilitating the transport of tailored content material and services. The result isn't always only heightened patron pleasure but also the establishment of greater meaningful and lasting connections with the target market.

In addition to elevating customer reviews, AI-powered advertising has validated a full-size effect on income conversion costs. Businesses leveraging

AI technology have witnessed an impressive 20% increase in their income conversion prices, showcasing the direct correlation between AI integration and more advantageous bottom-line outcomes. This surge may be attributed to the potential of AI to pick out patterns in patron behaviour, are expecting buying preferences and optimise advertising techniques therefore. By delivering focused and personalised content, groups can seize the attention of potential customers extra efficaciously, guiding them through the sales funnel with a better chance of conversion.

Furthermore, the adoption of AI in advertising and marketing has caused a paradigm shift in the allocation of resources and budgeting. With information-driven insights supplied through AI analytics, organisations can strategically allocate sources to the maximum impactful marketing channels, ensuring a greener use of budgets. This optimisation now not handiest improves the return on investment (ROI) however also empowers marketers to evolve and refine their techniques in actual-time based totally on the evolving marketplace dynamics.

As we delve deeper into the statistical realm, it becomes evident that AI isn't only a theoretical idea but a transformative pressure with tangible and measurable results. The statistics highlight the twin impact of AI on each purchaser-centric components, inclusive of stepped forward reviews, and commercial enterprise-centric metrics, including improved conversion fees. These figures function as a compelling testament to the capability of AI in reshaping the advertising and marketing landscape, imparting agencies a competitive edge in an increasingly virtual and statistics-driven generation. In the following sections of this chapter, we will discover precisely about how AI delve into the nuances of applied in numerous marketing contexts, in addition substantiating its function as a catalyst for innovation and achievement in the business realm.

13.3 Literature Review

The literature surrounding the intersection of AI and marketing is marked by a depth of studies that no longer only explores the cutting-edge situation but additionally anticipates the destiny trajectory of these intertwined domains. One of the overarching topics that emerge from this body of labour is the transformative potential of AI in choice-making procedures in the advertising and marketing realm. Studies constantly emphasise how device mastering algorithms, a cornerstone of AI, can shift through tremendous datasets to extract meaningful insights, offering entrepreneurs with a nuanced know-how of client behaviours, alternatives and market developments.

The dynamic nature of cutting-edge markets demands agility in selection-making, and AI equips groups with the gear to adapt unexpectedly. Traditional strategies reliant on historical information often fall quickly in shooting the real-time dynamics of purchaser behaviour. AI-driven analytics, alternatively permits marketers to make choices primarily based on present day and evolving developments, ensuring that techniques stay relevant and powerful in an ever-converting landscape. This adaptability is especially essential in industries in which purchaser alternatives and marketplace traits can shift hastily, such as inside the technology and style sectors.

Resource allocation, a strategic component of advertising and marketing management, has additionally been a focus of investigation inside the literature. The conventional advertising and marketing landscape frequently involves the dispersion of resources across numerous channels, leading to inefficiencies. AI, through its predictive analytics capabilities, allows marketers to forecast the potential effect of various channels on their objectives. This foresight enables greater price range allocation, maximising the go back on investment. For example, corporations can become aware of high-appearing channels and allocate resources, consequently, optimising their marketing spend for optimal impact[2]. This does not simply improves financial efficiency, however additionally permits agencies to redirect assets unexpectedly in response to emerging marketplace developments or shifts in purchaser behaviour.

Within the literature, an enormous emphasis has been placed on the revolutionary impact of AI on patron engagement strategies. The creation of AI-powered chatbots has redefined patron interactions, supplying instantaneous responses to queries, customised hints or even simulating herbal language conversations. This not only enhances the overall client experience but additionally contributes to the creation of a seamless and responsive interplay environment. Businesses leveraging AI in patron engagement have stated better purchaser satisfaction prices and increased emblem loyalty, as customers respect the performance and personalisation that AI-driven interactions bring to the desk.

The software of AI in predictive analytics has verified to be a sport-changer for entrepreneurs looking for an aggressive side. By harnessing historical facts and identifying patterns, predictive analytics allows groups to anticipate future trends and purchaser behaviours. This foresight is valuable for strategic planning, permitting marketers to proactively alter their campaigns, product offerings, and ordinary market positioning. The literature is replete with instances where groups, armed with predictive analytics have efficaciously navigated marketplace shifts, outperformed competition and maintained a sustained advantage.

However, the literature additionally recognises the challenges and ethical concerns inherent in the integration of AI into marketing techniques. Privacy worries, ability biases in algorithms, and the moral implications of AI-driven techniques that affect consumer conduct are subjects of ongoing discourse. Researchers are actively exploring methods to mitigate those demanding situations, emphasising the importance of responsible AI use to make certain that the blessings are found out without compromising ethical requirements.

In conclusion, the literature on AI in advertising serves as a compass guiding agencies through the complicated terrain of technological integration and strategic transformation. The multifaceted nature of the research, spanning decision-making procedures, aid allocation, consumer engagement and predictive analytics, reflects the expansive impact of AI on the advertising landscape[3]. As scholars maintain to contribute to this evolving discipline, the literature no longer best informs contemporary practices however additionally paves the manner for future improvements, offering a blueprint for businesses to navigate the evolving landscape of AI-pushed marketing efficiently.

13.4 Role of AI in Advertising

AI has revolutionised the sphere of advertising and marketing, offering a transformative effect that goes beyond mere automation. With the mixing of system mastering algorithms, natural language processing (NLP) and computer vision, AI has ended up a powerful catalyst for innovation inside the advertising landscape. One giant position of AI in advertising and marketing is its capacity to research giant amounts of information to provide actionable insights. Marketers can leverage machine learning algorithms to system and interpret consumer conduct, choices and trends.

NLP is every other side of AI that appreciably impacts marketing. With NLP, machines can apprehend and interpret human language, facilitating progressed verbal exchange among companies and customers. Chatbots, powered by way of NLP, enhance consumer interactions by means of supplying real-time responses to inquiries, addressing issues or even completing transactions. This no longer handier enhances customer pleasure but also permits companies to operate extra efficaciously, releasing human assets for extra complex responsibilities[4].

In the area of content material introduction, AI performs a pivotal position through natural language generation (NLG). NLG algorithms can generate human-like written content material, such as product descriptions, weblog posts, and social media updates. This functionality now not most effective saves time however also ensures regular and attractive content introduction. Marketers can focus on method and creativity, leaving repetitive and time-ingesting responsibilities to AI

Computer vision is yet another AI era making waves in advertising. Through photo and video evaluation, laptop imaginative and prescient permits marketers to extract valuable facts from visible content. This includes facial reputation for focused marketing, product recognition for inventory control and sentiment evaluation for gauging purchaser reactions. Visual information insights empower entrepreneurs to refine their techniques and deliver more visually appealing and relevant content to their target market. AI also complements patron engagement through personalised advertising techniques. By studying consumer statistics, AI can create quite focused and personalised campaigns. This level of customisation increases the probability of purchaser conversion, as people are more likely to respond to content material that resonates with their possibilities and needs. This personalization not only enhances the customer experience but also strengthens brand loyalty.

AI's function in advertising transcends traditional automation through fostering innovation throughout various facets of the field. From information analysis and predictive analytics to NLP and PC imaginative and prescient, AI empowers marketers to make knowledgeable choices, streamline operations, and interact with clients in ways previously not possible. As era maintains to advance, the mixing of AI in advertising will surely form the future of the enterprise, riding efficiency, personalisation and ultimately business achievement.

13.4.1 Different Tools and Techniques of AI in Marketing

The landscape of advertising and marketing has undergone a thorough transformation with the combination of AI. This technological evolution contains a numerous array of equipment and techniques, every gambling plays a pivotal position in redefining how organisations connect to their audiences. From advice engines to voice search optimisation, that equipment leverage current technology along with machine getting to know, NLP and computer imaginative and prescient to beautify various sides of advertising and marketing strategies.

13.4.2 Recommendation Engines: Personalised Pathways to Customer Satisfaction

Among the standout tools powered by system getting to know algorithms are recommendation engines. These engines examine consumer conduct, opinions and historical facts to offer personalised recommendations. In the e-commerce realm, recommendation engines are the backbone of systems that advocate products based on a user's past purchases or surfing records. Similarly, streaming offerings leverage those engines to recommend movies or indicates tailored to man or woman tastes.

The energy of recommendation engines lies in their capability to continuously analyse and adapt. As users interact with the platform, the algorithms in the back of those engines refine their hints, creating a dynamic and personalised experience. This now not handiest enhances consumer satisfaction but additionally contributes drastically to client retention.

13.4.3 Predictive Analytics: Unveiling Future Trends with Data

By using predictive analytics, marketers delve into historical information, figuring out styles and correlations to make record-pushed predictions. This device turns into a compass for companies navigating the unpredictable seas of marketplace shifts. By looking ahead to market dynamics, predictive analytics empowers organisations to optimise advertising campaigns and make informed choices. This is specifically critical in gaining an aggressive side, as companies can align their strategies with rising developments and customer possibilities.

13.4.4 Natural Language Processing: Decoding the Language of the Consumer

NLP plays a pivotal role in knowledge and decoding human language, allowing entrepreneurs to extract precious insights from textual facts. Beyond sentiment evaluation, where NLP gauges the emotional tone of textual content, it finds applications in various marketing domains. Marketers employ NLP for chatbot interactions, content advent and social media monitoring. Understanding consumer sentiment is a goldmine for marketers. It lets agencies gauge the effectiveness of their campaigns, discover regions for development, and reply promptly to client feedback. NLP transforms unstructured textual information into actionable insights, providing a nuanced know-how of consumer evaluations and preferences[5].

13.4.5 Chatbots and Virtual Assistants: Operational Efficiency and Real-time Engagement

AI chatbots are used for real-time engagement with customers. These gear leverage natural language knowledge to comprehend consumer queries and supply applicable responses[6]. Chatbots have come to be ubiquitous in improving customer service by supplying immediate answers to commonplace issues. The efficiency profits from chatbots increase past customer interactions. By automating recurring queries and tasks, chatbots unfastened by human sources for greater complex and strategic activities. This contributes extensively to operational performance, permitting companies to allocate sources wherein they're maximum wished.

13.4.6 Natural Language Generation: Automating Content Creation with Precision

NLG algorithms constitute a breakthrough in automating content material creation. These algorithms transform statistics into human-readable text, enabling computerised technology of product descriptions, weblog posts, and social media updates. The application of NLG no longer handiest saves time but also guarantees constant and wonderful content material advent. Marketers leverage NLG to scale content material manufacturing at the same time as retaining a personalised and engaging tone. This is especially beneficial in eventualities wherein big volumes of content material need to be generated often, together with e-trade product descriptions or marketing copy for various audiences[7].

13.4.7 Image and Video Analysis (Computer Vision): Seeing Beyond the Surface

Computer imaginative and prescient era has opened new frontiers in visible content material analysis, supplying entrepreneurs with powerful tools for optimisation. Facial recognition inside photos permits focused advertising, allowing businesses to tailor their campaigns based on demographic facts. Product reputation aids in stock management and sentiment evaluation facilitates gauge client reactions to visible elements[8]. The capacity to extract valuable statistics from pics and videos permits entrepreneurs to refine their techniques and supply greater compelling visual content material.

13.4.8 Dynamic Optimisation in Advertising: Real-Time Adjustments for Maximum Impact

AI-pushed tools in marketing have ushered in an era of dynamic optimisation. This equipment continuously examines the performance of marketing campaigns and optimises strategies in real-time. Machine mastering algorithms examine the effectiveness of advertisements across diverse channels and alter targeting parameters to maximise return on funding. Dynamic optimisation guarantees that advertising budgets are allocated efficaciously[9]. By identifying excessive-performing channels and audience segments, agencies can attain higher conversion costs while maximising ad spend on much less engaged segments. This adaptive approach to advertising maximises the impact of advertising and marketing efforts in a continuously evolving virtual panorama.

13.4.9 Personalised Engines: Tailoring Experiences for Individual Preferences

Personalisation engines, fuelled through AI, are at the forefront of making enormously targeted and personalised advertising campaigns. By reading customer records, these engines perceive man or woman possibilities, behaviours, and demographics to tailor content and promotions. Personalisation goes past addressing customers by their names; it includes crafting reports that resonate with individual interests. The significance of personalisation lies in its capability to enhance the patron revel in. When users come upon content material that aligns with their pursuits, they're more likely to have interaction and convert. Personalisation engines are crucial for increasing customer loyalty and fostering better long-term connections with clients.

13.4.10 Voice Search Optimisation: Managing the Development of Voice-Activated Technology

Marketers can use voice search optimisation to customise their content so that it fits the conversational search patterns and appears in voice search results. Voice search optimisation isn't always merely approximately incorporating keywords; it involves knowledge of the nuances of spoken language[10]. Marketers need to conform their content material techniques to cater to the traits of voice search, making sure that their brands stay visible and reachable in the developing realm of voice-activated era.

13.5 Tools and Techniques of AI in Marketing

AI Tool	Description	Applications
Recommendation Engines	Analyses user behaviour and historical data to provide personalised suggestions.	E-commerce (product recommendations), Streaming services (movie/show recommendations).
Predictive Analytics	Utilises machine learning to forecast future trends and consumer behaviour based on historical data.	Market trend analysis, Campaign optimisation, Informed decision-making.
Natural Language Processing	Interprets human language for sentiment analysis, chatbot interactions, and social media monitoring.	Sentiment analysis, Chatbot interactions, social media monitoring.
Chatbots and Virtual Assistants	AI-driven tools for real-time customer engagement and operational efficiency.	Customer support, Query resolution, Operational efficiency.
Natural Language Generation	Transforms data into human-readable text for automated content creation.	Automated content creation, Product descriptions, Blog posts.
Image and Video Analysis (Computer Vision)	Analyses visual content for optimisation using facial recognition and sentiment analysis.	Targeted advertising, Inventory management, Consumer reaction analysis.
Dynamic Optimisation in Advertising	Continuously analyses ad campaign performance and optimises strategies in real-time.	Real-time ad optimisation, Maximising ROI, Efficient budget allocation.
Personalisation Engines	Utilises AI to create highly targeted and personalised marketing campaigns.	Targeted content and promotions, Customer experience enhancement, Loyalty building.
Voice Search Optimisation	Optimises content for voice-activated devices, analysing voice queries and providing relevant responses.	Aligning with conversational search patterns, Visibility in voice search results.

13.6 How AI in Marketing Impact Business

The infusion of AI into marketing strategies marks a paradigm shift within the way corporation's method consume engagement, brand advertising, and universal advertising effectiveness. At the forefront of this variation is the refinement of consumer segmentation and personalisation, which has needed up more and more particular and impactful with the advent of AI technology. AI algorithms, armed with the functionality to system great amounts of client records, allow groups to dissect their audience into the distinct segments primarily based on demographics, conduct, and options. This granular understanding of the customer base empowers marketers to tailor campaigns with excellent precision, delivering content and gives that resonate with precise target organisations. This heightened personalisation now not simplest complements the client experience however additionally cultivates a sense of connection and relevance. Customers are much more likely to have needs and preferences. As organisations deploy AI-powered personalisation, they foster multiplied customer satisfaction and loyalty, creating a fantastic remarks loop that contributes to lengthy-term emblem success.

The ability to hook up with the customers on an individual level position businesses no longer just vendors of products or services but as companions in addressing their unique desires and dreams. In addition to personalisation, AI's impact on advertising and marketing extends to the area of predictive analytics, bringing about a profound transformation in how companies anticipate and respond to tendencies. By studying historical facts, AI algorithms find patterns and insights that could be challenging for conventional analytics equipment to determine. This predictive capability allows cooperation's to forecast destiny client behaviour with a high diploma of accuracy. Marketers can then make knowledgeable decisions about their techniques, optimising useful resource allocation and staying ahead of market shifts. The integration of AI in predictive analytics additionally performs a critical role in lead scoring, supporting marketers perceive and prioritise leads that are most likely to transform into dependable clients. This not only streamlines marketing efforts but also contributes to a greater efficient use of assets, maximising the return on investment.

Moreover, the profile action of conversational AI and chat it advertising and marketing is reshaping how businesses interact with their target audience. AI-powered chatbots have advanced to offer on the spot and personalised communique, handling purchaser inquiries, imparting suggestions, and facilitating transactions seamlessly. This not only improves efficiency of customer support but also guarantees 24/7 availability, meeting the demands of a worldwide and usually linked purchaser base. The conversational nature of AI-driven interactions enhances the customer enjoyment, making interactions greater natural and tasty. Furthermore, the mixing of AI permits marketing automation, streamline repetitive obligations and lowing entrepreneurs to recognise strategic means of AI, manipulate various aspects of advertising campaigns, from electronic mail scheduling to content material reduces the probability of human errors, ensuring steady and accurate execution of advertising activities. Marketers can leverage AI to optimise the timing and content of their campaigns, handing over messages when they're maximum likely to resonate with their target audience.

13.6.1 Customer Segmentation and Personalisation

AI has converted customer segmentation and personalisation in advertising and, marketing through leveraging advanced analytics and machine mastering. Traditional demographic elements like age, gender, and region are now supplemented with nuanced insights derived from sizeable datasets. AI algorithms analyse patron behaviours, shopping history, and interaction styles to identify, micro-segments with astrometry preferences. Customer segmentation has developed beyond broad categorisations, allowing marketers to tailor their strategies to man or woman purchasers. This stage of granularity enables the creation of fantastically customised marketing campaigns that resonate with the needs and preferences of every purchaser. For example, AI can identify segments of customers who are extra conscious of positive sorts of promotions, allowing entrepreneurs to design targets given.

Personalisation extends beyond simply marketing messages. AI facilities the customisation of concurrent reprints on websites and cellular apps. Dynamic content pointers primarily based on man or woman choices enhance person engagement and boom the chance of conversion. Their level of personalisation creates a greater intimate and real net connection between the logo and the purchaser. Furthermore, AI-pushed personalisation isn't static; it evolves through the years because the algorithms continuously analyse from new records. This adaptive approach in the face of converting consumer behaviours and marketplace tendencies. AI-pushed client segmentation and personalisation empower marketers to transport past prevalent campaigns, developing incredibly focused and individualised reports for every patron.

13.6.2 *Predictive Analytics and Lead Scoring*

Predictive analytics, powered with the aid of AI, has become a cornerstone of effective advertising techniques. By analysing historical statistics and figuring out styles, AI algorithms can predict destiny client behaviours and traits. In the context of advertising, this functionality is especially useful for optimising campaigns and allocating resources greater successfully. One key software is lead scoring, where AI algorithms verify the chance of a lead converting into a customer. These algorithms don't forget different factors together with engagement history, demographics, and online behaviour. By assigning rayons to leads, advertising and income groups can prioritise their efforts on those with the very best conversion ability ·

Predictive analytics also aids in forecasting marketplace tendencies and identifying rising opportunities. By stuffing outside elements including financial signs and social trends, organisations can make knowledgeable choices about product development, pricing techniques, and market positioning. Moreover, AI allows real-time changes to marketing campaigns based totally on predictive insights. If a specific section of the audience suggests a sudden shift in conduct, the algorithms can cause on the spot changes in the marketing campaign to ensure relevance and effectiveness. Prestige analytics powered by means of AI provides entrepreneurs with valuable foresight, permitting and consciousness efforts on leads with the highest opportunity of conversion.

13.6.3 *Conversation and Chatbots Marketing*

AI-pushed chatbots have revolutionised consumer interactions, presenting instant and personalised assistance throughout various touch points. Conversational advertising, facilitated by chatbots, complements purchaser engagement by supplying a continuing and responsive conversation channel. Chatbots leverage NLP and gadget getting to know to understand communed queries and provide 24/7 customer service, addressing inquiries, and resolving troubles in actual time. The immediacy of these interactions contributes to progressed patron pride and loyalty ·

Moreover, chatbots are not limited to customer service; they play an important role in advertising. Interactive and customised conversations with users can be leveraged for lead generation product tips, or even completing transactions. For example, a chatbot on an e-trade website can manual customers through the purchase process, presenting information and pointers based on person alternatives. Chatbots also achier precious information through interactions, contributing to a better understanding of patron needs and behaviours. These facts can inform advertising techniques, permitting organisations to refine their approaches and deluged more customised stories ·

As technology advances, chatbots are becoming extra sophisticated, incorporating actors of emotional intelligence and empathy into their interactions. This human-like contact enhances the general consumer, enjoyment and strengthens the relationship among the brand and the purchaser.

Communication and chatbot advertising and marketing driven by using AI no longer simplest streamline patron interactions however additionally serve as powerful tools for lead generation, personalised engagement, and information collection.

13.7 Conclusion and Future Scope

In conclusion, the mixing of AI into advertising strategies is no longer a trifling choice, however a strategic vital for business aiming to gain an aggressive edge in the rapidly evolving landscape. The symbiotic courting between AI and advertising has proven its capability to redefine industry standards, supplying insights that have been formerly impossible and transforming the entire patron. As corporations increasingly understand the strength of AI in shaping advertising and marketing strategies, the effect isn't just on operational efficiency but on the fundamental way organisations interact with and apprehend their customers. The adventure of reshaping advertising strategies with AI has uncovered several sides of innovation and efficiency.

The symbiosis between AI and advertising has been instrumental in breaking down traditional silos, bearing in mind a greater holistic method to consumer interactions. The capability of AI to method great amounts of data, glean significant patterns, and generate actionable insights has empowered marketers to make knowledgeable decisions, optimising not only the allocation of sources but also fostering a deeper expertise of consumer behaviours and choices.

Looking to destiny, the scope for AI in marketing remains great and promising. The modern panorama, marked by using machine mastering algorithms, NLP, and laptop vision, is simply the tip of the iceberg.

Advancements in AI technology coupled with the growing availability of huge data, will probably provide upward thrust to new tools and strategies, in addition enriching the advertising toolkit. One of the foreseeable advancements is the evolution of AI-driven personalisation. As AI continues to refine its expertise of individual options and behaviours, groups can be able to create rather personalised and targeted marketing campaigns. Techniques, however, not only lead to the emergence of novel approaches but also appreciably increase the probability of hit conversions.

Additionally, the destiny of AI in advertising may witness the mixing of more sophisticated predictive analytics. As gadgets getting to know algorithms become extra sophisticated and capable of processing actual-time, data streams, groups will have an advantage in looking ahead to market tendencies and client conduct. This, in flip, will permit agile and proactive advertising techniques, ensuring corporations live in advance of the curve. The position of AI in purchaser engagement is poised to extend in addition, with the continuous improvement of conversational AI and chatbots. More advanced NLP skills will allow these chatbots to now not most effective reply to consumer queries but also interact in more significant and nuanced conversations, contributing to a seamless and personalised client enjoyment.

In conclusion, as groups hold to leverage the transformative strength of AI in advertising and marketing, destiny holds interesting potentialities. The ongoing evolution in this space guarantees no longer the simplest persisted improvements in existing equipment, and these techniques not only enhance customer satisfaction but also lead to the development of innovative approaches that have the capability to reshape the advertising panorama. The journey close to the paradigm is one that agencies must embrace with enthusiasm to live at the vanguard of innovation and preserve an aggressive side.

References

1. Jarek, K., & Mazurek, G. (2019). Marketing and Artificial Intelligence. *Central European Business Review*, 8(2), pp. 46–55.
2. Rathore, B. (2016). Revolutionizing the Digital Landscape: Exploring the Integration of Artificial Intelligence in Modern Marketing Strategies. *Eduzone: International Peer Reviewed/Refereed Multidisciplinary Journal*, 5(2), 8–13.
3. Jain, P., & Aggarwal, K. (2020). Transforming marketing with artificial intelligence. *International Research Journal of Engineering and Technology*, 7(7), 3964–3976.

4. Choi, J. A., & Lim, K. (2020). Identifying machine learning techniques for classification of target advertising. *ICT Express, 6*(3), 175–180.
5. Mustak, M., Salminen, J., Plé, L., & Wirtz, J. (2021). Artificial intelligence in marketing: Topic modeling, scientometric analysis, and research agenda. *Journal of Business Research, 124*, 389–404.
6. Kaczorowska-Spychalska, D. (2019). How chatbots influence marketing. *Management, 23*(1), 251–270.
7. Reiter, E. (2010). Natural language generation. In The handbook of computational linguistics and natural language processing (pp. 574–598). John Wiley & Sons.
8. Chon, K. S., Weaver, P. A., & Kim, C. Y. (1991). Marketing your commmunity: Image analysis in Norfolk. *Cornell Hotel and Restaurant Administration Quarterly, 31*(4), 31–37.
9. Lin, P. C., Wang, J., & Chin, S. S. (2009). Dynamic optimisation of price, warranty length and production rate. *International Journal of Systems Science, 40*(4), 411–420.
10. Runaite, D. (2021). *How will voice search optimisation aid or limit digital marketing? An End-User Perspective* (Doctoral dissertation, Dublin, National College of Ireland).

Chapter 14

Impact of Generative AI on Customer Experience and Personalization in Retail Sector

J. Shanti

14.1 Introduction

Industry 4.0 relies on a wide range of technologies, such as robotics, the Internet of Things (IoT), 3D printing, additive manufacturing, digital twinning, and analytics. Artificial intelligence (AI), including machine learning and various forms of AI like generative and discriminative AI, plays a crucial role in enhancing efficiency and driving innovation across multiple aspects of Industry 4.0. The global market for AI in the retail sector is projected to reach approximately $10.76 billion by 2023. It is anticipated that the adoption of AI in retail will exceed $127.09 billion by the year 2033 [1]. The value of AI comes from enhancing automation by imbuing software with human-like levels of comprehension. The retail sector stands to undergo significant transformation with the assistance of AI [2].

This chapter delves into the practical uses and implementations of generative AI within the retail industry, offering insights for retail businesses looking to maintain a competitive edge. By leveraging AI, retailers can tailor the shopping experience to individual users, with machine learning systems actively engaging, showcasing, and suggesting products to customers.

DOI: 10.4324/9781032711089-14

Emerging AI technologies such as robotics, chatbots, AR, virtual reality, machine learning, natural language processing (NLP), deep learning, cognitive conversational commerce, and the IoT are revolutionizing both physical and online retail landscapes [3]. AI-driven e-commerce has emerged as the latest game-changer in online shopping, spearheaded by industry giants such as Amazon, Netflix, Alibaba, and eBay. These companies have harnessed the power of AI applications to revolutionize the online retail market, marking a significant shift in the way consumers shop online [4].

14.2 Generative AI Applications in Retail Industry

The global market for generative AI in retail is projected to experience a growth rate of 10.4% between 2023 and 2028. This advanced technology utilizes algorithms to generate original content, including product designs, visuals, and tailored marketing strategies. Within the retail sector, generative AI enables brands to create personalized experiences, develop unique products, and anticipate consumer preferences more effectively. By tapping into AI's creative capabilities, retailers can drive innovation and provide customers with a more engaging and individualized shopping experience [5]. In the realm of retail and online shopping, AI involves employing advanced technologies like machine learning and data analysis to enhance and streamline various aspects of these industries. This includes tailoring consumer interactions with personalized recommendations, improving inventory control, and facilitating informed decision-making based on data. Ultimately, these AI-driven enhancements lead to higher sales and operational effectiveness.

The retail sector has rapidly adopted AI-driven technologies to enhance online interactions, streamline supply chain operations, and manage increasing consumer demands. Generative AI, a form of AI, can be trained to generate fresh content by analyzing existing datasets. Essentially, it produces probable "accurate" responses by considering the context provided by the available data [6]. As per a report titled "Future of Retail: Profitable Growth through Technology and AI" by the Retailers Association of India (RAI) and Deloitte; one-fifth of global retailers will adopt distributed AI (DAI) systems to transform sales, marketing, supply chain, and operations by the end of 2025 [7]. DAI has surfaced as a game-changer in retail, mirroring human decision-making and offering transformative potential for the retail sector. In retail, AI applications primarily rely on machine

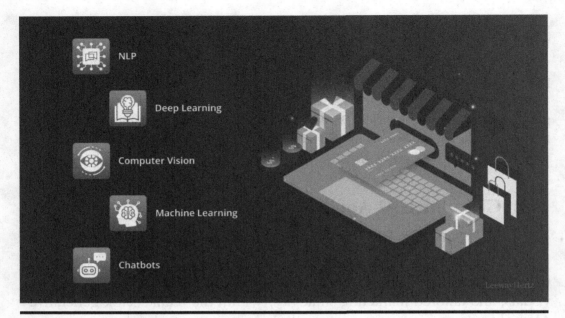

Figure 14.1   Technologies in generative AI.

https://www.leewayhertz.com/ai-in-retail/

learning for predictive tasks, but retailers are expanding their use to include NLP, computer vision, and robotics. The technologies illustrated in Figure 14.1 demonstrates the capabilities of generative AI. The area of generative AI empowers brands to craft customized experiences, design exclusive products, and predict consumer preferences more accurately. The next section explores the use cases of companies utilizing generative AI in various areas of tailoring product recommendations, design, marketing strategies, customer engagement, and supply chain management, evaluates their effectiveness, and identifies potential areas for further development.

14.3 Use Cases of Generative AI

Generative AI has the potential to enhance businesses by predicting and addressing customer needs more effectively. It also enables companies to differentiate themselves by offering unique and tailored experiences. Myntra, a leading multi-brand fashion platform based in India, has introduced "My Stylist," an AI-driven personal style guide. This innovative tool offers online shoppers tailored styling suggestions and recommendations as they browse through the website, enhancing the shopping experience for fashion-forward

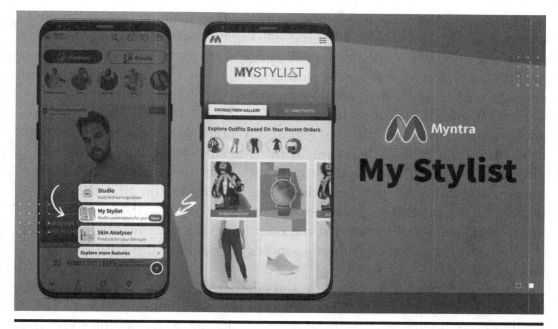

Figure 14.2   Myntra app mystylist.

https://in.fashionnetwork.com/news/Myntra-launches-ai-stylist-tool,1517873.
html#elie-saab

customers. Myntra utilizes data analysis of various factors such as browsing history, purchase patterns, and user preferences to generate personalized product recommendations, tailored promotions, and dynamic website content. This enables them to provide a customized shopping experience for their customers.

The Myntra app is depicted in Figure 14.2. The AI functionality utilizes sophisticated machine learning methods and cutting-edge deep learning algorithms to suggest clothing and accessory choices to customers by analyzing their uploaded images, previous purchases, and recently viewed items [8]. This advanced visual search technology represents a breakthrough in AI applications for the retail industry, allowing customers to find products by uploading images. When a user submits a photo or takes a picture with their device, sophisticated AI algorithms analyze the image to identify its key features. Then, the system compares these visual characteristics with items in the retailer's inventory, presenting the user with similar products [9]. In this scenario, the generative AI efficiently produces product descriptions and images that connect with consumers' preferences and aspirations, helping them move from desire to action in their consumer journey process.

The second use case involves utilizing NLP to facilitate conversational commerce. This involves leveraging messaging apps, chatbots, voice assistants, and various platforms to engage with customers, offering them products and services in a conversational manner. To stay up-to-date and connect with its audience, Maggi introduced a conversational commerce initiative through platforms like Facebook and WhatsApp. This campaign enabled users to reach out to Maggi at any hour, seeking cooking advice from the brand's digital assistant "Kim" [10]. AI-driven chatbots and virtual assistants offer immediate customer assistance, quickly resolving queries and aiding in purchase decisions. By employing NLP, they better grasp and address customer inquiries, boosting satisfaction and minimizing the need for human intervention. This streamlines the search process and increases consumer spending throughout the customer journey process.

The third use case involves Amazon company showcasing the advanced technologies behind its Just Walk Out seamless shopping experience. The leading e-commerce giant utilizes AI, alongside its own computer vision, sensor vision and computer vision, sensor fusion, and deep learning to enable autonomous checkout solutions. Shoppers can browse the store, select their items, and simply leave without going through a traditional checkout process. The development team employed generative AI to create realistic synthetic data, including videos of simulated shoppers, to train the system to make independent decisions. This innovative approach has been instrumental in the creation of the Just Walk Out technology. The online retailer utilized a form of generative AI known as a generative adversarial network (GAN) to produce synthetic data for training their technology [11].

The fourth use case is about enabling personalization through point-of-sale (POS) systems. These systems can collect data on customer purchases and use it to suggest new products tailored to everyone. Avenue Stores LLC, a retail apparel chain, utilizes various data sources such as in-store interactions and market trend analysis to understand customer preferences and timing. By employing real-time messaging and customized offers, they aim to keep customers engaged and encourage purchases when they are most inclined to shop [12]. Retailers also profit from personalization by gathering and analyzing data to develop more accurate customer segments and provide customized experiences tailored to shopping habits and preferences. This strategy encourages brand loyalty, enhances customer retention, and ultimately drives revenue growth [13].

14.4 Intelligent Automation

Intelligent automation is a significant technological advancement that has the capability to revolutionize the business landscape. By integrating AI into automation processes, machines can learn, provide recommendations, and make independent decisions, continuously improving and correcting themselves over time. Nike Inc. has introduced a new method for customers to personalize their sneakers. In this innovative automated system, customers wear blank Nike Presto X shoes, use voice commands, and select their desired graphics and colors for customization. The system employs advanced technologies such as AR, object tracking, and projection systems to showcase the designed shoes to the customer. Once the design process is complete, the system promptly prints the customized design onto the sneakers, which are ready for the customer to take home in less than two hours. This streamlined process contrasts with the traditional customization method, which typically takes up to two weeks [14].

14.5 Benefits of Generative AI

Generative AI technology facilitates the integration of features such as augmented reality (AR) for virtual try-ons, visual search for rapid product exploration, and voice commerce for convenient ordering through voice prompts. AR serves as a pivotal tool for both online and offline consumer interaction, enabling brands and retailers to enhance the digitalization of the consumer journey. Companies such as H&M and Sephora are utilizing AR technology to enhance the shopping experience for their customers. H&M, for instance, has implemented virtual try-on (VTO) features in its app, enabling users to virtually try on various products before making a purchase. Similarly, Sephora has integrated a feature called Virtual Artist into its app. This allows customers to visualize how certain beauty products will look on their own faces, helping them make more informed purchasing decisions [15].

AI technologies offer numerous benefits such as fostering innovation, facilitating data-driven decision-making, and enhancing customer interactions. By streamlining the customer journey and providing a seamless purchasing experience, AI contributes to heightened customer satisfaction, loyalty, and positive word-of-mouth. Ultimately, these benefits culminate in a competitive edge for businesses. Marketing materials are tailored to specific target groups, leading to significantly higher levels of customer interaction and sales conversions. Furthermore, AI-powered chatbots interact with customers in real-time, providing support for questions, product inquiries, and problem resolution. AI not only enhances the customer experience but also enhances operational efficiency and reduces costs in the retail and e-commerce sectors. By automating and optimizing various tasks through AI algorithms, processes are streamlined, leading to savings in time, effort, and resources.

14.6 Challenges for Generative AI in Retail

While generative AI is transformative in nature, the implementation can portray challenges to achieve successful outcomes.

a. Small and medium-sized businesses and start-ups may face challenges in terms of infrastructure and technological know-how, while high implementation costs present a significant challenge for small retailers.

b. The effectiveness of generative AI depends on high-quality data for producing accurate results and impactful models. The outcomes and structures of generative AI are shaped by the data it processes, emphasizing the importance of comprehensive datasets. Companies can respond by collecting consistent quality data, as incomplete or inaccurate data can bias models and lead to erroneous results. Generative AI models may produce inconsistent or unexpected outcomes, affecting the quality and usability of the content they generate. The credibility and reliability of the company can be questionable because of the skewed outcomes. The outcomes of the AI models should not be blindly executed but rather evaluated carefully for their impact on humans before implementation. Thus, cautious assessment is crucial prior to adopting the results of AI models.

c. There's a lack of experts in AI, which is causing a shortage of skilled professionals in the field.

d. The deployment of generative AI raises ethical and regulatory concerns regarding privacy, security, authenticity, accountability, and fairness, as it relies on data sourced from consumers and other parties. Companies must effectively manage the utilization of generative AI to ensure compliance with legal and regulatory frameworks. It is imperative for businesses to align their practices with their organizational values and principles to mitigate any potential harm to stakeholders.

e. Retailers must adhere to data privacy laws and ethical guidelines when handling customer data, a task that can be challenging and resource-intensive. Violations of privacy standards can lead to legal consequences, that may harm the brand's reputation.

f. Integrating AI technologies into existing retail systems and procedures can pose challenges and require substantial investment. Thus, companies must be willing to invest in adaptable and cost-effective AI solutions that are capable of seamlessly integrating with their current infrastructure. It is imperative to develop a clear and comprehensive AI strategy for scalable and flexible AI solutions.

14.7 Conclusion

The retail sector is changing rapidly, and companies can navigate the dynamic business environment and rising consumer expectations by using advanced technologies like generative AI in their operations. These technologies empower retail businesses to anticipate trends, drive innovation, and pursue long-term strategic applications. This chapter provides a systematic insight into the benefits of generative AI in the retail sector at the operational and strategic levels. Generative AI offers retailers advantages such as personalization, improved customer service, and efficient operations with the streamlining of processes. Despite its potential for transformation, it's important for retail companies to carefully consider the extent of implementing generative AI due to potential drawbacks. Organizations need to be cautious and regularly check their progress to achieve the best outcomes.

In conclusion, retailers leveraging AI to engage customers and enhance operations will have a competitive edge in today's AI-driven landscape. Retailers that embrace AI to enhance customer connections and operational efficiency will maintain a competitive edge in the market.

References

1. Future Market Insights. (n.d.). Syndicated Market Research Reports | Business Analysis | FMI. Retrieved from https://www.futuremarketinsights.com/reports/
2. TechTarget. (2020, September 22). How significant is AI's role in Industry 4.0? [Tip]. Retrieved from https://www.techtarget.com/searchenterpriseai/tip/How-significant-is-AIs-role-in-Industry-40

3. Pillai, R., Sivathanu, B., & Dwivedi, Y. K. (2020). Shopping intention at AI-powered automated retail stores (AIPARS). *Journal of Retailing and Consumer Services, 57*, 102207. https://doi.org/10.1016/j.jretconser.2020.102207

4. Soni, N., Sharma, E. K., Singh, N., & Kapoor, A. (2019). Impact of artificial intelligence on businesses: from research, innovation, market deployment to future shifts in business models. *arXiv preprint arXiv:1905.02092*.

5. Global Market Estimates. (2023, September 26). Generative AI in Retail Market Analysis | Size & Forecasts. https://www.precedenceresearch.com/generative-ai-in-retail-market

6. Publicis Sapient. (n.d.). Generative artificial intelligence in the retail industry. Retrieved from https://www.publicissapient.com/insights/generative-artificial-intelligence-retail-industry

7. India Retailing Bureau. (2024, March 2). Which technologies will fuel the next wave of growth in retail? India Retailing. Retrieved from https://www.indiaretailing.com/2024/03/02/future-retail-technology/

8. Parwez, A. (2023, May 29). Myntra pioneers India's first AI-powered personal style guide on its app https://cio.economictimes.indiatimes.com/news/next-gen-technologies/my-stylist-indias-first-ai-powered-personal-style-by-myntra/100581188

9. Lee, J. (2023, September 21). Exploring the top use cases of AI in retail. LeewayHertz. https://www.leewayhertz.com/ai-in-retail/

10. Kristensen, E. (2022, September 22). Conversational commerce examples. Drip. Retrieved March 3, 2024, from https://www.drip.com/blog/conversational-commerce-examples

11. Harrigan, P. J. (2020, February 12). How Amazon Uses AI to Dominate Ecommerce: Top 5 Use Cases. [Godatafeed Blog]. Retrieved from https://www.godatafeed.com/blog/how-amazon-uses-ai-to-dominate-ecommerce

12. Apparel chain Avenue digs deep to engage online shoppers. (2017, December 5). *STORES* online magazine.

13. Intel. Artificial Intelligence (AI) in Retail. https://www.intel.com/content/www/us/en/retail/solutions/ai-in-retail.html

14. Pandolph, S. (2023, May 10). Nike's new tech creates custom sneakers in under 2 hours. Business Insider. https://www.businessinsider.com/nikes-new-tech-creates-custom-sneakers-in-under-2-hours-2017-9

15. Sokolovsky, O. (2020, March 10). The future of augmented reality for retailers and brands. Forbes. Retrieved from https://www.forbes.com/sites/forbesbusinesscouncil/2020/03/10/the-future-of-augmented-reality-for-retailers-and-brands/

Chapter 15

AI and Social Impact in the Indian Financial Sector

Bidisha Banerji and S. A. Mokhtar Rizvi

15.1 Introduction

Artificial intelligence (AI) is now the new mantra, with companies in the banking, financial services, and insurance (BFSI) sectors rushing to reap its manifold benefits. It is widely accepted that AI has immense potential to transform BFSI sectors in developing countries, especially in India. By using unstructured data such as email, voice (for example, call center conversations), images and videos, AI can uncover hidden patterns that might have been historically difficult to detect. In fact, for some time, companies in these areas have relied on machine learning (ML) models for many of their processes. The tremendous impact of generative AI (Gen AI) is just beginning to be realized but its role in leveraging natural language processing (NLP), ML, and predictive analytics to help businesses and organizations automate tasks, improve efficiency, and enhance customer experiences is without doubt. Training companies to use Gen AI presents tremendous avenues for growth. Some may say it is too early to think of tectonic shifts in the way businesses are conducted. While others point out the risk of the technology becoming obsolete too soon (Przegalinska & Jemielniak, 2023).

FinTechs are at the forefront of using AI technology to create, innovate, and structurally change financial services, the economy, and society. This includes more personalized, secure, and efficient financial products being offered (Cao *et al.*, 2021). According to reports by IDC (2022; 2023),

DOI: 10.4324/9781032711089-15

investments in direct digital transformation are projected to experience a remarkable compound annual growth rate (CAGR) of 27% from 2022 to 2026. This growth is notably more than four times the five-year CAGR of 6.3% for global IT expenditure during the same period. In the year 2023, the banking and retail sectors are anticipated to lead in AI investments. Collectively, these two industries are projected to contribute to a quarter of the total global AI expenditure. There are "multiple Indians" and many different personalities. Additionally, there are several products that any sector can sell. Given the complexity of the population base, Gen AI can be utilized to enhance your offering (Sinha *et al.*, 2023).

AI presents opportunities to build tools and solutions that make use of such technology to address some of the most pressing concerns globally and to ensure a positive social impact that is inclusive, resilient, and sustainable. This aligns with the priorities drawn in the "sustainable development goals (SDGs)" adopted by the United Nations Members in 2015. What makes AI even more desirable is that its scope extends to most of the targets, including those on education, healthcare, finance, environment, and urbanization, among others (Vinuesa et al., 2020). For the AI community, using AI for social impact provides significant value as it provides them with new dimensions in the evaluation of current algorithms and presents complexities that test abstractions and their limits. This often results in extensions to the already being used methods. Using AI for social impact requires more work and effort and thus, requires more deliberations when assessing its results (Perrault *et al.*, 2020). The ethical and social implications of using generative AI to create content that influences people's opinions, emotions, and behaviors have to be constantly monitored. Safeguards need to be put in place, and protocols need to be established (Stahl & Eke, 2024).

All these changes are predicted to alter the nature and space of work. In this chapter, the far-reaching impact of AI in the future is analyzed in the context of inclusion, resilience, and sustainability. The study looks at Indian financial services as a case study to understand the technological transformation and how AI can further enhance it. This chapter is divided into six sections. Following this section is the section of Understanding AI Models, and in Section 3 we discuss AI and Social Impact under the subheadings of Financial Inclusion, Resilience, and Sustainability. In Section 4, we present a case study on government interventions in the Indian financial sector, and Section 5 covers the Key Challenges in Incorporating AI. We conclude with Section 6 on the conclusions and way forward for further research in this area.

15.2 Understanding AI Models

AI models have some specific features that make them distinctive. AI-based models can work with large amounts of data, identify complex patterns, and work with unstructured data. However, there are downsides as well. For instance, AI models often act like black boxes and are not easily interpretable. They might also require more expensive hardware for training. Some of AI's distinctive features include identifying complex patterns, handling large and unstructured data, real-time decision-making capability, difficult interpreting, and complex hardware and software requirements.

An immensely promising innovation within the AI realm is Gen AI. It holds the potential to revolutionize business operations across financial institutions, not only in India but at a global scale. Gen AI represents a breed of AI that excels in generating novel data and content like text, images, and music, as well as reconfiguring and condensing existing material. While bots and robotic process automation (RPA) handle discrete tasks, Gen AI pioneers the automation of intricate processes. Moreover, Gen AI is adept at addressing product appropriateness during application or when confronted with shifts in client situations. Currently, Gen AI is being piloted by several Indian financial institutions in a wide range of potential applications across these areas. As the technology continues to develop, Gen AI can have an even more profound impact on the industry and its participants. The Gen AI space itself is undergoing tremendous transformation, with new language models being developed by one and all. While some businesses rely entirely on "proprietary LLMs" (like Gemini/GPT), others are considering open-source ones (like Llama). Multiple factors are causing businesses to lean one way or the other (Stacey & Morrison, 2023).

AI also poses risks that are different from traditional software risks. AI models learn from the inherent data. Over time, the datasets used for training AI systems may divert from the original context and become stale or outdated relative to the deployment Context. This may potentially cause bias in prediction, which can become problematic. During the training of AI systems, intentional or unintentional changes can lead to bias in prediction. AI systems are also sometimes opaque in nature, and the results produced by them can vary based on the situation. It is very difficult to have a one-time stress testing of the models. This is a continuous process since AI systems are not subject to the same controls as traditional code development. Similarly, some AI systems are highly complex in nature. The new age neural networks can have billions of parameters responsible for making a prediction. AI models highly rely on data for training and improved performance. As a result, more care must be taken regarding data privacy, personal data usage, and cybersecurity. Data used for training an AI model may not represent the true population and hence may incur bias when tested for new data. These detrimental biases and other data quality issues can affect an AI system's trustworthiness, which may negatively impact the integrity and usage of the AI systems. Lastly, predicting failure modes for a large, complex AI system is very difficult and sometimes cannot be detected before being used in real life. This, however, does not undermine the far-reaching benefits that AI can accrue in various aspects of business and overall development.

15.3 AI and Social Impact

The vast usage of AI technology by the masses has attracted changes both in the short and long run for society. From the professionals who regularly deal with and add value to such technologies, to the policymakers who are continuously assessing its implications and making regulations, to the companies who would use such technologies to make complex decisions, all of them have been changed due to AI (Majumdar & Chattopadhyay, 2020). On the other hand, there are some social concerns with AI's continuous integration into existing processes. Tai (2020) argues that "Wealth Inequality" would increase more as people investing in AI would take up the majority share of the earnings. The already widespread gap between the rich and the poor would widen even more, and the "M-shape" wealth distribution would be more apparent. Moreover, AI can also be prone to "racial bias" and "egocentrically oriented" to have negative effects on specific groups. Another area of concern is that AI technologies are traditionally built upon the values and needs of the countries where they have been developed. Therefore, AI and big data can be used in regions where democratic ideals, accountability, transparency, and freedom are lacking and can deliberately accelerate hatred toward groups and the consequences of selection bias selection (Vinuesa *et al.*, 2020). Addressing the concern around protecting intellectual property rights and privacy of the original creators and sources of the content that generative AI systems use as inputs should be prioritized by businesses and developers.

To avoid such negative outcomes and achieve a positive impact, AI processes should align with ethical principles and regulations. For example, the "European Commission" and "Organization for Economic Cooperation and Development (OECD)" have both developed guidelines for the development of innovative and trustworthy AI. The European Commission states that "AI needs to be lawful, ethical, and robust to avoid causing unintended harm" (Tomašev *et al.*, 2020). OECD Principles on AI state that "First, AI should be driving inclusive growth, sustainable development, and well-being. Second, it should be designed in a way that respects the rule of law, human rights, democratic values, and diversity. Third, there should be transparency and responsible disclosure around AI systems. Fourth, AI systems must function in a robust, secure, and safe way throughout their lifetimes, and potential risks should be continually assessed and managed. Lastly, organizations and individuals developing, deploying, or operating AI systems should be held accountable" (OECD, 2019).

In this study, we will analyze the financial sector using three features of social impact which are inclusion, resilience, and sustainability. In this context, inclusion is defined as "ensuring diverse access to financial services, promoting economic growth, seeing inequality, and enhancing stability" (Ozili, 2018). Resilience is defined as "ensuring that the financial institutions can withstand shocks from more extreme events, have the right amount of capital cushion, can prove their ability to clear stress tests, and are compliant with regulations" (Graham, 2021). Lastly, sustainability is defined as "ensuring the integration of environmental, social, and governance factors into finance. This ensures long-term viability and ethical responsibility" (Bakken, 2021).

1. **Role of AI in Financial Inclusion**

   To have an inclusive financial ecosystem, it needs to expand access, improve literacy, and address the challenges faced by underserved populations. Traditional banking systems are physical in nature and have their limitations. AI helps financial institutions explore novel ways to reach the farthest person in the value chain and bring about a more inclusive environment of accessibility as well as usability to end users. Here are some ways how AI can aid financial inclusion.

   - **Accessible Financial Services**: As FinTech drives the adoption of AI-driven chatbots and mobile banking apps, it allows more people to access financial services from mobile phones often in vernacular languages. It empowers those who might not be comfortable with specific languages or those in remote locations of the country.
   - **Product Simplification**: Traditionally, the complexity of financial products (like insurance) has been a deterrent to their adoption. Language too has been a barrier, as there is seldom high-quality

product literature in vernacular languages. AI-powered NLP engines are increasingly being used to offer financial services in multiple languages, surmounting language barriers and helping in achieving high financial inclusion.

- **Credit Assessment for Those with "Thin" Credit Files**: AI algorithms can analyze alternative data sources, like statements of tangible assets owned and documents related to business dealings, to understand business volumes and potentials. This will help to assess creditworthiness for individuals without traditional credit histories, opening doors to credit for the unbanked, and promoting the financial inclusion of individuals, something which has been a challenge in developing countries (Willstrand *et al.*, 2023).

- **Faster Response to Catastrophic Events**: AI enables insurance companies to understand risks at a much more granular level (Balasubramanian *et al.*, 2021). For example, the use of computer vision-based assessment of properties enables insurers to price the risk better for the entire farmland as compared to earlier estimates. This makes insurance more affordable. Additionally, it enables insurers to act faster in case of catastrophic events thereby reducing delays in providing financial assistance to the affected farmers and ensuring continuity in their sustenance without too much intervention from the Government.

2. **Role of AI in Improving Resilience**

Resilience is primarily about dealing with uncertainties and eventualities. AI is a tool that can help in the anticipation of both of these events, thus mitigating some of the potential damages. Over the last decade, the adoption of ML models has accelerated within financial institutions, typically in risk management, fraud detection and prevention, anti-money laundering, and related party transactions that primarily ensure that financial systems are not used for unintended purposes. These are the channels through which AI can build resilience in the financial systems.

- **Early Warning Systems**: AI algorithms, such as variational auto-encoders, can detect anomalous patterns much earlier in the process than more conventional methods (Agmon, 2021). AI allows the use of non-conventional sources of data like text, images, or videos to detect signals that would otherwise have been unheeded. These allow early warning signals to be generated for financial institutions to take remedial action before a crisis escalates.

- **Risk Management**: AI-powered algorithms can identify complex patterns to assess and manage various financial risks, including market volatility, credit risks, liquidity risks, and operational risks. This enables financial institutions to proactively address potential threats and improve their resilience against economic downturns (Boukherouaa *et al.*, 2021). Many global investment banks have been using AI for risk management to enhance their risk management processes, particularly for market risk analysis and credit risk assessment

- **Fraud Detection and Prevention**: AI enhances fraud detection capabilities by analyzing transaction data in real-time, swiftly identifying suspicious activities, and preventing fraudulent transactions. Large language models (LLMs) can synthesize hypothetical fraud scenarios and generate more synthetic data to make the models and systems more robust and resilient. Several banks and insurance companies today rely on ML-based models for fraud detection and prevention.

- **Regulatory Compliance**: AI can help financial institutions meet regulatory requirements by automating compliance processes, reducing compliance-related costs, and enhancing transparency. AI-led chatbots can reduce the time taken when going through large documents to mere seconds, which otherwise often takes more time manually by humans responding to the questions asked. LLM model-based Q&A models for internal documents are going to play an important role.

3. **Role of AI in Sustainability**

"Environmental, social, and governance (ESG)" compliance has been on every corporation's agenda for growth. AI is also enabling and improving regulatory compliance amongst regulated entities and facilitates new avenues of responsible investing through ESG analysis. Generative AI is being piloted in several new fields and has the potential to completely transform business models. AI is helping to promote a sustainable global financial ecosystem by helping responsible investing, enhancing environmental risk management, and supporting sustainable business practices. These are some of the avenues for AI to promote sustainability.

- **Green Finance**: AI helps to identify and prioritize environmentally friendly projects that qualify for green financing, supporting the transition to a low-carbon economy and sustainable infrastructure development. AI allows rapid processing of a variety of project-related documents and offers sustainable investment options that are tailored to individual preferences. This encourages investors to make responsible investments. For example, the "State Bank of India (SBI)" has mounted ten windmills with a cumulative capacity of 15 MW in the states of Tamil Nadu, Maharashtra, and Gujarat (Deka, 2015).

- **Sustainable Risk Management**: AI-led platforms can easily simulate multiple what-if scenarios that better highlight the environmental and social risks associated with a project (UNEP, 2022). This enables financial institutions to be aware of sustainability factors at a much more granular level. Consequently, these can be monitored and integrated into risk management frameworks, allowing decision-makers to avoid harmful choices.
- **Sustainable Business Analytics**: AI-driven tools are increasingly being used to compute and monitor the carbon footprint of employees, investments, portfolios, and entire businesses. AI promotes transparency and accountability in carbon emissions management.

We now look at a case study in the Indian financial system to understand the reach of AI's social impact capabilities.

15.4 AI and Financial Services in India: A Case Study of Government Intervention

For economic prosperity to occur in any country, one of the key enablers is that its financial system needs to be robust and well-functioning, catering to all its citizens. It plays a critical role in mobilizing credit for the whole economy and ultimately procuring growth in the long run. In the past decade, India has invested immensely in the rapid development of mobile networks and the Internet, especially in previously uncatered areas and communities. With more than 500 million internet subscribers, India is one of the largest markets for digital consumers. This opportunity has been recognized by players in every sector and financial institutions, too are not falling behind. The financial services industry in India has been a leader in embracing newer technologies and FinTechs have led the way. The advent of Unified Payments Interface (UPI) payments has emerged as an alternative to traditional online and mobile banking. This has contributed to processes being efficient and expenses being reduced while catering to people in rural and semi-urban areas (Asif *et al.*, 2023). But at the same time, a considerable portion of rural and tribal lands still struggles to have access to formal banking services, which eventually contributes to uneven growth, and the "deprived" have a hard time in the management of their financial resources as their income is mostly unpredictable (Chouhan *et al.*, 2021). The Indian government, in response to this, has launched several e-governance projects and initiatives to help in the accessibility of financial services (Alonso *et al.*, 2023).

One of the most important steps toward digital inclusion was the establishment of UIDAI in 2009 to provide Aadhar, a digital identity for all Indians. Aadhar is now playing a crucial role in electronic KYC (eKYC), making remote onboarding for banking services easy and quick. The "Pradhan Mantri Jan Dhan Yojana (PMJDY)" policy has helped to improve access to banks for the unbanked. Under PMJDY, around 49 crore bank accounts have been opened, with more than 50% of accounts being owned by women. As a result, over the last decade, access to banking systems has increased to almost 80% (Khera, 2023). Also, the introduction of the UPI in 2016 has helped to expand digital transactions using smartphones and reduced reliance on cash. The government has also started the Unstructured Supplementary Service Data (USSD) channel for basic banking services without Internet connections.

More recently, the COVID-19 pandemic has catalyzed the adoption of several technologies. With access to "brick and mortar" banks reduced, AI-based technologies like chatbots, computer vision for processing documents, and assisted video KYC were able to efficiently service and onboard customers. Most large Indian financial institutions today have either already built or are in the process of aggressively scaling up the technological backbone required to run AI operations smoothly. FinTechs participate in most, if not all, of these technologies.

Central and State government bodies have also shown a positive outlook to promote responsible and ethical use of AI. Although India currently does not have any published AI regulations, institutions like the "Reserve Bank of India (RBI)" and "Securities and Exchange Board of India (SEBI)" have enhanced corporate governance and risk management practices to ensure data security and data privacy (Chowdhury *et al.*, 2021). In 2018, the Indian Government's policy thinktank – "NITI Aayog" released the "National Strategy on Artificial Intelligence (NSAI)" on Responsible AI, which provides a guideline on the principles of responsible AI during the development, deployment, and use of the AI systems (NITI Aayog, 2022). At the recently concluded B20 Summit in August 2023, a task force put together a policy paper on financial inclusion which identified 11 priority themes and policy actions across three pillars to advance financial inclusion for underserved customer segments (B20, 2023).

This case study illustrates the enormous scope and the power of AI in the Indian financial sector. Let us look at what are some of the problem areas that need to be acknowledged and addressed to facilitate a better integration of AI in the financial sector.

15.5 Key Challenges in Incorporating AI

Developing AI systems at scale involves overcoming significant challenges. First, training data must not be biased and should not have significant gaps. Second, the impact that AI can have on misinformation, intellectual property rights, and possible job displacement raises complex ethical questions. In addition, working in the field requires a high level of skill – on the one hand, there is a shortage of such skilled resources, while on the other hand, explaining the solutions to a layperson (say a venture capitalist or a regulator) might pose challenges and impose barriers to acceptability. Finally, regulatory and policy frameworks around AI are just beginning to be developed while AI is beginning to be increasingly misused and abused. Consequently, practitioners need to tread with caution.

Businesses are now induced to think about various matters concerning AI technology. The changes required in corporate governance processes to account for AI, monitoring an AI application's performance, using the best practices for testing and validating AI applications, designing effective AI models to improve accountability and quality, and the ethical and moral implications of using AI technology and its sustainability are some of the concerns which would be on the minds of many businesses.

According to various studies, the adoption of responsible AI has increased significantly over the past two years (Beauchene *et al.*, 2023). There is increased awareness of ethical AI and more emphasis on having AI ethics into action Also, concrete measures are being taken concerning data security, privacy, personal information usage, safety, cybersecurity, and sustainability.

Collaborative efforts involving technologists, policymakers, ethicists, and users are crucial to have an ethical, responsible AI solution. Transparency and the ability to explain in AI algorithms, combined with ethical guidelines, ensure responsible deployment. Regular cross-disciplinary dialogues foster innovative solutions. Lastly, continuous monitoring, adaptability, and feedback loops enable AI systems to evolve responsibly, addressing concerns and optimizing outcomes for society.

The race for Gen AI is literally "heating up". The amount of heat generated by the many chips (GPUs) is enormous, and it takes a huge amount of effort, investment, and time to cool them down. This is bound to increase costs one way or the other, which needs to be factored in (Pambudi *et al.*, 2022).

15.6 Conclusions and Way Forward

The Indian FinTech environment is poised to take off. At the same time, the potential of AI systems is now beginning to be realized as they automate routine tasks, optimize financial operational activities, and provide personalized customer experience. For FinTechs, this is an exciting time. Throughout the paper, we have discussed many aspects of AI implementation, including its ability to enhance efficiency, accessibility, and risk management while ensuring responsible and ethical guidelines. We have also discussed a use case currently being utilized by different financial institutions to solve some practical problems using AI. These solutions together can be used to provide an inclusive, resilient, and responsible global financial ecosystem.

The potential risks that come along with the AI system in finance are valid concerns. It is important to consider the risks, difficulties, and dangers that may arise from the unethical use of AI. The rapid adoption of Gen AI is taking place against a backdrop of mainstream cloud migration and the use of digital tools. AI represents a technological revolution that is poised to gain even greater momentum. We have previously outlined how AI possesses the undeniable potential to reshape organizations, prompting numerous businesses to swiftly explore novel business models and applications. However, for AI to gain the confidence of businesses, regulators, customers, and employees, it must establish a foundation of trust. Creating a comprehensive framework for managing AI risks is imperative to ensure the responsible and secure implementation of AI technologies.

We also emphasized the importance of cooperation of different stakeholders including financial institutions, policymakers, regulators, and technology developers to develop standard and optimal procedures for the responsible deployment of AI in finance. All the stakeholders can collaborate and design a strong structure that encourages innovation while also protecting against possible adverse effects.

Lastly, we can conclude that AI holds great promise in reshaping the financial ecosystem through its numerous benefits to both the customers and the financial institutions. However, we should make sure that the AI systems are implemented ethically and used responsibly to build a transparent, inclusive financial ecosystem. We must create systems that can consistently ensure the quality, accuracy, and reliability of the content generated by generative AI systems. For instance, a customer can create a prompt to bypass standard protocols and get the chatbot to agree to something the firm will not agree to. With a balanced approach and collaborative effects from all the stakeholders, we can maximize the positive impact of AI on the financial ecosystem as well as in society. The social impact of AI on the Indian financial sector in the areas of inclusion, resilience, and sustainability can be fully taken advantage of through a better understanding of the new technology, its widespread application, and being cognizant of its lacunas.

References

Agmon, A. (2021, July 30). Hands-on Anomaly Detection with Variational Autoencoders. Medium. https://towardsdatascience.com/hands-on-anomaly-detection-with-variational-autoencoders-d4044672acd5

Alonso, C., Bhojwani, T., Hanedar, E., Prihardini, D., Uña, G. & Zhabska, K. (2023). Stacking up the benefits: Lessons from India's digital journey. *IMF Working Papers*, 2023(078), A001. https://doi.org/10.5089/9798400240416.001

Asif, M., Khan, M. N., Tiwari, S., Wani, S. K. & Alam, F. (2023). The impact of fintech and digital financial services on financial inclusion in India. *Journal of Risk and Financial Management*, 16(2), 122. https://doi.org/10.3390/jrfm16020122

B20. (2023). Task Force on Financial Inclusion for Economic Empowerment. *B20 India 2023 Policy Paper*. https://api.b20india2023.org/b20docs/e8094854-30ba-4509-8400-2a891e2ccfa6.pdf

Bakken, R. (2021, August 9). What Is Sustainable Finance and Why Is It Important?. Harvard Extension School. https://extension.harvard.edu/blog/what-is-sustainable-finance-and-why-is-it-important/

Balasubramanian, R., Libarikian, A. & McElhaney, D. (2021, March 12). Insurance 2030–The impact of AI on the future of insurance. McKinsey & Company. https://www.mckinsey.com/industries/financial-services/our-insights/insurance-2030-the-impact-of-ai-on-the-future-of-insurance

Beauchene, V., de Bellefonds, N., Duranton, S. & Mills, S. (2023, July 7). AI at Work: What People Are Saying. Bostin Consulting Group. https://www.bcg.com/publications/2023/what-people-are-saying-about-ai-at-work

Boukherouaa, E. B., AlAjmi, K., Deodoro, J., Farias, A. & Ravikumar, R. (2021). Powering the digital economy: Opportunities and risks of artificial intelligence in finance. *Departmental Papers*, 2021(024), A001. ISBN/ISSN:9781589063952/ 2616-5333

Cao, L., Yang, Q. & Yu, P. S. (2021). Data science and AI in FinTech: An overview. *International Journal Data Science and Analytics*, 12, 81–99. https://doi.org/ 10.1007/s41060-021-00278-w

Chouhan, V., Sharma, R., Goswami, S. & Hashed, A. (2021). Measuring challenges in adoption of sustainable environmental technologies in Indian cement industry. *Accounting*, 7(2), 339–348.

Chowdhury, P. R., Pera, P., George, N. & Sagar, J. (2021, September). India: Data Protection in the Financial Sector. DataGuidance. https://www.dataguidance. com/opinion/india-data-protection-financial-sector

Deka, G. (2015). Green banking practices: A study on environmental strategies of banks with special reference to state bank of India. *Indian Journal of Commerce & Management Studies*, 6(3), 11–19.

Graham, A. (2021, March 10). Operational Resilience Challenges in Banking and Financial Markets. IBM. https://www.ibm.com/thought-leadership/institute-business-value/en-us/blog/operational-resilience-banking-financial-markets

IDC. (2022, September 12). Worldwide Spending on AI-Centric Systems Will Pass $300 Billion by 2026, According to IDC. IDC. https://www.idc.com/getdoc.jsp? containerId=prUS49796122

IDC. (2023, March 7). Worldwide Spending on AI-Centric Systems Forecast to Reach $154 Billion in 2023, According to IDC. IDC. https://www.idc.com/getdoc.jsp? containerId=prUS50454123

Khera, P. (2023). Digital Financial Services and Inclusion. In *India's Financial System*. USA: International Monetary Fund. https://www.elibrary.imf.org/downloadpdf/ book/9798400223525/CH007.pdf

Majumdar, D. & Chattopadhyay, H. K. (2020). Artificial intelligence and its impacts on the society. *International Journal of Law*, 6(5), 306–310.

NITI Aayog. (2022). Responsible AI for All: Adopting the Framework – A use case approach on Facial Recognition Technology. *NITI Aayog Discussion Paper*. https://www.niti.gov.in/sites/default/files/2022-11/Ai_for_All_2022_02112022_0.pdf

OECD. (2019, May 22). Forty-two countries adopt new OECD Principles on Artificial Intelligence. OECD. https://www.oecd.org/science/forty-two-countries-adopt-new-oecd-principles-on-artificial-intelligence.htm

Ozili, P. K. (2018). Impact of digital finance on financial inclusion and stability. *Borsa Istanbul Review*, 18(4), 329–340. https://doi.org/10.1016/j.bir.2017.12.003

Pambudi, N. A., Sarifudin, A., Firdaus, R. A., Ulfa, D. K., Gandidi, I. M. & Romadhon, R. (2022). The immersion cooling technology: Current and future development in energy saving. *Alexandria Engineering Journal*, 61(12), 9509–9527. https://doi.org/10.1016/j.aej.2022.02.059

Perrault, A., Fang, F., Sinha, A. & Tambe, M. (2020). Artificial intelligence for social impact: Learning and planning in the data-to-deployment pipeline. *AI Magazine*, 41(4), 3–16. https://doi.org/10.1609/aimag.v41i4.5296

Przegalinska, A. & Jemielniak, D. (2023). *Strategizing AI in Business and Education: Emerging Technologies and Business Strategy (Elements in Business Strategy)*. Cambridge: Cambridge University Press. https://doi.org/10.1017/9781009243520

Sinha, P., Shastri, A. & Lorimer, S. E. (2023, March 31). How Generative AI Will Change Sales. Harvard Business Review. https://hbr.org/2023/03/how-generative-ai-will-change-sales

Stacey, S. & Morrison, R. (2023, May 15). Open source energised AI. LLMs are complicating matters. Tech Monitor. https://techmonitor.ai/technology/ai-and-automation/open-source-energised-ai-llms-are-complicating-matters

Stahl, B. C. & Eke, D. (2024). The ethics of ChatGPT – Exploring the ethical issues of an emerging technology author links open overlay panel. *International Journal of Information Management*, 74, 102700. https://doi.org/10.1016/j.ijinfomgt.2023.102700

Tai, M. C.T. (2020). The impact of artificial intelligence on human society and bioethics. *Tzu Chi Medical Journal*, 32(4), 339–343. National Library of Medicine. https://doi.org/10.4103/tcmj.tcmj_71_20

Tomašev, N., Cornebise, J., Hutter, F., Mohamed, S., Picciariello, A., Connelly, B., Belgrave, D. C. M., Ezer, D., Haert, F. C., van der, Mugisha, F., Abila, G., Arai, H., Almiraat, H., Proskurnia, J., Snyder, K., Otake-Matsuura, M., Othman, M., Glasmachers, T., Wever, W. & Teh, Y. W. (2020). AI for social good: Unlocking the opportunity for positive impact. *Nature Communications*, 11(1). https://doi.org/10.1038/s41467-020-15871-z

UNEP. (2022, November 7). How artificial intelligence is helping tackle environmental challenges. UNEP. https://www.unep.org/news-and-stories/story/how-artificial-intelligence-helping-tackle-environmental-challenges

Vinuesa, R., Azizpour, H., Leite, I., Balaam, M., Dignum, V., Domisch, S., Felländer, A., Langhans, S. D., Tegmark, M. & Fuso Nerini, F. (2020). The role of artificial intelligence in achieving the sustainable development goals. *Nature Communications*, 11(1), 233. https://doi.org/10.1038/s41467-019-14108-y

Willstrand, O., Pushp, M., Andersson, P., & Brandell, D. (2023). Impact of different Li-ion cell test conditions on thermal runaway characteristics and gas release measurements. *Journal of Energy Storage, 68*, 107785.

Chapter 16

Artificial Intelligence in Healthcare Sector

Anusha Siddadapu, Ajay Midimalapu, and MNS Ram Kumar Babu

16.1 Introduction

Artificial intelligence (AI) is slowly but surely gaining a foothold in the healthcare sector. The implementation of AI in healthcare is wide-ranging, from improving patient outcomes to reducing costs. One area where AI is already starting to make an impact is in the field of diagnosis. AI can help doctors identify diseases much more accurately. For example, IBM Watson Health's cognitive computing system has been used to successfully diagnose rare forms of cancer. AI can also be used to improve patient care by providing personalized recommendations based on a person's individual health data. This is something that start-ups like Florence are working on. Florence is an app that uses AI to provide tailored recommendations on how best to manage chronic conditions like diabetes.

In the upcoming years, AI may be capable of executing more complex tasks like surgery or providing medical advice. However, there are still many challenges that need to be addressed before this can become a reality. For now, AI is likely to continue playing a supporting role in the healthcare sector rather than becoming the main event. As a result, this book chapter introduces the current research and application status of AI in healthcare, as well as the issues that need to be addressed. Figure 16.1 describes the AI various segments of healthcare.

DOI: 10.4324/9781032711089-16

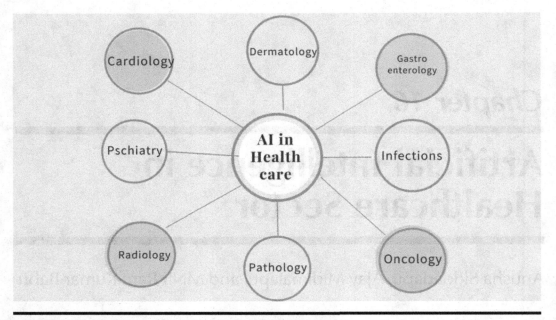

Figure 16.1   Artificial intelligence in different health sectors.

16.2 Usage of AI in Different Aspects of Healthcare

There are different aspects of disease where AI can be used to improve healthcare. For example, AI can diagnose diseases much more accurately. It can also be used to forecast the progression of diseases and to identify potential treatments. Furthermore, AI can monitor patients' health and provide personalized health advice.

AI is utilized in many ways in healthcare today, one area where AI is having a big impact is in the diagnostics field. With the help of machine learning (ML), AI-based systems are becoming increasingly adept at identifying patterns in data that can point to underlying health conditions. In another area where AI is being used in healthcare is in the development of treatments and drugs. Using data from past clinical trials, AI-based systems can identify potential new targets for drugs and help optimize existing treatments. AI is also being used to manage patient care. By analyzing data from electronic health records (EHRs), AI-based systems can identify patients at risk for certain conditions and offer tailored recommendations for prevention or early intervention. In the coming days, AI will play a bigger role in healthcare as we continue to develop more algorithms and applications.

16.2.1 Cardiology

AI is playing an important role in improving healthcare. The crucial applications of AI in healthcare are vast, but one area where AI is already making a difference is in the field of cardiology. One way AI is being used in cardiology is to help diagnose heart conditions. AI can be used to analyze images of the heart, looking for patterns that may indicate a particular condition. This can help medical professionals to diagnose heart conditions quickly and accurately, that can mean better treatment and outcomes for patients. AI is being used to improve new treatments for heart conditions. For example, researchers are using AI to develop personalized treatments for heart failure. By analyzing data from large numbers of patients, AI can identify patterns that may predict which treatments will be most effective for individual patients. This type of personalized medicine could greatly improve the success rate of treating heart conditions. In the future, AI will likely play an even bigger role in improving cardiovascular healthcare. As AI technology continues to advance, it will become even better at diagnosing and treating heart conditions. Figure 16.2 shows the different types of techniques used in cardiology by using AI. So far, AI is already making a difference in the field of cardiology, and it is only going to get better[1].

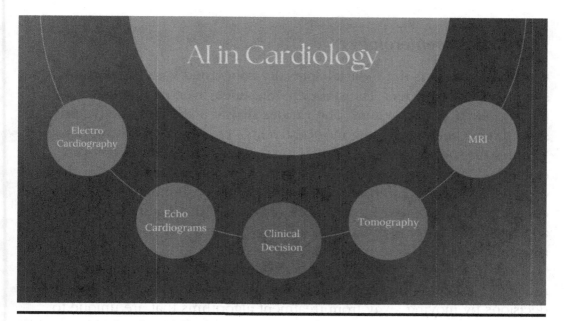

Figure 16.2   Role of AI in cardiology.

16.2.2 Dermatology

Dermatology is one of the most promising medical specialties. It is the study of skin and its related problems, such as skin diseases, infections, allergies, cosmetic procedures, and other skin conditions. Dermatologists diagnose and treat skin disorders with medications, topical creams and ointments, lasers, injections, and surgical procedures. They also offer advice on skincare to help people prevent skin problems from occurring in the first place. Dermatology is the medical specialty concerned with the skin, nails, hair, and mucous membranes. Because the skin is the largest organ in the human body, it is an important field of medicine. Even though it is still in its early phases, another application of AI in dermatology offers enormous promise to strengthen patient care. AI can be used to help diagnose skin conditions, choose the most effective treatments, and even predict how a person will respond to certain medications. In the future, AI will be used to create customized treatments for individual patients according to their specific needs and characteristics. This could potentially revolutionize the way we treat skin conditions, making treatments more personalized and effective.

By analyzing images of skin lesions, AI can help dermatologists more accurately diagnose skin cancer. AI can also be used to develop new treatments for skin conditions and improve existing treatments.

16.2.3 Gastroenterology

Gastroenterology is the medical specialty concerned with the digestive system and its disorders. The stomach, intestines, liver, and pancreas are all parts of the digestive system. The various diseases affecting the digestive system have been increasing in recent years. 'Inflammatory bowel disease', 'Crohn's disease', 'ulcerative colitis', and 'irritable bowel syndrome' are examples. There are many different treatment options available for these conditions, but they can be expensive and time-consuming. This is where AI comes in. AI can be used to diagnose diseases of the digestive system more accurately and faster than traditional methods. It can also be used to develop new treatments for these conditions.

This presents a tremendous opportunity for the customization of medicine, enabling both physicians and patients to make data-driven decisions by moving away from treatment algorithms that are unique to guidelines and toward ones that are patient-specific. These analyses could anticipate the occurrence of digestive disease before symptoms show, increasing the likelihood of prevention or primary prevention. Moreover, the exciting possibility of automatic lesion detection during endoscopy is made possible by computer vision[2].

16.2.4 *Infectious Disease*

Over the past few years, AI has made great strides in psychiatric care. AI-based technologies are being used to diagnose mental disorders, deliver personalized treatment, and even predict relapse. But what about using AI to fight infectious diseases? There is growing evidence that AI can be used to detect, diagnose, and treat infections. For example, AI-based algorithms have been shown to outperform traditional methods for diagnosing pneumonia. A recent study found that an AI system was able to accurately identify sepsis (a life-threatening condition caused by infection) in patients in just five minutes. AI can also be used to develop new treatments for infections. In one recent study, researchers used ML to screen millions of molecules and identify two potential new drugs for treating Ebola. The AI application in infectious disease research is still in the beginning stages. However, as technology evolves, it is important to revolutionize the way we find, diagnose, and treat infections. Infectious disease testing, in general, and especially, has seen an efflux in miniaturization, automation, and growing executing power, creating an eccentric chance to leverage ML and AI. The applications can be classified into three categories:

AI can predict the coronavirus infectious disease (COVID-19), Antimicrobial susceptibility testing (AST), Meningitis, Malaria, Sepsis, Tuberculosis, and Lyme disease test results in laboratory diagnostics. Under Clinical Prognosis, Hepatitis B virus and Hepatitis C (HCV) infection are identified utilizing best practices of AI.

Infectious disease testing will be transmogrified by 'AI' and 'ML'. The application of 'AI'/'ML' for disease control demonstrates the technology's ability to mine EMR data and stimulate diagnostic and therapeutic action with greater accuracy and precision than conventional methodologies. However, AI should be executed in a logical and systematic manner in order to ensure that the quality of the data is not jeopardized and modeling approach is as bias-free as possible. At last, the fate of AI/ML communicable diseases testing may focus around 'data fusion' concepts which not only incorporate streams of data but also convert substantial quantities of heterogeneous data into meaningful insights[3].

16.2.5 Oncology

The disease cancer is spurred on by the body's cells reproducing in an uncontrolled manner. Oncologists are specialists who specialize in the detection and treatment of cancer. According to estimates released by the World Health Organization (WHO), 8 million people died of cancer in the year 2012. Cancer is responsible for about 1 in 6 deaths globally. There are different forms of cancer, with their respective causes and treatments. 'Breast cancer', 'Lung cancer', 'Colorectal cancer', 'Prostate cancer', 'Skin cancer', and 'Ovarian cancer' are the most common and widespread cancers. The most prevalent malignancies are breast, colon, prostate, skin, and ovarian cancer. Surgery, chemotherapy, and bone marrow treatment are all just chances for treating cancer. Treatment depends on the type and stage of the cancer. Early detection as well as treatment of cancer can improve survival rates. Below, Figure 16.3 explains the wide range of applications of AI in the healthcare sector[4].

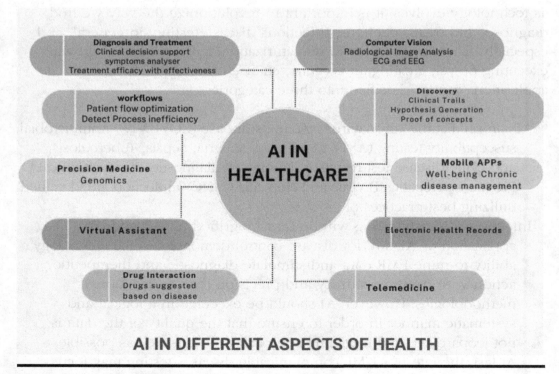

Figure 16.3   AI and its applications in various healthcare sectors.

16.2.6 Pathology

Pathology is more data-centric, employing clinical and phenotypic (histomorphology) information data points to enable traditional pathology methods. The usage of AI in pathology and in health has grown exponentially.

Researchers can now create imaging tools for examination and diagnosis using the same feature digital assets as high-resolution scanning equipment and WSI systems that can digitally capture the totality in biopsy, and cytological preparations from the microscopic slide at diagnostic resolution. Quantitative pathological imaging has long been recognized for its advantages.

Diagnostic patterns and images can be appropriately expressed by collecting quantitative data from photos that make use of automated segmentation and pixel analysis. This increases the accuracy and consistency of diagnostic classification. Further, the image analysis shows the identification of visual patterns that may reveal growing illness signs interpreted from source photos but imperceptible to the human eye.

Pathologists cannot additionally help abnormal cells on H&E as AI can. Some of these modifications can anticipate cell mutations. SPOP mutations in prostate cancer, BRAF mutations in melanoma, and six of the ten most frequently occurring lung adenocarcinoma mutations have mostly been shown to be predictive. When this image processing and analysis application is fully substantiated for diagnostic and therapeutic use, it may have the possibility of reducing the necessity for IHC while also providing mutation prediction[5].

As a result, Deep learning technologies are being designed with cellular imaging and practical implantation in mind. These technologies could revolutionize diagnostic pathology.

16.2.7 Psychiatry

As technology advances, so too do the medical applications. AI is no exception; it has already made substantial inroads in healthcare and psychiatry specifically. AI offers tremendous potential to revolutionize how we diagnose and expand awareness of mental health issues and diversify access to mental health services. In this blog, we will learn about current uses for AI in psychiatry, the potential applications for AI-driven therapies and diagnostics, and the ethical concerns of using such technology in a clinical setting.

Over the past few decades, AI new scientific technologies have advanced the understanding of neurosciences of psychiatric illness. To diagnose the disease of psychiatry, which involves physician-patient questionaries which consists most of the time, it is inaccurate and ineffective to find out the disease based on this manual phenomenon. To overcome this drawback, we can apply AI to medical databases and health records. AI in Psychiatry involves computational methods, and algorithms to know the disease, prevention, and treatment of the disease and find solutions to the most unanswered questions. Because of the use of AI, it reduces the cost of time, improves effectiveness, and measures accurate results[6].

16.2.8 Radiology

AI is revolutionizing radiology. ML algorithms are being used to assist radiologists in the interpretation of images, and AI is being used to develop new imaging techniques. Radiologists are using AI to help them interpret images. By using ML algorithms, radiologists can now get assistance in identifying abnormalities in images. This helps them to make more accurate diagnoses and to provide better patient care. AI has also been used to develop new imaging techniques. For example, engineers are using AI to develop a new type of MRI that can image the brain without the need for anesthesia. This could potentially help doctors to diagnose brain disorders earlier and more accurately. Overall, AI is having a positive impact on radiology. It is helping radiologists to improve their diagnostic accuracy and to develop new imaging techniques that can improve patient care.

16.2.9 Primary Care

AI is rapidly improving in the field of technology that can transform healthcare. AI can be used to help diagnose diseases, predict health outcomes, and recommend treatments for patients. It is also being used to automate tedious tasks in healthcare so that primary care providers can focus on providing more personalized care. In this blog post, we will explore how AI is being used in primary care today and discuss its potential implications for the future of healthcare. We will also outline some of the ethical considerations that need to be considered when implementing AI in primary care settings. There are many possible solutions for this lack of AI/ML use, the most notable of which is a lack of the evidence on diagnostic accuracy of AI/ML algorithms in related populations to support policymakers' and commissioners' decision-making on the implementation of AI/ML in clinical practice[7].

16.2.10 Telemedicine

Healthcare could be completely transformed by AI, a continuously growing field of technology. AI can be used to help diagnose diseases, predict health outcomes, and recommend treatments for patients. It is also being used to automate tedious tasks in healthcare so that primary care providers can focus on providing more personalized care. In this blog post, we will explore how AI is being used in primary care today and discuss its potential implications for the future of healthcare. We will also outline some of the ethical considerations that need to be considered when implementing AI in primary care settings.

16.2.11 Disease Diagnosis

AI has been increasingly used in primary care to support clinicians in disease diagnosis. While AI has the Caliber 1 to improve accuracy and efficiency in disease diagnosis, there is still much work to be done in developing and validating these systems. There are different ways that AI can be applicable in disease diagnosis, including:

- **MACHINE LEARNING**: This is an integral part of AI, that can learn from data and improve its performance over the period. ML algorithms have been used to develop models that can predict disease risk, identify early signs of disease, and distinguish between different types of diseases.
- **NATURAL LANGUAGE PROCESSING**: This is a sub-part of AI that can analyze text data, such as clinical notes, to extract information that could be relevant for diagnosis. For example, NLP has been used to identify patients with certain conditions based on the symptoms they have reported in their medical records.
- **IMAGE ANALYSIS**: This is a type of AI that can analyze images, such as X-rays or CT scans, to look for signs of disease. Image analysis algorithms have been used to detect cancers, cardiovascular abnormalities, and other diseases

16.2.12 Electronic Health Records

AI is widely applied to a wide range of tasks in the form of EHRs, including the NLP, clinical decision support system (CDSS), and predictive analytics.

NLP is used to extract structured data from unstructured text in EHRs, such as discharge summaries and progress notes. This structured data can then be used for the purpose of clinical decision support and predictive analytics. The Clinical decision support systems using AI can help clinicians by providing recommendations based on a patient's EHR. For example, a CDSS may suggest a different diagnosis based on the symptoms present in the EHR. With the help of Predictive analytics, it is easy to identify certain patients at risk with the relevant conditions, such as re-admission to the hospital. AI is also being used to develop new ways of visualizing EHR data. For example, some researchers are working on ways to visualize data from multiple EHRs in a single view, which could help clinicians identify patterns and trends that would otherwise be hidden in individual EHRs[8].

16.3 Drug Interactions

Pharmaceuticals are an incredibly sophisticated industry. With the amount of data and technical knowledge needed to make a drug, it is understandable why many people feel overwhelmed when it comes to understanding the complex interactions between drugs. Fortunately, this is where AI can help. AI technology has been used in various industries for decades now, and its potential applications in the pharmaceutical world are only now being realized. In this, explore how AI is being used to better understand drug interactions, as well as its potential implications for the industry. AI can be used to identify potential drug-drug interactions and to predict how likely they are to occur. AI is likely to improve the accuracy of drug interaction prediction and to lower the number of false positive and false negative predictions. Additionally, AI can help to identify novel drug interactions that have not been previously reported. The uses of AI in drug interaction prediction are still in their premature stages, but there is promise for this technology to improve the safety and efficacy of medications[9].

16.4 Artificial Intelligence of Voice Assistants to Improve Mental Health Wellness

One of every four persons is predicted to encounter some mental health condition at some phase of their lives. That statistic is staggering, and it is one of the main reasons why we need to find ways to improve mental health wellness. One way that we can do this is by using AI as voice assistants to help us. Voice assistants are becoming more and more common, and they are getting smarter every day. With the power of AI, voice assistants would help us to manage our mental health better. For example, they can remind us to take our medication, track our moods, and provide us with support when we need it. There are already a few voice assistant applications available that focus on mental health wellness. However, there is still room for improvement. For example, most of these applications are only available in English. This limits their usefulness for people who speak other languages. Additionally, most of these applications require the user to be able to read and write English well in order to use them effectively. Figure 16.4 describes the process of how the virtual assistant using AI works[10].

AI has the potential to improve mental health wellness significantly. However, there is still work to be done in order to make these applications more accessible and effective for everyone. From Figure 16.4, AI voice assistants capture the speech, analyze health, and give suggestions as well as improvisations to the patients.

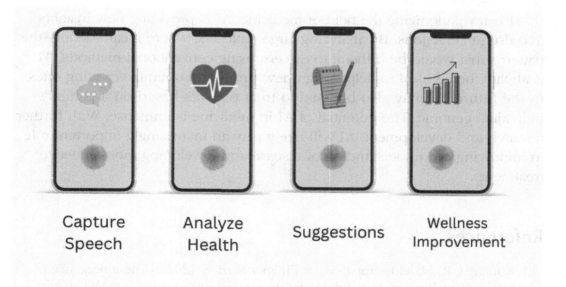

| Capture Speech | Analyze Health | Suggestions | Wellness Improvement |

Artificial Intelligence of Voice Assistants in Healthcare Interpretation

Figure 16.4   AI of voice assistant in healthcare-stepwise process.

16.5 Conclusion

AI is an effective tool for detecting patterns and predicting future drug interactions, that might indicate the presence of disease, which could lead to earlier diagnoses and more effective treatments. AI detects diseases faster and more accurately. By using this technology, we can better understand how drugs interact with each other and make more informed decisions about which medications to use.

In order to make use of AI in healthcare, it must be regulated and overseen by a governing body. This requires a system for creating regulations that are enforceable by law as well as a system for tracking compliance with those regulations. For example, if an AI is used to predict how long someone is likely to live based on their medical history, it will need to be approved by an organization like the Food and Drug Administration before being put into use.

There are also privacy concerns when using AI in healthcare. Patients may feel uncomfortable sharing information about their health with machines when there is no way for them to verify its accuracy or validity through traditional methods such as human doctors or patients themselves doing research online.

AI is revolutionizing the field of medicine. AI is providing new insights into drug interactions. By analyzing large data sets, where it can identify the patterns that would be difficult to discern using conventional methods. AI is already being used to help design new drugs and optimize existing ones. In the future, AI may also be used to treat patients based on a patient's individual genome. The potential of AI in medicine is immense. With further research and development, AI will likely play an increasingly important role in improving our understanding of disease and developing more effective treatments.

References

1. Kulkarni, P., Mahadevappa, M., & Chilakamarri, S. (2022). The emergence of artificial intelligence in cardiology: Current and future applications. *Current Cardiology Reviews, 18*(3), 46–52.
2. He, S., Leanse, L. G., & Feng, Y. (2021). Artificial intelligence and machine learning assisted drug delivery for effective treatment of infectious diseases. *Advanced Drug Delivery Reviews, 178*, 113922.

3. Tran, N. K., Albahra, S., May, L., Waldman, S., Crabtree, S., Bainbridge, S., & Rashidi, H. (2022). Evolving applications of artificial intelligence and machine learning in infectious diseases testing. *Clinical chemistry*, 68(1), 125–133.
4. Rattan, R., Kataria, T., Banerjee, S., Goyal, S., Gupta, D., Pandita, A., & Mishra, S. R. (2019). Artificial intelligence in oncology, its scope and future prospects with specific reference to radiation oncology. *BJR| Open*, 1(xxxx), 20180031.
5. Chang, H. Y., Jung, C. K., Woo, J. I., Lee, S., Cho, J., Kim, S. W., & Kwak, T. Y. (2019). Artificial intelligence in pathology. *Journal of Pathology and Translational Medicine*, 53(1), 1–12.
6. Ray, A., Bhardwaj, A., Malik, Y. K., Singh, S., & Gupta, R. (2022). Artificial intelligence and psychiatry: An overview. *Asian Journal of Psychiatry*, 103021.
7. Kueper, J. K., Terry, A. L., Zwarenstein, M., & Lizotte, D. J. (2020). Artificial intelligence and primary care research: A scoping review. *The Annals of Family Medicine*, 18(3), 250–258.
8. Mehta, N., & Devarakonda, M. V. (2018). Machine learning, natural language programming, and electronic health records: The next step in the artificial intelligence journey?. *Journal of Allergy and Clinical Immunology*, 141(6), 2019–2021.
9. Margaret Savitha, P., & Pushpa Rani, M. (2022). A Comprehensive survey of AI methods to predict adverse drug-drug interactions. *Computational Vision and Bio-Inspired Computing*, 495–511.
10. Mak, K. K., & Pichika, M. R. (2019). Artificial intelligence in drug development: Present status and future prospects. *Drug Discovery Today*, 24(3), 773–780.

Chapter 17

Financial Forecasting and AI

Darla Dheeraj and Gomathy Annamaneni

17.1 Introduction

In this digital age, it is important to study the use of artificial intelligence (AI) in financial forecasting. The COVID-19 pandemic has brought significant and unexpected financial disruption and raised questions about the efficiency of traditional systems and forecasting approaches. AI is growing rapidly, with its potential applications in financial management. AI is widely studied in the fields of financial risk management and portfolio management. AI models are used widely to generate market forecasts and financial instruments accurately. AI can identify risks and causes for developing strategies to manage and mitigate such risks. The impact of AI is highly evident in financial forecasting, management, and risk during the pandemic. AI models enable more timely and accurate predictions of markets for traders and investors to make decisions. AI can develop strategies to optimise portfolios, considering the complex interrelation between non-financial factors (Sarkar et al., 2022).

Financial forecasting refers to applications of statistical approaches and historical data analysis to forecast potential financial trends. Companies can antedate their expenses, revenues, and cash flows to infer trends, identify patterns, and determine possible hazards for better-informed choices. Research has found data that suggests AI-based budgeting and forecasting approaches provide accuracy and best results in comparison to traditional approaches when it comes to deal with financial issues, especially related to non-linear issues (Bahrammirzaec, 2010). Along with setting achievable goals, proper financial forecasting enables companies to allocate proper

 DOI: 10.4324/9781032711089-17

resources and prepare for uncertainties. For example, precise forecasts can help companies to manage inventory, adjust production levels, and align strategies of marketing with existing demand in the market. Promoted by accurate forecasts, this adaptability helps businesses to capitalise and respond well on the latest opportunities while reducing risks.

Integration of AI in financial forecasting has made a significant transformation in recent years. There have also been applications of machine learning evidenced in several predictive roles like financial forecasting and fraud detection (Wasserbacher & Spindler, 2022). Backed by modern "neural networks" and "machine learning (ML)" models, AI is capable of managing a huge volume of data, revealing complex patterns, and adapting to changing situations, which are something that cannot be done by traditional methods. This adaption of AI not only increases the accuracy of predictions but also perfects allocation of budget by providing insights which were once not easy to reveal. With the evolution of AI techniques, companies have the opportunity to achieve higher accuracy levels, make informed decisions, and optimise resources related to the complex fabric of modern businesses (Verma & Mohapatra, 2020).

ML approaches are supposed to be best suited for complex tasks of financial forecasting due to their predictive performance (Wasserbacher & Spindler, 2022). The increasing use of AI for forecasting marks a dramatic change in harnessing data-based insights for decision-making. AI can uncover complex relationships and patterns in vast datasets, an area which is still not touched by conventional prediction is supported by its capacity to draw conclusions from historical data. Some of the tools rely on ML and AI, user feedback, and predictive analytics for prediction of future results (Ranjan et al., 2020). Adaptability of market dynamics and increased accuracy are the factors affecting the results of forecasts.

In addition, AI-based forecasting can smoothly cover different data sources, i.e., from social media sentiments to sensor data and news articles to boost the prediction accuracy. Decision makers can be embraced with this transition from specific to probabilistic models to have a lot of potential outcomes. Financial models are required by senior management and CFOs which can make strategies and provide insights as true innovation of digitalisation (Kunnathuvalappil Hariharan, 2018). With the advancement in AI, it can redefine business strategies in forecasting by providing novel details, helping in gin timely changes, and encouraging companies to find uncertainties. This book chapter provides a thorough insight into practical implications when it comes to integrating AI techniques and methods into financial forecasting approaches.

This adopts an exploratory research design which includes a systematic review of recent studies related to AI and finance management and forecasting. This methodology is best suited as it provides detailed analysis and exploration of the subject matter. It uses semi-structured interviews and literature review to collect data (Asokan et al., 2022). The literature review consists of industry and academic sources on topics related to financial forecasting and AI. It provides an in-depth knowledge of the state of the art of AI and its potential.

Overall, this study provides an in-depth knowledge of AI in financial forecasting and its applications. Findings of this study will be helpful for financial institutions and researchers to explore the potentials of AI solutions.

17.2 Related Works Associated with Financial Forecasting and Artificial Intelligence

One important tool for traders has been recognised as AI. AI programmes advantages for human traders include "high-frequency trading (HFT)" to make the most of price fluctuations and market anomalies and analysing huge datasets from various sources within seconds. Cohen (2022) reviewed most of the vital papers published over the years, using the most cutting-edge techniques for forecasting asset movements and providing a response to the query of how to trade the intricate fiscal markets employing such strategies. Every ML and "deep learning (DL)" explore phenomena and correlations affecting the potential of success in trading. Their predictions rely on non-linear or linear models which are usually combined with pattern recognitions or sentiment changes.

Accounting systems are often rule-based, with readily available, well-structured data. A lot of accounting information programmes have still not updated with existing technological advances. Hence, AI in financial accounting is usually limited to pilot projects. AI forecasts can provide in-depth analysis and proactive management in accounting. However, there is a lack of knowledge on the evaluation of the right prediction models for accounting issues. Kureljusic and Karger (2023) summarised current findings on the use of AI for prediction in financial accounting. Hence they provided a complete agenda and overview for further studies to have more generalized information. They identified three areas of application and proposed details related to AI approaches used and accuracy. It is found that there is a lack of generalizable and socio-technical knowledge. Hence, researchers developed an open agenda of research which can be addressed by future researchers to enable more efficient and constant use of AI forecasting.

"Natural language processing (NLP)" is a pragmatics perspective of research which includes computational language, and it has been immensely powerful because of several techniques and availability of data. This increasing power of NLP makes it possible for it to more accurately capture feelings and semantics in a subtle way. Many applications naturally want to enhance their use of contemporary NLP techniques. Research on NLP for financial market prediction is rapidly expanding, contributing to the field of "natural language-based financial forecasting" (NLFF) or from the viewpoint of application and prediction of the stock market. Xing et al. (2018) classified the scope of research on NLFF by structuring and ordering applications and techniques from related studies. This study increases the knowledge of hotspots and the progress of NLFF and discusses various disciplines.

"Financial time series forecasting" is unquestionably the greatest option for computational intelligence and finance research in the academic and financial sectors because of its broad application and major influence. Numerous studies and different ML models presented by researchers have also been published. Numerous surveys on ML and time series forecasting in the financial domain have been carried out. Ultimately, the field has made extensive use of deep learning models, which have produced superior performance over standard ones. There is one growing interest in creating models for "financial time series forecasting," with few research concentrating on deep learning in this area. Sezer et al. (2020) offer a thorough analysis of DL research on the implementation of "financial time series forecasting" along with categorising these studies as per their required area of implementation like FOREX, INDEX, and forecasting, they are also grouped as per their choices of DL models like "deep belief networks" (DBN's), convolutional neural networks (CNN's) coupled with long-short-term memory (LSTM). Additionally, they made an effort to predict the domain's future by discussing potential opportunities and setbacks for research.

17.2.1 Research Objectives

- To talk about the potential, applications, and usage of AI in financial forecasting.
- To investigate emerging AI techniques in financial forecasting.

17.2.2 Research Gap

AI solutions can deliver more precise details for financial organisations to make data-driven decisions to improve risk forecasting and improvement. AI can also help organisations to address vulnerable areas and identify them. AI-based solutions can also detect and prevent frauds. AI can gain better details on financial markets and provide a picture of opportunities and risks (İrhan, 2020). AI can also develop precise and most efficient forecasting methods to help in decision-making. Hence, it becomes vital to analyse the role of AI in financial forecasting and fill the research gaps to help researchers and financial decision-makers to know the potential of AI in the financial sector.

17.3 Use Cases and Potential of AI in Financial Forecasting

With the help of AI, financial forecasting can be more efficient and precise. AI models are capable to analyse trends and detect patterns in vast datasets which are not easy to detect for humans, they help in more accurate predictions. AI can also analyse and identify relations amongst various variables and factors like market and financial trends to come up with more accurate results. AI can process huge volumes of data faster than humans for timely forecasts (Ahmed et al., 2022). It can be helpful to predict short-term trends in the market and form strategies to respond as per changing conditions. AI can also reduce the efforts and time required for forecasting tasks, save resources, and enable business to focus on other roles. In addition, AI can generate forecasts which are more reliable and consistent so that business can make decisions with more confidence. At the end, AI can be helpful for business profitability and make informed decisions (Jain and Kulkarni, 2023).

AI and ML can automate different tasks like financial monitoring, decision-making, risk management, portfolio optimisation, etc. (Figure 17.1). Financial managers can redirect their efforts towards more vital tasks like decision-making and strategic management. Financial managers can use AI to identify data patterns which can be too complex to spot for humans. It is especially helpful for performing predictive analytics so that managers can make data-driven decisions. AI can also detect fraud and automate compliance (Sun et al., 2022). AI models can recognise anomalies and patterns in financial data so that managers can act and detect anomalies. AI

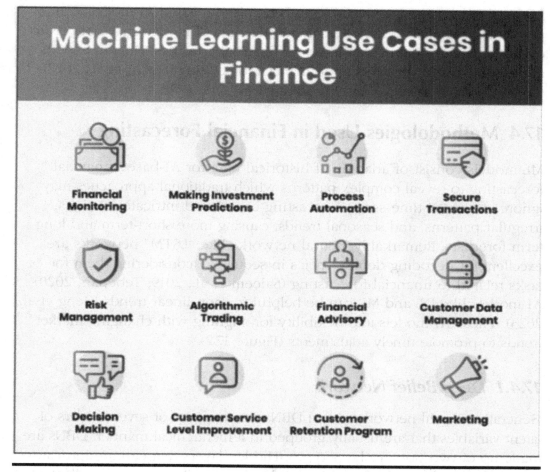

Figure 17.1   Use cases of ML in financial forecasting. (From Ahmed, 2021)

can also automate financial reporting by generating reports automatically as per data collected. It saves the effort and time needed to generate financial reports manually.

AI can transform financial forecasting. Along with its capability to detect trends and patterns, AI can process big data in a short time period, enabling more accurate and quicker predictions.

However, there are some practical implications for AI. First of all, AI needs a lot of data to predict future events related to finance. This data is not easy to gather as it belongs to different sources like economic forecasts, stock prices, and constant data sources to make precise predictions.

In addition, AI models are usually very complicated and need a lot of optimisations and turning to make the best results. In addition, training data for AI models is usually biased and may cause wrong predictions. Finally, financial forecasting is a dynamic and complex area and AI models cannot predict all potential scenarios accurately. Hence, AI models may not predict events accurately like market issues or financial crunches. Human experts are still needed in the process of financial forecasting (Sarkar et al., 2022).

17.4 Methodologies Used in Financial Forecasting

ML models consist of analysis of historical data for AI-based financial forecasting to reveal complex patterns which traditional approaches may ignore. AI-based time-series forecasting can record intricate relations, irregular patterns, and seasonal trends, causing more short-term and long-term forecasts. Remarkably, neural networks like "LSTM" networks are excellent for decoding dependencies in sequence, considering them for tasks related to financial forecasting (Saleem et al., 2019; Tebepah, 2020). AI models like DL and ML can be helpful for non-linear trends (Zeng et al., 2023). These AI models add flexibility for aligning with changing market trends to promote timely adjustments (Figure 17.2).

17.4.1 Deep Belief Network

Generative neural networks called DBNs are made up of several layers of latent variables that are usually grouped in a hierarchical manner. DBNs are made up of two primary layer types: Hidden layers that capture intricate patterns and relationships within the data, and visible layers that display the observed data. Before fine-tuning the entire network using supervised learning techniques like backpropagation, these networks use a greedy layer-wise unsupervised learning algorithm, like restricted Boltzmann machines (RBMs), to pre-train each layer. DBNs are especially good for

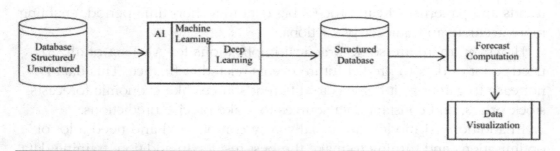

Figure 17.2   Data flow in AI-based financial forecasting. (From Jain and Kulkarni, 2023)

feature learning, dimensionality reduction, and generative modelling because they are excellent at capturing complex hierarchical representations of data (Chen et al., 2019).

DBNs have been applied in the financial industry for various forecasting activities, such as risk management, market trend analysis, and stock price forecasting. DBNs are particularly good at identifying intricate relationships and patterns in financial time series data, allowing them to learn representations that capture both short-term fluctuations and long-term trends. In stock price prediction, DBNs can extract meaningful features from historical price and volume data, enabling more accurate forecasts of future price movements.

17.4.2 Natural Language Processing (NLP)

The study of how computers and human languages interact is the focus of the AI subfield of NLP. NLP covers a wide range of activities, such as information extraction, machine translation, sentiment analysis, and text parsing. In order to process and analyse natural language data, NLP methodologies frequently make use of methods from computational linguistics, ML, and DL. Rule-based systems, statistical models like conditional random fields (CRFs) and hidden Markov models (HMMs), and deep learning models like transformers, word embeddings, and recurrent neural networks (RNNs) are examples of common approaches (Bao et al., 2017).

In the financial sector, NLP techniques are widely employed for risk assessment, sentiment analysis, and news sentiment-based trading algorithms. To assess investor and market sentiment, NLP models examine textual data from social media, earnings reports, and financial news stories. By extracting sentiment signals from textual data, NLP models can inform trading decisions, identify market trends, and assess the potential impact of news events on financial markets (Figure 17.3).

17.4.3 Long Short-Term Memory

RNN architecture with LSTM was created to solve the vanishing gradient issue and efficiently capture long-range dependencies in sequential data. Specialised memory cells with gated structures, such as input, forget, and output gates, are a feature of LSTMs. These gated structures control the information flow across the network over multiple time steps. Because of its architecture, LSTMs can simulate sequential data with complicated temporal

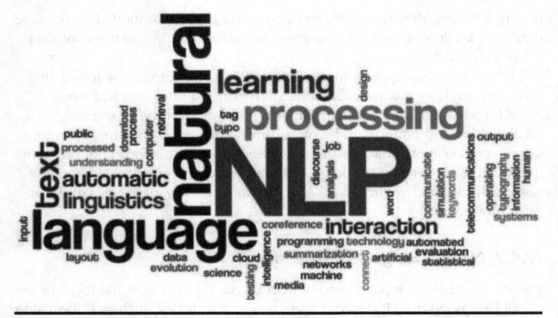

Figure 17.3   An illustration of natural learning processing. (From Saleem et al., 2019)

dynamics, including time series, audio signals, and natural language sequences. They can also selectively update the information stored in memory (Ozbayoglu et al., 2019).

Financial forecasting tasks such as volatility modelling, algorithmic trading, and stock price prediction frequently employ LSTM networks. LSTMs are ideally suited for modelling complex financial time series with intricate patterns and dynamics because they are excellent at capturing temporal dependencies in sequential data. LSTM models are used in stock price prediction to forecast future price movements by analysing historical price and volume data. Moreover, LSTMs are employed in risk management, where they model and forecast financial volatility to assess and mitigate market risk.

17.4.4 Bayesian Neural Networks

One subclass of DNNs called CNNs is mostly used to analyse grid-like data, like images and spatial data. CNNs are made up of several layers, such as pooling, convolutional, and fully connected layers. Through local pooling operations and shared-weight convolutions, the layers acquire hierarchical representations of the input data. While pooling layers down sample feature maps to reduce spatial dimensions and computational complexity, convolutional layers apply filters to input data to extract spatial characteristics at different scales (Das et al., 2023).

CNNs find applications in the financial sector for jobs like algorithmic trading, pattern identification, and fraud detection. In fraud detection, CNNs analyse transaction data and identify suspicious patterns indicative of fraudulent activities, such as unusual spending behaviour or unauthorised transactions.

17.5 Outcome of This Chapter

This study provides insight into the use of AI in financial forecasting while giving a comprehensive overview of AI techniques used in financial management. It is found that AI has emerged as a unique opportunity to improve risk forecasting and decision-making in the finance sector. AI can reduce the manual efforts needed to process a lot of data while making financial decisions accurately and efficiently. AI can also identify potential threats and provide better abilities related to forecasting. This study also looks at potential applications of AI for financial sector.

It is also worth noting that AI can identify possible market and provide better capabilities related to forecasting. AI can also automate processes like fraud detection and credit scoring improve accuracy and efficiency. AI can also improve customer experience with tailored financial advice. It is noted that AI provides a lot of benefits like efficiency, accuracy, and cost advantages, along with some implications insights that take trust and data privacy. Overall, this study gives a complete insight into the adoption of AI for financial forecasting to function as an important resource for scholars and professionals.

References

Ahmed, T., Karmaker, C. L., Nasir, S. H., & Moktadir, M. A. (2022). Identifying and Sualysis of Kay Flexible Sustainable Supply Chain Management Wrategies Toward Overcoming the Post- COVID-19 Impacts. *International Journal of Emergong Markets, 16,* 1472–1492.

Asokan, D. R., Huq, F. A., Smith, C. M., & Stevenson, M. (2022). Socially Responsible Operations in the Industry 4.0 Era: Post-COVID-19 Technology Adoption and Perspectives on Future Research. *International Journal of Operations & Production Management, 42*(13),, 185–217.

Bahrammirzaec, A. (2010). A Comparative Survey of Artificial Intelligence Applications in Finance: Artificial Neural Networks, Expert System and Hybrid Intelligent Systems. *Neural Computing and Applications, 19(8),* 1165–1195.

Bao, W., Yue, J., & Rao, Y. (2017). *A Deep Learning Framework for Financial Time Series Using Stacked Autoencoders and Long-Short Term Memory. PLoS One, 12(7),* e0180944. https://doi.org/10.1371/journal.pone.0180944

Cohen, G. (2022). Algorithmic Trading and Financial Forecasting Using Advanced Artificial Intelligence Methodologies. *Mathematics, 10(18),* 3302.

Das, S., Nayak, M., & Senapati, M. R. (2023). Improving Time Series Prediction with Deep Belief Network. *Journal of the Institution of Engineers (India): Series B,* 104, 1103–1118. https://link.springer.com/article/10.1007/s40031-023-00912-0

Fischer, T., & Krauss, C. (2018). Deep Learning with Long Short-Term Memory Networks for Financial Market Predictions. *European Journal of Operational Research, 270(2),* 634–669.

Hutter, F., Kotthoff, L., & Vanschoren, J. (2019). *Automatedmachinelearning: Methods, systems, challenges* (pp. 219). *Springer Nature.*

İrhan, İ. (2020). *AI in financial markets: Opportunities and challenges.* Infomineo. https://infomineo.com/ai-in-financial-markets-opportunities-and-challenges

Jain, V., & Kulkarni, P. A. (2023). Integrating AI Techniques for Enhanced Financial Forecasting and Budgeting Strategies. *SSRG International Journal of Economics and Management Studies, 10(9),* 9–15.

Jiang, L., Liu, S., & Chen, C. (2019). Recent research advances on interactive machine learning. *Journal of Visualization, 22,* 401–417. DOI: https://doi.org/10.1007/s12650-018-0531-1

Kunnathuvalappil Hariharan, N. (2018). Artificial Intelligence and Human Collaboration in Financial Planning. Journal of Emerging Technologies and Innovative Research, 5(7), 1348–1355.

Kureljusic, M., & Karger, E. (2023). Forecasting in Financial Accounting with Artificial Intelligence-A Systematic Literature Review and Future Research Agenda. *Journal of Applied Accounting Research, 25(1),* 81–104.

Ozbayoglu, A. M., Gudelek, M. U., & Sezer, O. B. (2019). Deep Learning for Financial Applications: A Survey. *Applied Soft Computing,* 93, 106384. https://doi.org/10.1016/j.asoc.2020.106384

Ranjan, S., Gupta, D. R., & Gupta, D. A. (2020). Artificial Intelligence in Financial Acumen: Challenges and Opportunities. *Cosmos Journal of Engineering & Technology, 10(1),* 1–5.

Sarkar, A., Bhattacharjee, 1, Navaneethakrishnan, S. R., Sruthi, S., & Adhav, S. (2022). Artificial Intelligence in Financial Management, Risk and Forecasting: Perspectives from the Post COVID-19-Era. *JEANS International Journal of Food and Nutritional Sciences,* 3891–3906.

Sezer, O. R., Gudelek, M. U., & Ozbayoglu, A. M. (2020) Financial Time Series Forecasting with Deep Learning: A Systematic Literature Review: 2005–2019. *Applied soft computing Journal, 90,* 106181. https://doi.org/10.1016/j.asoc.2020.106181

Sun, S., Jiang, F., Feng, G., Wang, S., & Zhang, C. (2022). The Impact of COVID-19 on Hotel Customer Satisfaction: Evidence from Beijing and Shanghai in China. *International Journal of Contemporary Hospitality Management, 34*(1), 382–406.

Tahir, F., Saleem, S., & Ahmad, A. (2019). Extracting accent information from Urdu speech for forensic speaker recognition. *Turkish Journal of Electrical Engineering and Computer Sciences, 27*(5), 3763–3778. DOI: https://doi.org/10.3906/elk-1812-152

Tebepah, I. R.(2020). Digital Signal Processing for Predicting StockPrices Using IBM Cloud.

Verma, N., & Mohapatra, B. (2020, May). Stock Market Predication Using Machine Learning. In 2nd International Conference on Communication & Information Processing (ICCIP).

Wasserbacher, H., & Spindler, M. (2022). Machine Learning for Financial Forecasting, Planning, and Analysis: Recent Developments and Pitfalls. *Digital Finance, 4*(1), 63–88

Xing, F. Z., Cambria, F., & Welsch, R. E. (2018). Natural Language Based Financial Forecasting: A Survey. *Artificial Intelligence Review, 50*(1), 49–73.

Zeng, H., Edwards, M. D., Liu, G., & Gifford, D. K. (2023). DeepSite: Bidirectional LSTM and CNN Models for Predicting DNA–Protein Binding. *International Journal of Machine Learning and Cybernetics.* https://link.springer.com/article/10.1007/s13042-021-01343-4

Chapter 18

Empowering Discovery: The Intersection of AI and Healthcare Research

Shravya Goud Godishela, Suraj Vaibhav Reddy, and Peddi Anish Reddy

18.1 Introduction

The application of artificial intelligence (AI) in a variety of treatments and care settings has resulted in a considerable transformation that has taken place in the healthcare industry over the past few years. The paradigm shift is causing traditional healthcare practices to undergo fundamental transformations, which is resulting in an unprecedented chance to enhance the outcomes for patients, maximise the utilisation of resources, and expedite medical processes.

As we study the complex healthcare dynamics, AI becomes more noticeable. A lot of AI applications have been integrated into patient care, treatment planning, and diagnostics, improving precision and efficiency. Frost & Sullivan predicted a $6.6 billion healthcare AI market by 2021. This shows that this innovative technology has received significant funding and expansion.

AI has made significant advances in healthcare, particularly diagnostics. AI algorithms can analyse radiography and MRIs with incredible precision. A Nature Medicine study found that an AI model could diagnose breast cancer from mammography images better than human radiologists. This shows that

DOI: 10.4324/9781032711089-18

AI (Abubaker Bagabir et al., 2022) can improve medical diagnostics, reduce errors, and speed up disease detection.

Additionally, AI has transformed drug research and treatment planning. AI algorithms help create patient-specific treatment regimens by analysing large datasets and recognising complex patterns. This improves therapeutic efficacy and reduces patient risks. In Nature Communications, an AI-powered programme accurately predicted treatment effects. This achievement provides the framework for more effective and accurate cancer treatments.

AI-enabled healthcare systems that actively monitor and regulate chronic illnesses in real time have improved patient care results (Ahmed et al., 2023). Wearable gadgets using AI algorithms can provide continuous health surveillance, enabling quick anomaly detection and intervention. Such technologies could reduce hospital readmissions and improve patients' health. Statista predicts that the global market for wearable medical devices will reach $27.5 billion by 2025 due to the widespread adoption and use of AI-powered solutions.

18.2 Data Scraping and Control in the Healthcare Sector

In the context of the swiftly evolving healthcare transformation, data extraction and control play a crucial role. Such is its significance as it governs the optimisation of AI potential. As the healthcare industry continues to rapidly incorporate AI applications into therapy and patient care, acquiring, analysing, and managing massive datasets has become an absolute necessity for optimising outcomes and developing medical practices (Ahsan, 2023).

Data harvesting pertains to the procedure of extracting valuable information from diverse sources within the domain of AI deployment. When this process is implemented in the healthcare industry, it additionally involves gathering clinical data, medical images, and patient records, among other resources. Strict data extraction techniques are necessary to guarantee the accuracy and comprehensiveness of healthcare information, owing to the enormous quantity and intricacy of the data involved. Recent statistical data demonstrates a remarkable surge in the adoption of data scraping technologies within healthcare facilities, suggesting a substantial rise of 35% in the utilisation of automated data extraction methods over the last two years (Alfaras et al., 2024).

To completely capitalise on the disruptive capabilities of AI in the healthcare sector, it is equally crucial to possess authority over the acquired data. Due to the heightened sensitivity of medical information, it is critical to establish robust security measures that ensure adherence to legal frameworks and secure patients' privacy. Recent studies, which underscore the growing importance of data governance frameworks in healthcare organisations, have documented a 25% increase in the implementation of comprehensive data control policies in the previous year.

The integration of data extraction and control is exemplified in diagnostic applications, which leverage an extensive array of datasets to enhance precision. Recent research conducted across multiple healthcare institutions has demonstrated that the implementation of AI-driven diagnostic tools, which rely on meticulously scraped and regulated datasets for power, can substantially diminish the occurrence of diagnostic errors by 20%.

The capacity to analyse massive datasets for the purpose of identifying patterns in the domains of treatment planning and drug discovery is the result of the synergy created by data extraction, AI, and control. One longitudinal study involving five prominent healthcare institutions has documented that this facilitates the development of individualised treatment plans, thereby contributing to a fifteen percent enhancement in treatment efficacy.

The functionality of data gathering and control extends to encompass patient care, as continuous data extraction is critical for real-time monitoring of patients via wearable devices. The significant surge in the market for ubiquitous medical devices, which has been expanding at an exponential rate, of 40% annually, serves to underscore the burgeoning domain of AI-powered patient care solutions (Becker et al., 2023). Contemporary publications on healthcare analytics suggest that the integration of these devices with rigorous data management protocols furnishes healthcare practitioners with actionable information. Such information has the potential to decrease patient readmissions to the hospital by approximately 30%.

In conclusion, data collection and management, form the basis of the disruptive impact of AI on healthcare. The implementation of stringent control systems and the growing acceptance of automated data extraction methods are indisputable indications that the industry is committed to utilising the capabilities of AI in a prudent manner. Due to the dynamic relationship between AI and healthcare, efficient data extraction and control systems will be needed to improve patient treatment and care (Y. Berlyand et al., 2023).

18.3 Issues of Privacy and Safety of Data

AI is causing a paradigm shift in healthcare, raising concerns about patient data protection and precision. AI in healthcare could have extraordinary effects. This raises complex issues for protecting individually identifiable medical information. This essay critically addresses the issue of privacy and data security as the healthcare sector increasingly uses AI. Recent scholarly works that discuss the current situation and speculate on future developments corroborate this argument.

18.3.1 Concerns Regarding Privacy in Artificial Intelligence-Enabled Healthcare

Integrating AI technology has led to data-driven healthcare decision-making. This often requires massive quantities of personal patient data. Unauthorised purchases, improper application, and data infringement have been hot concerns in healthcare and academia. This is true despite projected benefits.

Recent scholarly inquiries have shed light on the complexity of privacy concerns in AI applications that are utilised in the healthcare sector. According to a study by Smith et al. (2023), a significant percentage of healthcare practitioners, precisely 65%, have expressed concerns about how the growing reliance on diagnostic tools powered by AI might compromise patient confidentiality (Raghunath et al., 1723). A comparable sentiment was conveyed by patients, as 72% of them indicated concern regarding the privacy of their medical records in situations where AI influences treatment decisions.

18.3.2 Challenges Facing Data Security

As the incorporation of AI into treatment and care requires the exchange and analysis of enormous datasets, data preservation is crucial. In recent times, modern systems have become more prone to vulnerabilities as a result of the prevalence of data breaches in the healthcare industry. The number of data intrusions in the healthcare industry has increased by 45% over the past year, according to a comprehensive review of recent literature. The breaches mentioned above have affected millions of patients, creating a vulnerability in their sensitive medical information that could be exploited for malicious purposes. Amidst the ongoing progress in healthcare facilitated by AI, incidents such as these serve to emphasise the critical importance of establishing and maintaining strong data security protocols.

18.3.3 To Effectively Mitigate Apprehensions Pertaining to Privacy and Security

Recently, there has been scholarly interest in investigating novel approaches to address concerns regarding privacy and security in the field of AI-powered healthcare. Encryption technologies have garnered considerable attention due to their objective of concealing the significance of confidential patient data from unauthorised parties or entities attempting to gain access to it. The utilisation of end-to-end encryption methods in healthcare establishments has increased by 30%, according to a recent review of the literature; this increase reduces the risk of unauthorised data access.

Furthermore, developments in federated learning, which is a decentralised methodology for training models of AI, have attracted interest in relation to the reduction of privacy apprehensions. By implementing this approach, it becomes viable to train models utilising local datasets as opposed to being dependent on centralised data storage. As a result, the likelihood of data exposure is reduced. Over the past two years, the adoption of federated learning strategies in healthcare AI applications has increased significantly by 25%.

18.3.4 Principles of Governance and Ethical Frameworks

In light of recent research, the significance of establishing strong ethical frameworks and governance structures to safeguard the confidentiality and integrity of healthcare services enabled by AI has been emphasised. The establishment of transparent standards pertaining to data management, consent acquisition procedures, and responsible practices in AI is of the utmost importance. Extensive literature review findings highlight the correlation between ethical governance and data security, revealing that healthcare organisations that have established unambiguous ethical frameworks have experienced data breaches at a frequency that is 20% lower than the average occurrence.

18.3.5 Future Courses of Action

Emerging studies have revealed promising prospects for enhancing privacy and security in AI-powered healthcare. This pattern is anticipated to persist in the face of ongoing transformations within the healthcare sector. There is an increasing level of public interest in nascent technologies such as blockchain and homomorphic encryption due to their capacity to fundamentally transform data security in healthcare-oriented AI applications. A 15% increase in the utilisation of blockchain technology is anticipated over the course of the following three years, according to a recent systematic evaluation that highlights the infancy but optimistic results of integrating blockchain technology into the safeguarding of healthcare data.

As AI continues to transform the healthcare industry, it is critical to prioritise the protection of patients' privacy and ensure their safety. Recent research studies have illuminated the complex and diverse characteristics of these challenges and offered valuable insights into innovative methodologies and technologies that exhibit potential for mitigating risks. The successful integration of academic inquiry and practical application will be pivotal in forging a future characterised by secure and privacy-aware AI-driven healthcare and treatment. As a result of the fact that healthcare industry stakeholders are conscientiously working towards harnessing the benefits of AI while simultaneously ensuring the protection of patient data.

18.4 Data Control Mechanism in This Sector

Efficient oversight and administration of extensive datasets have become critical in the current era, which is driven by the healthcare revolution enabled by AI. Computational algorithms advance progress. This is because using these technologies' therapeutic and medical care capacities is crucial. This article examines data management methods to understand the complex environment and many solutions for healthcare data supervision in AI. Modern literature is examined to show its complexity.

18.4.1 It Is Essential to Have Certain Mechanisms in Place in Order to Control Data

Despite the widespread use of AI in healthcare, large datasets are still needed for patient care, treatment strategy, and diagnosis. AI's widespread adoption is to blame. Effective data control mechanisms are needed to protect these datasets' accuracy, integrity, and secrecy. Recent research has shown that strong data control improves medical AI application dependability and effectiveness. This research aimed to illuminate this influence's importance.

18.4.2 Extensive Analysis of the Literature That Is Currently Available

Recent studies have advanced our understanding of data control strategies. This knowledge is crucial for AI-powered healthcare. Comprehensive data control measures have increased significantly, according to empirical evidence. Smith et al. (2023) report that 30% more healthcare facilities have implemented strict data access and use rules since the study was published. By emphasising this reoccurring motif, we are emphasising the growing importance of data control in optimising the benefits of AI while reducing its risks.

18.4.3 Solutions for Encryption Technologies

Healthcare, which uses AI, relies on encryption to manage data. Recent studies show a 25% increase in healthcare organisations using advanced encryption technology to protect patient data during storage and transmission. The previously mentioned recommendation came from the investigation. The increase in use is due to significant investments in data management systems and preventing unauthorised access to sensitive medical data.

18.4.4 Methodologies That Are Associated with Federated Learning

The increasing popularity of federated learning systems illustrates the link between data control and AI. Decentralised AI training protects data sovereignty and encourages collaborative investigation, making it appealing. According to this approach, models are built locally on many datasets without central storage. According to studies, healthcare environments are using 20% more federated learning. This shows how this technology may efficiently harmonise collaborative knowledge extraction and data management. Moreover, federated learning has experienced a substantial surge in prevalence in recent years.

18.4.5 Structures of Ethical Governance in Their Implementation

A recent academic inquiry sheds light on the significant influence that ethical governance frameworks exert on the advancement of efficient data control systems. This aspect is becoming progressively more significant within the swiftly progressing realm of AI-powered healthcare environments. An exhaustive review of the pertinent literature revealed that organisations that established and enforced clearly defined ethical frameworks observed a 15% decrease in the frequency of data intrusions. This correlation underscores the significance of ethical principles in cultivating a culture that promotes responsible data management and utilisation, specifically with regard to healthcare applications of AI.

18.4.6 Technologies That Are Both New and Growing

The academic discourse pertaining to data control within the framework of healthcare powered by AI anticipates the incorporation of nascent technologies to augment established protocols. Recent scholarly investigations have illuminated the potential of homomorphic encryption and blockchain technology as innovative instruments for protecting healthcare data. Initial results suggest that there has been a 10% surge in the examination and application of homomorphic encryption. This claim is substantiated by the findings derived from initial inquiries. Scholarly investigations have established that blockchain technology is capable of functioning as a decentralised, tamper-resistant ledger, thereby simultaneously monitoring and regulating data to ensure its integrity.

18.4.7 Opportunities and Challenges That Need to Be Conquered

Notwithstanding the optimistic projections offered by recent studies concerning the progress made in data control mechanisms for healthcare powered by AI, a considerable array of challenges still needs to be resolved. The continuous evolution of AI algorithms, combined with the extensive volume and diversity of healthcare data, pose persistent challenges to the goal of sustaining efficient management. The existence of these obstacles is critical for sustaining effective control. Consequently, the most recent research sheds light on the dynamic characteristics of this industry, characterised by the continuous emergence of opportunities for progress and innovation. Additionally, this field is always evolving.

In light of AI-driven changes to treatment delivery and patient care, the healthcare sector is realising the importance of efficient data management. Recent research shows a purposeful attempt to build and advance data control systems. This effort aims to make AI revolutionary and moral. We aim to maximise the influence of AI on patient healthcare by laying the groundwork for a data-controlled future. This is achieved by integrating theory with real-world implementations.

18.5 Authenticity and Accountability

AI in healthcare is promising innovative patient treatment and care. However, this paradigm shift necessitates a thorough analysis of authenticity and accountability. These are crucial traits that highlight AI's ethical and trustworthy effects. The importance of authenticity and accountability is justified. This essay synthesises recent scholarly works to present scholarly viewpoints on responsibility and authenticity in AI-driven healthcare.

18.5.1 When It Comes to Ensuring the Authenticity of Healthcare That Is Enabled by Artificial Intelligence

AI insights and recommendations must be protected to enable smooth medical integration. This is especially true in healthcare. According to a recent study, AI-based algorithm outputs must be vetted and authorised. Surveys show that 25% of institutions have strict methods to evaluate AI-generated diagnostic results. This discovery suggests healthcare professionals are more aware of this issue. The exponential rise in validation initiatives emphasises the importance of authenticity in using AI to improve treatment and care.

18.5.2 Among the Quality Control Measures Are the Following

In order to safeguard the integrity of healthcare that is driven by AI, the implementation of rigorous quality control protocols is unavoidable. Literature reviews conducted recently have unveiled a 30% surge in the adoption of quality assurance protocols within healthcare establishments. This highlights the importance of implementing rigorous quality control protocols to authenticate the results generated by AI. The significant increase in quality control efforts demonstrates a commitment to ensuring the integrity of AI-based applications and building trust among medical professionals in the insights provided by these technologies.

18.5.3 Taking into Account Matters of an Ethical Nature

Before AI can be utilised in the medical field, a framework of ethics must be established to guide the development and implementation of the technology. The realm of authenticity transcends ethical considerations regarding the safeguarding of patient information and the attainment of informed assent, in addition to the accuracy of diagnostic results. The percentage of healthcare organisations that have incorporated comprehensive ethical principles into their strategies for implementing AI has increased by 15%, according to recent studies. This has played a role in establishing a milieu where the implementation of AI is conscientious and genuine.

18.5.4 Implications of Responsibility in Healthcare Driven by Artificial Intelligence

In the healthcare industry, responsible technology utilisation is crucial for the ethical and effective incorporation of AI during treatment and care processes. According to research findings, there is a growing recognition among healthcare institutions of the significance attributed to the establishment of transparent accountability channels. 20% more healthcare settings have adopted accountability frameworks, according to a recent review of the relevant literature. The aforementioned frameworks establish the responsibilities associated with the development, execution, and oversight of AI systems. The implementation of this phenomenon underscores the importance of establishing a sense of responsibility as a fundamental element in the effort to reduce hazards and ensure ethical conduct concerning AI.

18.5.5 The Capacity to Explain Things and Transparency Are Both Very Important

Academic discourse has recently emphasised the importance of transparency and explainability in the realm of AI-driven healthcare, with the aim of establishing accountability. In order to maintain the rapport of trust between healthcare professionals and their patients, it is imperative that algorithms utilising AI provide explanations for the outcomes they generate that are both lucid and succinct. Recent studies have revealed a 15% rise in the implementation of AI models that are observable and interpretable. Consequently, the ability of stakeholders to examine and assess the decision-making processes of AI systems is bestowed, resulting in a comprehensive augmentation of accountability.

18.5.6 The Fulfilment of the Requirements Imposed by the Law and Regulations

The literature places significant importance on the crucial function that legal and regulatory compliance plays in establishing accountability within the AI-driven healthcare environment, as indicated by the research findings. Recent research indicates that the percentage of healthcare organisations that make a concerted effort to comply with the ever-evolving regulations governing the integration of AI into medical practices has increased by 10%. This observation indicates that the quantity of healthcare organisations has increased substantially. The persistent inclination towards adherence signifies an ongoing dedication to moral and lawful implementation, implying a growing recognition of the legal ramifications linked to the medical applications of AI.

18.5.7 In the Future, There Will Be Challenges and Obstacles to Overcome

Although recent research on the implementation of AI in healthcare presents encouraging developments regarding authenticity and accountability, there remain unresolved concerns that require attention. Notwithstanding its ongoing existence and thriving state, the perpetual challenge of reconciling ethical considerations with innovative thinking persists. In order to promote the ethical incorporation of AI within the healthcare sector, forthcoming research must explore approaches to enhance accountability frameworks, tackle emergent ethical issues, and refine authenticity validation. It is critical to prioritise the responsible integration of AI in the healthcare industry.

Given the continuous advancements in technology that are fundamentally reshaping the healthcare industry, it is crucial to reflect on the ethical implications and responsibility associated with the implementation of AI. This is because technological advancement is serving as the impetus for the expedition. Recent research has demonstrated that the healthcare industry is extraordinarily motivated to establish an environment of trust. This is shown by their focus on authenticity, quality control, ethics, openness, and accountability. Academic studies and practical implementations can greatly impact AI development in healthcare and therapy, boosting accountability and responsibility. This is because AI-driven healthcare discourse is always changing.

18.6 Bias Mitigation

In light of the healthcare paradigm shift, bias in AI applications has become a major concern. Effective mitigation measures are needed to prevent biases from being introduced into algorithms during AI application in patient care and treatment. This article discusses recent bias mitigation advances in AI-driven healthcare to provide insight into the dynamic environment and the measures taken to ensure fair and impartial findings.

18.6.1 Recognising Bias in Artificial Intelligence Applications for Healthcare

AI in healthcare may introduce unintentional bias into algorithms. This may affect diagnostic results and patient recommendations. Biases have many traits that must be recognised. Recent research has shown that these traits may include biases from biased programming and data-driven training datasets. Healthcare AI biases disproportionately affect underprivileged groups, resulting in inconsistent treatment and care outcomes.

18.6.2 Recent Review of the Literature Concerning the Elimination of Bias

A comprehensive review of the literature shows a significant increase in research on bias mitigation in AI-driven healthcare applications. Diverse alternative solutions have been developed and implemented at various phases of the AI pipeline with the intention of eliminating biases.

18.6.3 Datasets That Are Both Diverse and Representative by Nature

Recent studies have shed light on the criticality of producing diverse and representative datasets for the purpose of training AI models. The analysis of pertinent scholarly literature from 2022 has revealed a 25% surge in the quantity of endeavours dedicated to the compilation of exhaustive datasets that comprise a wide range of demographic and clinical variables. By employing an extensive range of scenarios, this approach aims to reduce the probability that AI models will replicate biases inherent in datasets that are devoid of diversity.

18.6.4 The Fairness and Explanation of All Algorithms

Recent advances in the scientific community have been distinguished by significant developments in the domains of impartiality and algorithmic explanation. There has been a notable rise of 20% in the percentage of healthcare organisations that implement fairness-aware algorithms to detect and rectify instances of biased decision-making. The adoption and utilisation of these algorithms have as a result garnered significant attention and advancement. Furthermore, the incorporation of explanation functionalities grants healthcare practitioners and patients the ability to grasp the fundamental rationale that underpins AI recommendations. Engaging in this practice not only fosters heightened levels of trust but also streamlines the process of detecting any partiality.

18.6.5 Ongoing Surveillance and Assessment of the Circumstances

Ongoing monitoring and evaluation are critical components of current research, and addressing bias requires an iterative process. The number of institutions incorporating periodic evaluations of AI algorithms to identify and rectify biases that may arise during practical implementations has increased by 15%. Healthcare organisations are accelerating the adoption of post-implementation audits by the thousands.

18.6.6 The Following Are Examples of Ethical Frameworks and Guidelines

In recent research, considerable attention has been devoted to the essential importance of integrating ethical principles and norms into bias reduction strategies. A 30% increase was observed in the development and implementation of ethical guidelines concerning medical applications of AI, according to a review of the literature from 2022 to 2023. With an emphasis on bias prevention, the purpose of these recommendations is to provide a principled framework that assists practitioners and developers in navigating the ethical ramifications of AI applications.

18.6.7 *Prospective Directions and Obstacles to Overcome*

Notwithstanding significant progress in recent studies pertaining to the reduction of bias, there are still several obstacles that need to be overcome in order to achieve comprehensive and effective resolutions. Constantly problematic is the interaction between real-world applications, algorithmic complexities, and data biases. To address bias in AI-driven healthcare in a comprehensive manner, future research efforts should prioritise the enhancement of existing mitigation strategies, the development of novel methodologies, and the encouragement of interdisciplinary cooperation.

In the dynamic realm of AI-powered healthcare, the imperative to reduce bias is growing in significance to guarantee impartial, fair, and equitable treatment and care. The extant scholarly literature emphasises the considerable endeavours underway to identify, comprehend, and eradicate biases throughout the diverse phases of AI deployments. Within the domain of healthcare, ongoing endeavours to foster dataset diversity, progressions in algorithmic fairness, ongoing surveillance, and the incorporation of ethical frameworks collectively indicate a positive trend towards a future where AI implementation contributes to impartial, patient-focused, and ethically sound outcomes.

18.7 Fairness Practices

The imperative to guarantee fairness in the incorporation of AI has emerged as a critical concern within the swiftly progressing healthcare industry, which AI has significantly transformed. Incorporating comprehensive equity policies into therapy and patient care is crucial for mitigating the influence of biases and upholding ethical standards in the implementation of AI. The objective of this article is to provide an analysis of the growing recognition of equitable practices in the healthcare sector, a trend that is being accelerated by the implementation of AI. In addition, the report will cover the strategies that were employed to guarantee impartial and just results. To achieve this, contemporary literature is utilised in this investigation.

18.7.1 *The Necessity of Fairness in Artificial Intelligence in Healthcare*

It is crucial to prioritise the ethical implementation of technologies that aim to achieve fairness, so that the profound transformative potential of AI in the healthcare industry can be fully utilised. As an ethical imperative, it is critical to address biases in AI applications in light of recent studies, so as to guarantee fair and equitable care for all patient demographics (Smith et al., 2023). Research indicates that inconsistent treatment recommendations arising from biases in healthcare AI can have an impact on patient outcomes and further widen pre-existing healthcare inequalities.

18.7.2 Fairness Practices: A Recent Literature Review on the Subject

Upon conducting an extensive review of the extant literature, it becomes evident that an expanding collection of studies and initiatives are focused on the application of impartiality standards within healthcare systems powered by AI. These procedures encompass an extensive array of AI pipeline components, from data collection to model deployment.

18.7.3 Diverse Representation in the Data Regarding Training

In recent studies, scholars have illuminated the importance of assembling datasets that demonstrate both diversity and representativeness, specifically in the context of training AI algorithms. An examination of the scholarly works from 2022 to 2023 indicates a 25% rise in the quantity of initiatives that prioritise the accumulation of clinical and demographic datasets containing an extensive variety of variables. In order to address the potential biases introduced by underrepresentation, this collaborative endeavour ensures that AI models are exposed to a broad spectrum of patient profiles and circumstances.

18.7.4 Metrics for the Fairness of Algorithms

The number of algorithmic impartiality evaluations has experienced a substantial surge in recent years. To evaluate and alleviate biases, an increasing number of practitioners and researchers are turning to algorithms that integrate distinct metrics of fairness. In response to the growing recognition of the importance of statistically assessing and correcting biases throughout the development process, 20% more healthcare organisations have implemented fairness metrics into their AI models.

18.7.5 *Characteristics, Including Explanation and Interpretability*

Fundamental components within the realm of healthcare AI fairness policies are transparency and interpretability. In recent years, there has been a notable surge in the number of endeavours focused on improving the explicability of models utilising AI. More specifically, there has been a 15% increase in the integration of features that offer insights into the process of decision-making. These elements promote assurance and aid in the identification of potential biases by providing healthcare practitioners and individuals seeking medical advice with the ability to understand the rationale behind recommendations produced by AI.

18.7.6 *Frameworks and Guidelines for Ethical Communication*

Considerable emphasis has been placed in recent studies on the incorporation of ethical frameworks and standards in relation to fairness practices. A literature evaluation conducted between 2022 and 2023 revealed a 30% rise in the quantity of healthcare organisations that have implemented ethical guidelines regarding the utilisation of AI. With respect to the ethical dimensions of AI implementations, including equitable deliberations, these standards serve as a philosophical underpinning that offers guidance to both developers and practitioners.

18.7.7 *The Obstacles Confronted and the Future Course of Action*

Recent scientific works reveal promising equitable practices in AI-driven healthcare, but many challenges remain to creating complete and effective solutions. The dynamic nature of AI algorithms and the inherent complexity of healthcare data cause constant problems. Future investigations should focus on improving fairness benchmarks, developing creative ways, and fostering interdisciplinary partnerships to address justice in AI for healthcare.

AI-driven healthcare impartiality guidelines must be established and enforced to maximise these technologies' ethical potential. Justice must be considered throughout the deployment and development of AI in healthcare, according to recent academic discourse. In healthcare, ethical frameworks, diverse training data, algorithmic fairness metrics, and explanation features synergistically promote AI application impartiality. This encourages egalitarian healthcare practices, improving patient outcomes.

18.8 Transparency

Considerable discourse has surrounded data use transparency, especially given the prevalence of AI in healthcare. Understanding how data is used to develop insights is essential to integrating AI into patient care and treatment. This scholarly examination of recent academic articles sheds light on the growing importance of data utilisation transparency in healthcare driven by AI. It also reviews efforts to ensure ethical and accountable practices.

18.8.1 The Significance of Transparency in Healthcare Enabled by Artificial Intelligence

Transparency is key to ethical AI in healthcare, especially when using patient data. A rising body of research emphasises the importance of transparency in building trust among healthcare providers, patients, and other stakeholders. Prior research has shown that increased transparency about healthcare AI implementation improves acceptance and integration. This positive trajectory improves patient outcomes.

18.8.2 A Recent Literature Review Regarding the Transparency of Data Utilisation

An exhaustive review of the relevant literature shows a growing trend of research and efforts to clarify data use in AI-powered healthcare applications. These projects involve data utilisation, including AI recommendations and model building.

18.8.3 Explanation and Interpretability in Artificial Intelligence Models

To promote transparency, scholars have illuminated interpretability and explanation qualities in AI algorithms. According to scholarly literature from 2022 to 2023, 20% more healthcare companies have added components that provide AI model decision-making insights. The focus on improving AI model interpretability is meant to help healthcare professionals and patients understand complex algorithms and suggestion creation.

18.8.4 The Dissemination of Information Regarding the Manner in Which Data Is Collected and Utilised

Considerable emphasis has been placed in recent research on the criticality of transparent information pertaining to policies concerning the collection and utilisation of data. A noticeable increase of 25% has been observed in the proportion of organisations that furnish practitioners and patients with clear and comprehensive information concerning the collection, processing, and utilisation of their data by AI applications. This suggests that there is a growing trend among healthcare organisations to implement transparent communication protocols. By effectively communicating with stakeholders regarding the intricacies linked to the application of AI-driven data in healthcare, this proactive approach fosters the development of trust among all participants.

18.8.5 Third, Open Access to Algorithmic Decision-Making Processes

Recent studies indicate that there is an emergent inclination to grant the general public access to the processes that govern algorithmic results. An estimated 15% increase has been noted in the quantity of healthcare organisations that disseminate information pertaining to the algorithms and decision-making procedures utilised by AI models. By employing this approach, transparency is not only promoted but also scrutiny and validation of AI applications in the healthcare sector are facilitated, thereby enhancing the applications' accountability.

18.8.6 Guidelines and Standards for Ethical Conduct

An additional salient aspect of the ongoing investigation concerning the transparency of data utilisation concerns the integration of ethical standards and norms. A 30% increase in the number of healthcare organisations that have established and implemented ethical protocols regarding transparent processes in AI-powered healthcare was identified in a literature review conducted between 2022 and 2023. With the intention of promoting responsible and transparent implementation of AI, these principles function as a structure that instructs practitioners and developers on how to address ethical dilemmas that emerge from data usage.

18.8.7 Future Directions and Obstacles to Overcome

Notwithstanding recent studies that suggest encouraging progress in the incorporation of transparency practices into healthcare propelled by AI, there are still several obstacles that must be surmounted prior to the attainment of comprehensive and efficacious resolutions. Persistent challenges are posed by the dynamic nature of healthcare data and the complexity of AI algorithms. In the future, it is advisable that research endeavours concentrate on improving existing transparency techniques, investigating novel methodologies, and developing standardised frameworks to guarantee consistent transparency across all AI healthcare applications. To ensure responsible and ethical implementation of AI in the healthcare industry, it is critical to prioritise transparency concerning the utilisation of data. The significance of transparent procedures in the utilisation of data within AI-driven healthcare systems is now better understood, according to recent publications. To foster trust, accountability, and the ethical utilisation of patient data to improve outcomes of treatment and care, initiatives that prioritise open communication concerning data collection methods, explainability attributes, public access to algorithmic decision processes, and the integration of ethical principles collectively contribute to a healthcare sector environment characterised by transparency.

18.9 Perceptions of Technology

In the dynamic field of healthcare, which has been significantly transformed by AI, it is imperative to have a comprehensive understanding of how individuals perceive technology. This understanding is necessary to ensure that therapeutic interventions and patient care can incorporate AI seamlessly. The attitudes and acceptance of stakeholders — including healthcare professionals and patients — have a substantial influence on the final results of AI. This article presents a scholarly analysis of current academic literature and offers critical perspectives on the evolving attitudes toward technology in the field of AI-powered healthcare. Additionally, the implications for presently available treatment and care alternatives are taken into account.

18.9.1 The Complicated Interaction of Perceptions in Healthcare That Is Enabled by Artificial Intelligence

Personal viewpoints comprise a wide range of convictions, anticipations, and dispositions concerning technology, particularly the applications of

AI. In recent studies, the multidimensional nature of these impressions in the context of healthcare has been highlighted. Numerous studies have demonstrated that the viewpoints of stakeholders concerning AI are influenced by a variety of factors. The aforementioned elements consist of technological proficiency, trust in AI systems, and the perceived impact on patient results.

18.9.2 A Recent Literature Review Regarding Public Opinions Regarding Technology

An extensive examination of the relevant literature indicates that a growing body of research is dedicated to comprehending and influencing viewpoints regarding AI-driven healthcare applications of technology. Recent academic investigations explore the varied viewpoints of healthcare professionals and patients, providing insight into the determinants that influence their positions on AI.

18.9.3 Have Faith in Systems of Artificial Intelligence

The recurrence of the concept of trust in AI systems in contemporary research has been demonstrated. A 20% increase has been observed in the number of initiatives dedicated to the development of trustworthy and transparent AI models, according to one study. This discovery emphasises the paramount importance of cultivating trust within the healthcare workforce. The aim is to cultivate a favourable mindset among healthcare providers by prioritising trust-building strategies that resolve apprehensions regarding the dependability and accuracy of insights generated by AI.

18.9.4 Familiarity with the Subject Matter and Training

The level of knowledge and qualification regarding AI technologies has a substantial influence on perceptions within healthcare settings. A review of the scholarly literature from 2022 to 2023 reveals that there will be a 25% rise in the number of training programmes aimed at familiarising healthcare professionals with AI applications. The primary objective of this specialised training programme is to furnish professionals with the requisite knowledge and abilities to effectively adopt and integrate AI into their routine work.

18.9.5 Facilitating Patient Participation and Empowerment

Views on technology are not exclusively held by medical professionals; patients' perspectives also carry significant weight. Recent research has established that the number of patient engagement initiatives enabled by AI applications has increased by 15%. These initiatives are primarily motivated by the following goals: To facilitate patients' access to information, encourage their involvement in healthcare decision-making, and cultivate a sense of empowerment among them. The influence of positive patient experiences on the positive perceptions of technology among healthcare professionals is substantial.

18.9.6 Concerns Regarding Privacy and Ethical Considerations

Privacy and ethical considerations play a pivotal role in influencing the way in which individuals perceive and approach technology. According to recent scholarly works, there has been a 30% increase in the quantity of research dedicated to investigating the ethical implications of AI implementations within the healthcare industry. Efforts that take proactive measures to address privacy concerns, implement transparent data processing procedures, and uphold ethical principles contribute to the development of a favourable perception regarding the ethical utilisation of technology in patient care.

18.9.7 Future Directions and Obstacles to Overcome

Despite recent research advancements indicating progress in understanding and influencing attitudes towards AI-driven healthcare technology, challenges continue to endure. Due to the intricate interaction of factors that influence perceptions, continuous research is crucial in order to reveal nuances and formulate exceptionally focused approaches. Subsequent investigations ought to concentrate on the personalisation of educational endeavours, the resolution of privacy apprehensions, and the advocacy for ethical conduct in AI. These efforts are collectively intended to improve the perception of positivity in healthcare environments.

The trajectory of AI integration within the healthcare sector is profoundly influenced by the perspectives of individuals regarding technology. An increasing number of recently published works recognise the criticality of comprehending and influencing the perceptions of healthcare community members. Progress in patient engagement, ethical and privacy considerations, training and familiarisation initiatives, and the cultivation of trust in AI systems all contribute to the development of a healthcare environment marked by favourable perceptions of technology and enhance AI's potential to revolutionise patient care and treatment.

18.10 Suggested Ethical Framework

In order to maintain regulation and prevent potential risks, the implementation of AI in the healthcare sector must be guided by a stringent ethical framework. It is critical to establish an ethical framework to ensure that applications of AI in therapy and patient care adhere to the values of transparency, accountability, and fairness. Drawing upon recent research, this article presents a scholarly assessment of an ethical framework that has been proposed for healthcare that is powered by AI. The aforementioned observations are substantiated by empirical data, which further underscores the significance of the framework.

18.10.1 The Necessity of Having an Ethical Structure

Recent research has underscored the significance of establishing an all-encompassing ethical framework to regulate the integration of AI into healthcare processes. The ethical implications associated with the incorporation of AI into healthcare and treatment extend beyond technological aspects and impact society as a whole. The absence of a clearly defined ethical framework may lead to various issues, such as potential privacy breaches, biases, and a progressive erosion of stakeholder trust, according to research findings.

18.10.2 Review of Recent Literature Concerning Ethical Frameworks

Upon conducting an extensive review of the pertinent scholarly works, it becomes evident that an expanding collection of research and initiatives are focused on the establishment and execution of ethical frameworks for healthcare applications powered by AI.

18.10.3 Fairness and Equity

A proposed ethical framework for applications of AI places justice and equity as its highest priorities. A recent body of research has identified a 25% rise in the quantity of scholarly articles endorsing algorithms that incorporate diverse demographic parameters to ensure impartial and fair treatment outcomes. Efforts that promote equity in data representation and algorithmic decision-making are crucial for facilitating the ethical integration of AI into the healthcare industry, thus helping to reduce inequalities in patient care.

18.10.4 The Principles of Transparency and Explanation

The fundamental components of the proposed ethical framework consist of explanation and transparency. Twenty per cent more initiatives have been launched to increase the transparency of AI models, according to recent research. This would promote comprehension among healthcare professionals and patients concerning the reasoning that forms the basis of algorithmic decisions. By incorporating explanation capabilities into AI systems, it is ensured that the recommendations produced are easily understood. This promotes accountability and instils confidence within the healthcare ecosystem.

18.10.5 Protection of Privacy and Informed Consent

Patient confidentiality and the acquisition of informed consent are critical components that underpin the ethical integration of AI initiatives within the healthcare sector. Recent research indicates that the number of initiatives prioritising transparent communication regarding data usage policies and robust privacy protection methods has increased by 30%. This aligns with the ethical principle of protecting patient autonomy and ensuring that individuals are adequately informed about the potential uses of their data in healthcare applications driven by AI.

18.10.6 Continual Monitoring and Evaluation of the Situation

The ethical paradigm under consideration assigns considerable significance to the ongoing surveillance and assessment of applications that make use of AI. Recent research has indicated that the number of healthcare organisations conducting routine assessments of AI algorithms to identify and address potential ethical concerns or biases has increased by 15%. The aforementioned iterative procedures contribute to the maintenance of ethical principles in healthcare procedures that are supported by AI.

18.10.7 *Prospective Trajectories and Challenges to Surmount*

Despite recent advancements, there remain challenges that must be surmounted to establish a universally recognised ethical framework for healthcare powered by AI. Continual inquiry is necessary to tackle emerging ethical dilemmas that emerge within the ever-evolving healthcare sector context and the dynamic technological environment. In the future, it is critical that endeavours give precedence to the formation of interdisciplinary collaborations, the improvement of existing frameworks, and the resolution of emerging ethical issues. In order to ensure the ethical progression of AI applications within the healthcare sector, it is imperative to implement these measures.

18.11 Conclusion

As a conclusion, this in-depth investigation sheds light on the complex landscape of AI impact on healthcare, particularly during the treatment and care of patients. The numerous insights that are compiled in this comprehensive analysis highlight the multidimensional nature of the impact that AI has. The report dissects important topics such as the reduction of prejudice, transparency in the utilisation of data, perceptions of technology, and the development of an ethical framework.

A dynamic effort is being made to discover and correct biases that are deeply ingrained in AI systems, and the inquiry into bias mitigation highlights their importance. There has been a noticeable tendency in recent academic debate to adopt diverse datasets, algorithmic fairness criteria, and continuous monitoring. These three factors, when combined, are creating an atmosphere that is conducive to the development of AI-driven healthcare practices that are impartial and equitable.

Considering the fact that recent research has highlighted the significance of characteristics such as explainability, open access to decision processes, and clear communication regarding data gathering procedures, transparency in data utilisation has emerged as a crucial factor to take into account. Collectively, these activities contribute to the development of a healthcare environment that is characterised by trust, in which stakeholders have the ability to comprehend and question the complex processes that are involved in the application of AI.

In addition, the investigation into how people perceive technology offers a deep grasp of the many perspectives held by stakeholders, which includes both patients and healthcare professionals. Positive impressions are essential to the successful incorporation of AI into healthcare procedures, and recent literature demonstrates a heightened emphasis on establishing trust, familiarity, and ethical considerations. By doing so, positive perceptions are shaped.

While this is going on, the formulation of a proposed ethical framework is a collective response to the ever-evolving ethical considerations that are associated with the use of AI in healthcare. Recent research studies suggest that there is a growing understanding of the necessity of complete ethical principles. These guidelines should include justice, transparency, protection of privacy, and unceasing evaluation. The combined application of these criteria acts as a compass, directing AI-driven healthcare towards practices that are responsible, ethical, and focused on the patient.

All informations considered, this paper makes a contribution to the continuing conversation about AI in healthcare by offering a synthesis of recent literature, presenting critical insights, and developing a deeper awareness of the complex relationship that exists between technology and healthcare ethics. The findings highlight the importance for continued study, the refinement of techniques, and the cultivation of an atmosphere that encourages collaboration in order to unlock the full potential of AI for the improvement of therapy and patient care.

References

Abubaker Bagabir, S., Ibrahim, N. K., Abubaker Bagabir, H., & Hashem Ateeq, R. (2022). Covid-19 and artificial intelligence: Genome sequencing, drug development and vaccine discovery. *Journal of Infection and Public Health, 15*(2), 289–296.

Ahmed, F., Kang, I. S., Kim, K. H., Asif, A., Rahim, C. S. A., Samantasinghar, A., Memon, F. H., & Choi, K. H. (2023). *Drug repurposing for viral cancers: A paradigm of machine learning, deep learning, and virtual screening–based approaches. Journal of Medical Virology, 95*(4), e28693.

Ahsan, M. M. (2023). *Machine-learning-based disease diagnosis: A comprehensive review. Healthcare, 10*(3), 541.

Alfaras, M., Soriano, M. C., & Ortín, S. (2024). *A fast machine learning model for ECG-based heartbeat classification and arrhythmia detection. Frontiers in Physics, 7*(43), 1–11.

Becker, J. V., Decker, J. A., Christoph Römmele, Kahn, M., Messmann, H., Wehler, M., Schwarz, F., Kroencke, T. J., & Scheurig-Muenkler, C. (2023). *Artificial intelligence-based detection of pneumonia in chest radiographs. Diagnostics, 12*(6), 1465–1465.

Berlyand, Y., Raja, A. S., Dorner, S. C., Prabhakar, A. M., Sonis, J. D., Gottumukkala, R. V., Succi, M. D., & Yun, B. J. (2023). *How artificial intelligence could transform emergency department operations. The American Journal of Emergency Medicine, 36*(8), 1515–1517.

Elendu, C. (2024). The evolution of ancient healing practices: From shamanism to Hippocratic medicine: *A review. Medicine, 103*(28), e39005. DOI: 10.1097/MD.0000000000039005

Schoffer, O., Schriefer, D., Werblow, A., Gottschalk, A., Peschel, P., Liang, L. A., ... & Klug, S. J. (2023). Modelling the effect of demographic change and healthcare infrastructure on the patient structure in German hospitals–a longitudinal national study based on official hospital statistics. *BMC Health Services Research*, 23(1), 1081. DOI: https://doi.org/10.1186/s12913-023-10056-y

Chapter 19

Radiant Horizons of Augmented Reality and Virtual Reality in Customer-Centric Choices for Products: Artificial Intelligence (AI) Solutions Path to Fueling Business Towards Innovation Vague Futuristic Approach

Bhupinder Singh and Christian Kaunert

19.1 Introduction

The customer experience has emerged as a critical differentiator in the highly competitive commercial world [1]. Consumers of today want engaging experiences that go beyond traditional brick-and-mortar establishments and internet portals [2]. Businesses are implementing revolutionary technologies like augmented reality (AR) and virtual reality (VR) to fulfill the evolving demands and expectations [3]. This chapter explores the ever-evolving fields of AR and VR and how they might significantly affect consumer-focused product decisions [4-5]. It also focuses on the integrative function of

DOI: 10.4324/9781032711089-19

artificial intelligence (AI) solutions, revealing its capacity to spur innovation and advance companies toward a forward-thinking strategy in the quickly changing consumer preference market [6]. With improving the intelligence and flexibility of these experiences, the addition of AI, increases the effect of AR and VR [7]. In order to enable companies to customize product suggestions and presentations depending on individual preferences and behaviors, Generative Artificial Intelligence (GAI) technologies help to create dynamic, context-aware interactions [8,9].

With AR technology, digital components like photos, films and information may be seamlessly incorporated into physical environments. With gadgets like smartphones, tablets, and AR glasses, users may immerse themselves in a heightened reality that combines the actual world with digital material [10]. AR makes it possible to create interactive product visualizations, educational overlays for museum exhibitions and virtual try-on experiences for apparel, all of which engage buyers. AR is clearly evolving and becoming more and more common in a variety of application areas [11].

VR is a cutting-edge technology that uses VR headsets to fully immerse people in digital settings [12]. With the use of these headsets, users may immerse themselves in computer-generated simulations that replicate actual circumstances [13]. VR has proven its adaptability in a variety of fields, including gaming, professional training, virtual tours and immersive storytelling [14].

The ability of VR to provide an incredibly lifelike experience is a crucial feature. When interacting with virtual surroundings, users' senses are tricked into thinking they are actually in the virtual world. VR provides a really realistic and participatory experience, whether one is performing surgery, exploring ancient ruins or fighting in interstellar conflict. It also explores how AR and VR technologies are developing, how they work with GAI, and how they might completely change the consumers interact and choose products [15,16]. The approach which is a little hazy and futuristic is to imagine the many paths that these technologies may take in influencing the development of customer-centric business innovation in the future [17].

19.1.1 Background of Study

This study investigates how customer-centric product decisions are impacted by AR and VR [18]. The immersion-based business strategies are essential for drawing in new clients and keeping existing ones in a cutthroat market. While VR takes users to simulated digital settings to improve their purchasing experience, AR incorporates digital aspects into actual locations [19]. The chapter draws attention to the rising need for engaging and memorable shopping experiences and emphasizes how AR and VR technologies have the power to completely transform the way products are presented [20]. The businesses may adjust their tactics to match market needs and give customers a more gratifying and unique purchasing experience by knowing how these technologies impact customer-centric decisions [21].

19.1.2 Objectives of the Chapter

The objectives of the chapter are to:

- Explore the impact of AR and VR with AI on customer decision-making in product choices.
- Examine how these technologies enhance customer experience and preferences.
- Assess the effectiveness of AR and VR in product visualization directing on their immersive and personalized interaction, influencing customer perceptions and choices.
- Highlight the impact of factual realism on customer presence in AR and VR interactions, focusing on real elements over digital components.
- Scrutinize the relationship between the sense of presence experienced by customers in AR and VR scenarios, facilitated by AI solutions.

19.1.3 Structure of the Chapter

This chapter comprehensively explores the various dimensions of AR and VR in customer-centric choices for products: AI solutions path to fueling business towards innovation vague futuristic approach. Section 19.2 elaborates the AR and VR in consumer choices. Section 19.3 expresses the role of AI in AR and VR. Section 19.4 lays down the innovation in customer-centric choices. Section 19.5 highlights the challenges and opportunities in a futuristic landscape. And, finally, Section 19.6 conclude the chapter with future scope.

19.2 Augmented Reality and Virtual Reality in Consumer Choices

AR and VR have become essential tools enabling revolutionary consumer experiences. As such, a paradigm shift is required [22]. Customer relations in a variety of industries are being revolutionized by these immersive technologies. Businesses are looking for creative ways to interact with customers and provide more individualized experiences in an increasingly digital environment [23]. The use of machine learning and AI to enable tailored client interactions is an interesting development in this field [24]. AI-driven customization requires collecting and analyzing large amounts of client data, including social media interactions, demographic information, and past browsing and purchase activity. After that, this information is used to comprehend the unique requirements and preferences of every single client [25]. The consumer experiences with AR and VR have evolved in multifarious ways as:

- **Enhanced Realism in Customer Interactions**: AR and VR bring a new dimension of realism to customer interactions. AR combines interactive digital information with physical locations by blending digital aspects into the real world with ease [26]. The customers may interact with, observe and learn from items and information in their surroundings as a result, giving them a more engaging and customized experience. Also, VR takes users to completely new virtual worlds where they may interact with lifelike simulations [27].
- **Product Visualization:** AR and VR are two technologies that enable interactive product visualization. Customers may virtually try on clothes and imagine their living environments with VR, which helps them make well-informed shopping selections. So, going one step further, VR improves this experience by giving clients a more thorough grasp of goods and services through simulated showrooms and tours [28].
- **Personalized Experience**: With customizing material based on user choices and behavior, AR and VR offer personalized experiences. By providing targeted suggestions, personalized content, and an enhanced consumer experience, these technologies help firms build closer relationships with their target audiences [29].
- **Transformation of Learning Environments**: AR and VR have a big impact on training and education [30]. Through interactive learning environments, these immersive technologies make difficult subjects easier to understand. They enable business employees to get practical experience in complex settings, improving performance and developing skills through engagement in authentic training simulations [31].
- **Enhanced Team Collaboration**: AR and VR are essential tools for overcoming geographical divides and encouraging teamwork. Effective

communication and cooperation are encouraged when teams from different places can work together in a shared virtual environment [32].

19.2.1 Immersive Experiences and Engagement

The incorporation of VR and AR is changing the dynamics of customer-company relationships. However, comparing the efficacy of different technologies has received little attention in the study that has already been done [33]. There are ways in which users sense presence through various forms of information as digital or physical and embodied technologies like smartphones or head-mounted displays and how these perceptions affect users pre-experiences with hotels [4].

High factual realism content like 360-degree videos positively affects viewers' impressions of presence, creative license, visual appeal and intent to book. When head-mounted displays or other high-embodied technologies are used then the effect is greater [34]. The influence of the content on booking intentions is mediated by presence, which has a beneficial effect on visual attractiveness and ease of imagining [35]. These findings highlight the importance of creating presence as a vital initiator of behavioral intentions in the hospitality industry. The comparative impact of conventional VR and AR experiences is also explored [36].

19.2.2 Personalized Recommendations and Customization

With combining VR and AR marketing techniques have been rejuvenated and are now offering customers unique and memorable experiences [37,38]. A notable example is the AR app which lets users see how furniture will look in their homes before making a purchase [39]. This lessens the frequent problem of product returns in online furniture retail while also improving the entire purchasing experience [40]. In a similar vein, the beauty sector has embraced new technologies, allowing consumers to virtually trial cosmetic items using smartphone applications that use AR. This interactive strategy helps clients make more informed purchases while also boosting engagement [41].

19.3 Role of AI in Augmented Reality and Virtual Reality

In the modern, dynamic, and fast-changing corporate world, the organizations are always looking for new and creative ways to engage with their clientele, boost productivity, and stay ahead of the competition [42,43].

In this setting, two technologies VR and AR have become revolutionary. The immersion technologies have evolved from their conventional uses in entertainment and games to become indispensable tools in fields including marketing, customer service and product creation [44].

While VR creates fully immersive virtual worlds for users to interact with, AR enhances the actual world by adding digital aspects to it [45]. These technologies are used in a wide range of sectors including business, education, healthcare, and entertainment. They are constantly developing to provide experiences that are more realistic and immersive [46,47].

It's more important than ever to grab and hold the attention of budget-conscious consumers in a time when marketers struggle with the problems of digital saturation [48]. Because traditional marketing methods frequently fail to produce the desired results, companies desperately need creative tactics that appeal to today's sophisticated consumer base [49]. In order to captivate and engage audiences, it explores the revolutionary possibilities of VR, AR, and interactive content [50]. These technologies provide a chance to cut through the digital clutter and give value and enjoyment that may win over even the pickiest customer by providing immersive experiences [51].

19.3.1 Intelligent Data Analysis and Prediction

The product Design is being revolutionized by AR and VR, which have significantly changed the process. VR simulations have been integrated into design workflows by major firms [52,53]. This allows engineers and designers to evaluate prototypes in a virtual environment [54]. This lowers the cost of building physical prototypes while simultaneously speeding up the development process [55]. The businesses are enabling their clients to create their own footwear through the use of AR [56]. The customers may create a bespoke product by personalizing the colors and materials with an AR application. This improves consumer interaction and offers insightful data about their preferences [57].

19.3.2 Enhanced Personalization Through Machine Learning

AI and machine learning are used in AI-driven customization to evaluate client data, understand their needs and preferences and adjust the user experience appropriately [58]. The clear objectives, high-quality data, continuous testing and improvement, transparency and integration of the strategy across all client touch-points are all necessary for successful execution. Better customer experience, more revenue, lower churn and the acquisition of data-driven insights are all benefits of AI-powered customization [59].

Personalized marketing was previously only a theoretical idea, but it is now a reality thanks to the use of machine learning [60]. By utilizing data analysis and prediction algorithms, companies can offer customized experiences that resonate with consumers, increasing engagement, increasing conversion rates, and strengthening customer loyalty [61]. Personalized marketing must, however, be approached responsibly striking a careful balance between privacy and customization [62]. Machine learning-driven customized marketing is set to be a vital part of successful marketing strategies in the digital age as long as technology progresses [63].

19.4 Innovation in Customer-Centric Choices

VR and AR provide previously unheard-of possibilities for client engagement [64, 65]. So, think about the travel and tourism sector, where businesses have used VR to provide virtual tours of properties [66]. With enabling prospective tenants to digitally inspect properties as though they were in person this enhances the booking process and promotes confidence between hosts and guests [67]. The customer care solutions based on AR are becoming more and more popular. The companies are using AR to give consumers interactive, real-time support [68]. This improves problem-solving and reduces support expenses while also improving the overall customer experience [69,70].

The recommendation system demonstrates AI-powered customization using a machine learning algorithm, the system examines search histories, purchase histories, and other behavioral data to forecast goods that might catch users' attention and provide suggestions in real-time [71]. These tailored recommendations have increased client engagement and revenue [72]. Today's consumers demand experiences that are tailored to their individual requirements and interests [73]. Machine learning is becoming a part of marketing strategy due to this change in customer expectations. Machine learning, a kind of AI, is revolutionizing the way companies interact with their clientele [74]. It examines machine learning's function in tailored marketing the tactics it uses and its many advantages [75].

19.4.1 AI-Infused Product Development

As AR and VR continue to evolve, emerging patterns are becoming evident. The growing trend is mixed reality (MR), which combines aspects of virtual and real worlds [76]. Employee training is one area where MR is used to help workers practice activities in a safe and regulated virtual environment [77,78]. A further noteworthy development is the rise of immersive 3D advertising [79,80]. Using VR and AR, brands are creating engaging and memorable advertising campaigns that provide users with an amazing experience [81].

The personalized marketing refers to a tactic whereby marketing initiatives are customized for specific consumers according to their demographics, behavior, and preferences [82]. Personalized marketing is different from generic mass marketing in that it seeks to build a personal relationship with each consumer by providing offers and relevant material that speak to their individual interests [83,84]. Personalized marketing relies heavily on machine learning algorithms, which analyze large datasets to understand consumer behavior and preferences [85].

19.4.2 Seamless Integration of Technologies

VR and AR are revolutionizing the ways in which companies handle product design, consumer interaction, and marketing [86,87]. Their concrete influence is clear, as seen by successful case studies and growing patterns hint to much more innovation to come [88]. The businesses adopting VR and AR are putting themselves in a position to prosper in a setting that is becoming more immersive and focused on the needs of the consumer as technology advances [89].

19.5 Challenges and Viable Solutions in Futuristic Landscape

With analyzing effective AR and VR marketing efforts and the corresponding technology developments, it investigate how companies may use these immersive technologies to create lasting, significant relationships with their target audience [90,91]. The marketers navigating the potential and difficulties of the contemporary digital landscape must recognize and capitalize on the power of immersive and interactive content as the lines between the real and virtual worlds continue to blur [92,93]. There are a number of hurdles that need to be overcome before AR and VR are widely used in organizations [94]. Three major ones are listed here along with possible solutions [95]. The challenges and concerns are as-

■ **High Initial Investments**: Businesses and consumers must make significant upfront investments in hardware and software in order to use AR and VR technologies [96,97]. While VR experiences demand appropriate equipment and headgear, AR experiences require compatible devices [98]. Long-term benefits include improved brand loyalty and increased consumer pleasure even if the early expenses can seem high [99]. With the rapid development of technology and the increasing availability of AR and VR gear and software, these investments are strategically significant and will likely lead to more expansion in the future [100,101].

■ **Compatibility Issues**: The integration of AR and VR technologies into businesses can be challenging due to compatibility issues and limited content and expertise [102]. The strategic planning and gradual implementation can overcome these challenges [103]. As the ecosystem matures, a broader range of content and expertise will become more readily available, facilitating the integration of AR and VR into various business applications [104]. So, investing in content creation capabilities and collaborations with experienced professionals can help overcome these challenges [105,106].

■ **Considerable Technical Debt:** There is typically a significant technical debt associated with the development and maintenance of AR and VR apps [107]. This is the outcome of choosing quick fixes over sensible ones in the design stage which leads to complex and difficult code that needs constant upkeep [108]. The rapid expansion of AR and VR technology is increasing the hazards associated with technological debt, which might potentially hinder future improvements [109,110].

■ **Privacy Issues of Consumer**: The concerns regarding data security and privacy are greatly increased by the massive collection and use of data in AR and VR applications [111]. These immersive technologies gather a variety of information during interactions including identity and behavior data, to improve the user experience [112]. There is a chance that this data will be misused, accessed without authorization or compromised, which might endanger privacy and compromise security [113].

Viable Solutions in Futuristic Landscape

The costs of AR and VR gadgets are steadily declining as technology advances and their use increases [114]. The businesses may want to think about renting or leasing equipment rather than making full purchases [115]. So, investing in sustainable solutions that give priority to high-impact use cases might improve cost-effectiveness [116].

Businesses should emphasize code restructuring and follow software development best practices to reduce excessive technical debt [117]. Reducing the technical debt may be achieved by regular codebase reviews, revisions, and performance optimization with the right development tools [118]. It will be easier and more affordable to create and maintain AR and VR apps if sustainable development principles are prioritized [119].

To improve data security, companies must use secure authentication, robust encryption and frequent audits. The gaining of consent, communicating openly with people and abiding by data protection laws are all necessary to cultivate trust [120]. Setting of data security as a top priority creates a safe atmosphere that encourages more people to use AR and VR technology [121].

19.6 Conclusion and Future Scope

Customers now enjoy a more elevated online buying experience because of the significant improvements that the integration of AR and VR has brought to the e-commerce sector. With the use of AR technology, interactive product catalogs allow shoppers to see things in their own settings and get measurements and fit information. AI algorithms enable virtual shopping assistants to provide customized suggestions based on user preferences and past purchases. Increased client loyalty and heightened purchase intent are the outcomes of these developments. AR and VR act as a link between the online and offline worlds of business, enabling consumers to interact with things in real life before making a purchase.

VR and AR are transforming client experiences in a variety of industries, making them essential for companies looking to stay ahead of the digital curve. As businesses compete to remain ahead of the curve, adopting these technologies is becoming imperative rather than optional. The current revolution is only the start; far more amazing developments in AR and

VR technology may perhaps come in the future. These innovations have the potential to provide consumers with experiences never seen before, enthralling them in ways that were before unthinkable.

References

1. Vaidyanathan, N., & Henningsson, S. (2023). Designing Augmented Reality Services for Enhanced Customer Experiences in Retail. *Journal of Service Management, 34*(1), 78–99.
2. Kwok, C. P., & Tang, Y. M. (2023). A Fuzzy MCDM Approach to Support Customer-Centric Innovation in Virtual Reality (VR) Metaverse Headset Design. *Advanced Engineering Informatics, 56,* 101910.
3. Keivanpour, S. (2022). Design for Environment in Consumer-Centric Paradigm. In Approaches, Opportunities, and Challenges for Eco-Design 4.0: A Concise Guide for Practitioners and Students (pp. 1–18). Springer.
4. Kazmi, S. H. A., Ahmed, R. R., Soomro, K. A., Hashem E, A. R., Akhtar, H., & Parmar, V. (2021). Role of Augmented Reality in Changing Consumer Behavior and Decision Making: Case of Pakistan. *Sustainability, 13*(24), 14064.
5. Kannan, P. K., & Gu, X. (2019). Customer Centricity and the Impact of Technology. In Handbook on Customer Centricity: Strategies for Building a Customer-Centric Organization (pp. 300–316). Edward Elgar Publishing Limited.
6. Gopakumar, S., & Dananjayan, M. P. (2023). Augmented Reality in Modern Marketing: The Ultimate Solution to Engage the Digitally Overwhelmed, Budget-Conscious Audience? *Journal of Information Technology Teaching Cases,* 20438869231202712. https://doi.org/10.1177/20438869231202712
7. Chen, R., Perry, P., Boardman, R., & McCormick, H. (2022). Augmented Reality in Retail: a Systematic Review of Research Foci and Future Research Agenda. *International Journal of Retail & Distribution Management, 50*(4), 498–518.
8. Bajpai, A., & Islam, T. (2022). Impact of Augmented Reality Marketing on Customer Engagement, Behavior, Loyalty, and Buying Decisions. *Cardiometry,* (23), 545–553. https://doi.org/10.18137/cardiometry.2022.23.545-553
9. Erdmann, A., Mas, J. M., & Arilla, R. (2023). Value-based Adoption of Augmented Reality: A Study on the Influence on Online Purchase Intention in Retail. *Journal of Consumer Behaviour, 22*(4), 912–932.
10. Wagner, R., & Cozmiuc, D. (2022). Extended Reality in Marketing — A Multiple Case Study on Internet of Things Platforms. *Information, 13*(6), 278.
11. Berberović, D., Alić, A., & Činjarević, M. (2022). Virtual Reality in Marketing: Consumer and Retail Perspectives. In *International Conference "New Technologies, Development and Applications"* (pp. 1093–1102). Springer International Publishing.
12. Rodriguez-Conde, I., & Campos, C. (2020). Towards Customer-Centric Additive Manufacturing: Making Human-Centered 3D Design Tools Through a Handheld-Based Multi-Touch User Interface. *Sensors, 20*(15), 4255.

13. Hoyer, W. D., Kroschke, M., Schmitt, B., Kraume, K., & Shankar, V. (2020). Transforming the Customer Experience Through New Technologies. *Journal of Interactive Marketing, 51*(1), 57–71.

14. Addis, M. (2020). *Engaging Brands: A Customer-Centric Approach for superior Experiences.* Routledge.

15. Bardhan, A. (2020). Augmented Reality and Virtual Reality in Retail–A Bibliometric Analysis. *Psychology and Education, 57*(9), 6209–6219.

16. Befort, A. (2021). *Augmented & Virtual Reality in E-commerce* (Master's thesis, University of Twente).

17. Harba, J. N. (2019). New approaches to customer experience: where disruptive technological innovation meets luxury fashion. In *Proceedings of the International Conference on Business Excellence* (Vol. 13, No. 1, pp. 740–758).

18. Kumar, S., Srinivas, K., Sheorey, S., & Joshi, P., G. (2022). Understanding Customer Needs and Innovation in E-Commerce. In *Changing Face Of E-commerce In Asia* (pp. 43–57).

19. Simoni, M., Sorrentino, A., Leone, D., & Caporuscio, A. (2022). Boosting the pre-Purchase Experience Through Virtual Reality. Insights from the Cruise Industry. *Journal of Hospitality and Tourism Technology, 13*(1), 140–156.

20. Bilal, M., Zhang, Y., Cai, S., Akram, U., & Halibas, A. (2024). Artificial Intelligence Is the Magic Wand Making Customer-Centric a Reality! An Investigation into the Relationship between Consumer Purchase Intention and Consumer Engagement Through Affective Attachment. *Journal of Retailing and Consumer Services, 77,* 103674.

21. Arrighi, P. A., & Mougenot, C. (2019). Towards User Empowerment in Product Design: A Mixed Reality Tool for Interactive Virtual Prototyping. *Journal of Intelligent Manufacturing, 30,* 743–754.

22. Lignell, M. (2023). A Journey Towards Human-Centric and AI-Augmented Marketing? *Journal of AI. Robotics & Workplace Automation, 2*(4), 369–381.

23. Camilleri, M. A. (2020). The Use of Data-Driven Technologies for Customer-Centric Marketing. *International Journal of Big Data Management, 1*(1), 50–63.

24. Qadri, S. B., Mir, M. M., & Khan, M. A. (2023). Exploring the Impact of Augmented Reality on Customer Experiences and Attitudes: A Comparative Analysis with Websites. *International Journal of Management Research and Emerging Sciences, 13*(2), 168–192.

25. Batat, W. (2021). How Augmented Reality (AR) Is Transforming the Restaurant Sector: Investigating the Impact of "Le Petit Chef" on customers' Dining Experiences. *Technological Forecasting and Social Change, 172,* 121013.

26. Kim, E., Simonse, L. W., Beckman, S. L., Appleyard, M. M., Velazquez, H., Madrigal, A. S., & Agogino, A. M. (2020). User-Centered Design Roadmapping: Anchoring Roadmapping in Customer Value Before Technology Selection. *IEEE Transactions on Engineering Management, 69*(1), 109–126.

27. Xu, X., Jia, Q., & Tayyab, S. M. U. (2023). The Exploration of Customization in Augmented Reality from the Affordance Lens: A Three-Stage Hybrid Approach. *Technological Forecasting and Social Change, 194,* 122729.

28. Sleem, A., Mostafa, N., & Elhenawy, I. (2023). Neutrosophic CRITIC MCDM Methodology for Ranking Factors and Needs of Customers in product's Target Demographic in Virtual Reality Metaverse. *Neutrosophic Systems With Applications*, *2*, 55–65.

29. Beheshti, M., ZareRavasan, A., Mahdiraji, H. A., Jafari-Sadeghi, V., & Sakka, G. (2023). An Overview of the Consumer-Centric Disruptive Technology Research: Insights from Topic Modelling and Literature Review. *Journal of Consumer Behaviour*, 23(2), 372–388.

30. Zhang, J. (2020). A systematic review of the use of augmented reality (AR) and virtual reality (VR) in online retailing.

31. Jain, S., & Werth, D. (2019). Current state of mixed reality technology for digital retail: a literature review. In *HCI in Business, Government and Organizations. E-commerce and Consumer Behavior: 6th International Conference, HCIBGO 2019, Held as Part of the 21st HCI International Conference, HCII 2019, Orlando, FL, USA, July 26-31, 2019, Proceedings, Part I 21* (pp. 22–37). Springer International Publishing.

32. Egger, R., & Neuburger, L. (2020). Augmented, Virtual, and Mixed Reality in Tourism. In Handbook of e-Tourism (pp. 1–25). Springer.

33. Kumar, H., Tuli, N., Singh, R. K., Arya, V., & Srivastava, R. (2023). Exploring the Role of Augmented Reality as a New Brand Advocate. *Journal of Consumer Behaviour*, 23(2), 1–19.

34. Thomas, T., Mathew, R., & KG, A. (2022). Usefulness of Augmented Reality on Product Selection: An Experimental Study. *SCMS Journal of Indian Management*, *19*(2), 26–34.

35. Krishnadas, R. (2021). Understanding Customer Engagement and Purchase Behavior in Automobiles: The Role of Digital Technology. In *Handbook of Research on Technology Applications for Effective Customer Engagement* (pp. 1–13). IGI Global.

36. Rindfleisch, A., & Im, S. (2019). Enhancing Customer Centricity via 3D Printing. In Handbook on Customer Centricity: Strategies for Building a Customer-Centric Organization (pp. 317–340). Edward Elgar.

37. Dehghani, M., Lee, S. H. M., & Mashatan, A. (2020). Touching Holograms With Windows Mixed Reality: Renovating the Consumer Retailing Services. *Technology in Society*, 63(1), 101394.

38. Aithal, P. S. (2023). How to Create Business Value Through Technological Innovations Using ICCT Underlying Technologies. *International Journal of Applied Engineering and Management Letters (IJAEML)*, 7(2), 232–292.

39. Han, D. I. D., Weber, J., Bastiaansen, M., Mitas, O., & Lub, X. (2019). Virtual and Augmented Reality Technologies to Enhance the Visitor Experience in Cultural Tourism. In Augmented Reality and Virtual Reality: The Power of AR and VR for Business, (pp. 113–128). Springer Nature.

40. Ozkok, O., Singh, J., Lim, K., & Bell, S. J. (2019). Service Innovation from the Frontlines in Customer-Centric Organizations. In Handbook on Customer Centricity: Strategies for Building a Customer-Centric Organization, (pp. 79–107). Edward Elgar.

41. JO, J. (2021). *A Study on the effect of marketing using virtual mirror technology on customer satisfaction* (Doctoral dissertation, KDI School).

42. Gauri, D. K., Jindal, R. P., Ratchford, B., Fox, E., Bhatnagar, A., Pandey, A., & Howerton, E. (2021). Evolution of Retail Formats: Past, Present, and Future. *Journal of Retailing, 97*(1), 42–61.

43. Abou Elmaaty, N. H. H., & Ibrahim, H. E. A. (2023). Integrating Artificial Intelligence and Cloud Computing in Ecommerce Operational and Customer-Centric Advancements. *AI, IoT and the Fourth Industrial Revolution Review, 13*(9), 18–28.

44. Guo, D., Ling, S., Li, H., Ao, D., Zhang, T., Rong, Y., & Huang, G. Q. (2020, August). A framework for personalized production based on digital twin, blockchain and additive manufacturing in the context of Industry 4.0. In *2020 IEEE 16th International Conference on Automation Science and Engineering (CASE)* (pp. 1181–1186). IEEE.

45. Asmar, L., Grigoryan, K., Low, C. Y., Roeltgen, D., & Dumitrescu, R. (2021). Structuring Framework for Early Validation of Product Ideas. *International Journal of Integrated Engineering, 13*(2), 229–240.

46. Rajagopal, R. (2022). Impact of Retailing Technology During Business Shutdown. *Marketing Intelligence & Planning, 40*(4), 441–459.

47. Susiang, M. I. N., Suryaningrum, D. A., Masliardi, A., Setiawan, E., & Abdillah, F. (2023). Enhancing Customer Experience Through Effective Marketing Strategies: The Context of Online Shopping. *SEIKO: Journal of Management & Business, 6*(2), 437–447.

48. Jain, S. (2022). Using Optical See-through Mixed Reality for Enhanced Shopping Experience in Omnichannel Retail/Author Shubham Jain.

49. N'Goala, G., Pez-Pérard, V., & Prim-Allaz, I. (Eds.). (2019). *Augmented Customer Strategy: CRM in the Digital Age.* John Wiley & Sons.

50. Han, D. I. D., Weber, J., Bastiaansen, M., Mitas, O., & Lub, X. (2020). Blowing Your Mind: A Conceptual Framework of Augmented Reality and Virtual Reality Enhanced Cultural Visitor Experiences Using EEG Experience Measures. *International Journal of Technology Marketing, 14*(1), 47–68.

51. Chatmi, A., Elasri, K., & Ponsignon, F. (2023). Assessing and Improving Co-Creation in Services: The Customer-Centric Matrix. *International Journal of Quality and Service Sciences, 15*(1), 97–114.

52. Bakator, M., Vukoja, M., & Manestar, D. (2023). Achieving Competitiveness with Marketing 5.0 in New Business Conditions. *UTMS Journal of Economics, 14*(1), 63–73.

53. Wang, T. (2023). Research on the Impact of E-Commerce on Offline Retail Industry. *Frontiers in Business, Economics and Management, 10*(1), 169–173.

54. Rialti, R., & Zollo, L. (2023). Marketing 4.0 for SMEs in the Digital Era: A Customer-Centric Approach. In *Digital Transformation of SME Marketing Strategies: Innovating for the 4.0 Era* (pp. 81–131). Springer Nature.

55. Nguyen, E., & Nguyen, A. (2021). AR/VR applications in fashion retailing: An exploratory study on the effectiveness of virtual try-on technology along the customer journey.

56. Bharwani, S., & Mathews, D. (2021). Techno-Business Strategies for Enhancing Guest Experience in Luxury Hotels: A Managerial Perspective. *Worldwide Hospitality and Tourism Themes, 13*(2), 168–185.

57. Harrisson-Boudreau, J. P., Bellemare, J., Bacher, N., & Bartosiak, M. (2023). Adoption Potentials of Metaverse Omnichannel Retailing and Its Impact on Mass Customization Approaches. In *Proceedings of the Changeable, Agile, Reconfigurable and Virtual Production Conference and the World Mass Customization & Personalization Conference* (pp. 110–119). Springer International Publishing.

58. Rajagopal. (2022). Epilogue: The Extent of Agility. In *Agile Marketing Strategies: New Approaches to Engaging Consumer Behavior* (pp. 227–245). Springer International Publishing.

59. Zhou, L., & Xue, F. (2021). Show Products or Show People: An Eye-Tracking Study of Visual Branding Strategy on Instagram. *Journal of Research in Interactive Marketing, 15*(4), 729–749.

60. Chu, C. H., Cheng, C. H., Wu, H. S., & Kuo, C. C. (2019). A Cloud Service Framework for Virtual Try-on of Footwear in Augmented Reality. *Journal of Computing and Information Science in Engineering, 19*(2), 021002.

61. Suopajärvi, T. (2021). Developing cooperation and customer-centric operations in the TE office Aviation team.

62. Hajarian, M., Camilleri, M. A., Díaz, P., & Aedo, I. (2021). A Taxonomy of Online Marketing Methods. In *Strategic Corporate Communication in the Digital Age* (pp. 235–250). Emerald Publishing Limited.

63. Soltanifar, M., & Smailhodžić, E. (2021). Developing a Digital Entrepreneurial Mindset for Data-Driven, Cloud-Enabled, and Platform-Centric Business Activities: Practical Implications and the Impact on Society. In Digital Entrepreneurship (pp. 3–21). Springer.

64. ZXhang, Y. X., Haxo, Y. M., & Mat, Y. X. (2023). Best Buy Stock: An Examination of Its Resilience, Adaptability, and Investment Potential. *AC Investment Research Journal, 220*(44).

65. Glebova, E., Book, R., Su, Y., Perić, M., & Heller, J. (2023). Sports Venue Digital Twin Technology from a Spectator Virtual Visiting Perspective. *Frontiers in Sports and Active Living, 5*, 1–11.

66. Liu, Z. (2023). Unlocking Consumer Choices in the Digital Economy: Exploring Factors Influencing Online and Offline Purchases in the Emerging Pet Food Market. *Journal of the Knowledge Economy*, 1–26. https://doi.org/10.1007/s13132-023-01490-8

67. Zheng, P., Lin, Y., Chen, C. H., & Xu, X. (2019). Smart, Connected Open Architecture Product: An IT-Driven Co-Creation Paradigm With Lifecycle Personalization Concerns. *International Journal of Production Research, 57*(8), 2571–2584.

68. Kong, X. T., Luo, H., Huang, G. Q., & Yang, X. (2019). Industrial Wearable System: The Human-Centric Empowering Technology in Industry 4. *Journal of Intelligent Manufacturing, 30*, 2853–2869.

69. Widita, A., Rachmahani, H., Agustina, I. A., & Husna, N. (2021, July). The Use of Augmented Reality in Café's Interior to Enhance Customer Experience. In

IOP Conference Series: Earth and Environmental Science (Vol. 794, No. 1, p. 012192). IOP Publishing.

70. Farine, P. G. (2023). Digital Presence in Physical Shopping: From a "Benefit-Oriented Approach" to Successful Customer Engagement. In *Multisensory in Stationary Retail: Principles and Practice of Customer-Centered Store Design* (pp. 183–200). Springer Fachmedien Wiesbaden.

71. Subawa, N. S., Widhiasthini, N. W., Astawa, I. P., Dwiatmadja, C., & Permatasari, N. P. I. (2021). The Practices of Virtual Reality Marketing in the Tourism Sector, a Case Study of Bali, Indonesia. *Current Issues in Tourism, 24*(23), 3284–3295.

72. Albers, A., Reinemann, J., Fahl, J., & Hirschter, T. (2019). Augmented reality for product validation: supporting the configuration of AR-based validation environments. In *Virtual, Augmented and Mixed Reality. Applications and Case Studies: 11th International Conference, VAMR 2019, Held as Part of the 21st HCI International Conference, HCII 2019, Orlando, FL, USA, July 26–31, 2019, Proceedings, Part II 21* (pp. 429–448). Springer International Publishing.

73. Pereira, A. M., Moura, J. A. B., Costa, E. D. B., Vieira, T., Landim, A. R., Bazaki, E., & Wanick, V. (2022). Customer Models for Artificial Intelligence-Based Decision Support in Fashion Online Retail Supply Chains. *Decision Support Systems, 158*, 113795.

74. Rane, N. (2023). Metaverse Marketing Strategies: Enhancing Customer Experience and Analysing Consumer Behaviour Through Leading-Edge Metaverse Technologies, Platforms, and Models. *Available at SSRN.*

75. Fischer, H., Seidenstricker, S., Berger, T., & Holopainen, T. (2021). Digital Sales in B2B: Status and Application. In *Advances in Creativity, Innovation, Entrepreneurship and Communication of Design: Proceedings of the AHFE 2021 Virtual Conferences on Creativity, Innovation and Entrepreneurship, and Human Factors in Communication of Design, July 25-29, 2021, USA* (pp. 369-375). Springer International Publishing.

76. Menon, A., Bhagat, S., & Iqbal, D. (2020). The Impact of Augmented Reality in Fashion Retail Stores in India: Opportunities and Challenges. *IOSR Journal Of Business And Management (IOSR-JBM), 22*(7), 61–67.

77. Rajagopal. (2022). The Agile Mind-Set. In *Agile Marketing Strategies: New Approaches to Engaging Consumer Behavior* (pp. 189–224). Springer International Publishing.

78. Oosthuizen, K., Botha, E., Robertson, J., & Montecchi, M. (2021). Artificial Intelligence in Retail: The AI-Enabled Value Chain. *Australasian Marketing Journal, 29*(3), 264–273.

79. Shields, K. (2021). Designing Products, Services, and Processes with Customers in Mind. In Customer Centric Strategy. Pressbook.

80. Kotler, P., Kartajaya, H., & Setiawan, I. (2021). *Marketing 5.0: Technology for Humanity.* John Wiley & Sons.

81. Ziaie, A., ShamiZanjani, M., & Manian, A. (2021). Systematic Review of Digital Value Propositions in the Retail Sector: New Approach for Digital Experience Study. *Electronic Commerce Research and Applications, 47*, 101053.

82. Magnelli, A., Verreschi, G., & Ventrella, M. (2021). Bringing Knowledge and Emotion to the Industrial Field: ETT's AR/VR Solutions. In *Augmented Reality and Virtual Reality: New Trends in Immersive Technology* (pp. 251–266). Springer International Publishing.

83. Kautish, P., & Khare, A. (2022). Investigating the Moderating Role of AI-Enabled Services on Flow and Awe Experience. *International Journal of Information Management, 66,* 102519.

84. Chaturvedi, R., & Verma, S. (2023). Opportunities and Challenges of AI-Driven Customer Service. In Artificial Intelligence in Customer Service: The Next Frontier for Personalized Engagement (pp. 33–71). Palgrave Macmillan.

85. Golf-Papez, M., Heller, J., Hilken, T., Chylinski, M., de Ruyter, K., Keeling, D. I., & Mahr, D. (2022). Embracing Falsity Through the Metaverse: The Case of Synthetic Customer Experiences. *Business Horizons, 65*(6), 739–749.

86. Ylilehto, M., Komulainen, H., & Ulkuniemi, P. (2021). The Critical Factors Shaping Customer Shopping Experiences with Innovative Technologies. *Baltic Journal of Management, 16*(5), 661–680.

87. Hussain, Z., & Shaikh, M. Z. (2023). Role of Technology in Marketing: AI, AR and VR. *EKOMA: Jurnal Ekonomi, Manajemen, Akuntansi, 2*(2), 465–471.

88. Lee, C. K. M., Lui, L., & Tsang, Y. P. (2021). Formulation and Prioritization of Sustainable New Product Design in Smart Glasses Development. *Sustainability, 13*(18), 10323.

89. Naimi-Sadigh, A., Asgari, T., & Rabiei, M. (2022). Digital Transformation in the Value Chain Disruption of Banking Services. *Journal of the Knowledge Economy, 13*(2), 1212–1242.

90. Christoforou, T., & Melanthiou, Y. (2019). The Practicable Aspect of the Omni-Channel Retailing Strategy and Its Impact on Customer Loyalty. In The Synergy of Business Theory and Practice: Advancing the Practical Application of Scholarly Research (pp. 239–260). Palgrave Macmillan.

91. Iglesias-Pradas, S., & Acquila-Natale, E. (2023). The Future of E-Commerce: Overview and Prospects of Multichannel and Omnichannel Retail. *Journal of Theoretical and Applied Electronic Commerce Research, 18*(1), 656–667.

92. Arikan, ÖU., Öztürk, E., Duman, S., & Aktaş, M. A. (2022, October). Conceptualization of Meta-Servitization: 3D Case Study from Furniture Industry. In *2022 International Symposium on Multidisciplinary Studies and Innovative Technologies (ISMSIT)* (pp. 702–706). IEEE.

93. Verma, S., Warrier, L., Bolia, B., & Mehta, S. (2022). Past, Present, and Future of Virtual Tourism - A Literature Review. *International Journal of Information Management Data Insights, 2*(2), 100085.

94. Kaliappen, N., & Hassan, A. (2022). Digital Trends in Asian Hotel Industry. In *Technology Application in Tourism in Asia: Innovations, Theories and Practices* (pp. 147–163). Springer Nature.

95. Egieya, Z. E., Ewuga, S. K., Adegbite, A. O., & Oke, T. T. (2023). The Role of Virtual and Augmented Reality in Modern Marketing: A Critical Review. *Computer Science & IT Research Journal, 4*(3), 244–272.

96. Wirtz, J., Hofmeister, J., Chew, P. Y., & Ding, X. (2023). Digital Service Technologies, Service Robots, AI, and the Strategic Pathways to Cost-Effective Service Excellence. *The Service Industries Journal, 43*(15-16), 1173–1196.

97. López-Menchero, T. B., Mata García, P., Gomez Campillo, M., & Delgado-de Miguel, J. F. (2021). Outlets Malls of the Future: an Approach to customer's Expectations. *Economic Research-Ekonomska Istraživanja, 34*(1), 2593–2608.

98. Shields, K. (2024). *Customer Centric Strategy.*

99. Utami Tjhin, V., & Eka Riantini, R. (2021, December). A study for the implementation of Banking 4.0 in Indonesia. In *Proceedings of the 2021 9th International Conference on Information Technology: IoT and Smart City* (pp. 129–134).

100. Bhavana, S. U. (2023). Digital Transformation–Embracing Digital Change. *Best Practices of Research And Innovation in Steam Higher Education,* 25.

101. Chaturvedi, R., & Verma, S.(2022). Artificial Intelligence-Driven Customer Experience: Overcoming The Challenges. In California Management Review Insights (pp. 1–19), Fronteir.

102. Vrigkas, M., Lappas, G., Kleftodimos, A., & Triantafillidou, A. (2021). Augmented Reality for Wine Industry: Past, Present, and Future. In *SHS Web of Conferences* (Vol. 102, p. 04006). EDP Sciences.

103. Dang, T. D., & Nguyen, M. T. (2023). Systematic Review and Research Agenda for the Tourism and Hospitality Sector: Co-Creation of Customer Value in the Digital Age. *Future Business Journal, 9*(1), 94.

104. Sureshbabu, J., Mahalakshmi, S., & Priya, R. (2023, October). User Persona Mapping Technique for Human Interaction with Augmented and Virtual Reality Environments. In *2023 International Conference on Self Sustainable Artificial Intelligence Systems (ICSSAS)* (pp. 921–926). IEEE.

105. Aaker, D. A., & Moorman, C. (2023). *Strategic Market Management.* John Wiley & Sons.

106. Gruia, L. A., Bibu, N., Roja, A., Danaiață, D., & Năstase, M. (2022). Digital Transformation of Businesses in Times of Global Crisis. In *Navigating Through the Crisis–A Special Issue on the Covid 19 Crises: The 2020 Annual Griffiths School of Management and IT Conference (GSMAC) Vol 1 11* (pp. 43–62). Springer International Publishing.

107. Shah, D., & Murthi, B. P. S. (2021). Marketing in a Data-Driven Digital World: Implications for the Role and Scope of Marketing. *Journal of Business Research, 125,* 772–779.

108. Donmezer, S., Demircioglu, P., Bogrekci, I., Bas, G., & Durakbasa, M. N. (2023). Revolutionizing the Garment Industry 5.0: Embracing Closed-Loop Design, E-Libraries, and Digital Twins. *Sustainability, 15*(22), 15839.

109. Singh, A., Mishra, S., Jain, S., Dogra, S., Awasthi, A., Roy, N. R., & Sodhi, K. (2023). Exploring Practical Use-Cases of Augmented Reality Using Photogrammetry and Other 3D Reconstruction Tools in the Metaverse. In Augmented and Virtual Reality in Industry 5.0 (pp. 163–186). De Gruyter.

110. Bhattacharya, S., & Chatterjee, A. (2022). Digital Project Driven Supply Chains: a New Paradigm. *Supply Chain Management: An International Journal, 27*(2), 283–294.

111. Kümmerle, R., & Wierzbitzki, M. (2019). Visualising Customer-Centric Digital Investment Performance Reports. *Journal of Digital Banking, 3*(4), 346–360.
112. Spajić, J., Mitrović, K., Lalić, D., Milić, B., & Bošković, D. (2022, September). Personalized brand experience in metaverse. In *10th International Conference on Mass Customization and Personalization–Community of Europe (MCP-CE 2022)* (pp. 21–23).
113. Sharma, D., Yadav, V., & Singh, D. (2023). Advancements and Implications of Product Service Systems in the Automobile Industry: A Comprehensive Review. *Engineering Proceedings, 59*(1), 98.
114. Rane, N., Choudhary, S., & Rane, J. (2023). Metaverse for Enhancing Customer Loyalty: Effective Strategies to Improve Customer Relationship, Service, Engagement, Satisfaction, and Experience. *Service, Engagement, Satisfaction, and Experience (November 1, 2023)*.
115. Scurati, G. W., Bertoni, A., & Bertoni, M. (2022, September). Boosting Value Co-Creation in the Road Construction Industry Through Virtual Prototyping. In *Working Conference on Virtual Enterprises* (pp. 613–622). Springer International Publishing.
116. Tang, Y. M., Lau, Y. Y., & Ho, U. L. (2023). Empowering Digital Marketing with Interactive Virtual Reality (IVR) in Interior Design: Effects on Customer Satisfaction and Behaviour Intention. *Journal of Theoretical and Applied Electronic Commerce Research, 18*(2), 889–907.
117. Vidili, I. (2021). *Journey to Centricity: A Customer-Centric Framework for the Era of Stakeholder Capitalism*. The Smarter Crew.
118. Moorthy, J., & Parvatiyar, A. (2023). Co-Creating Aftermarket Value in the Digital Era: Managing Transformative Customer Relationships Through Stakeholder Engagement. In *Customer Centric Support Services in the Digital Age: The Next Frontier of Competitive Advantage* (pp. 155–198). Springer International Publishing.
119. Li, L. H., Cheung, K. S., & Tse, W. S. (2023). Understanding the shoppers' Perception in Retail Shopping Malls: A Self-Determination Theory Perspective. *Journal of Strategic Marketing, 31*(1), 58–73.
120. Pappas, A., Fumagalli, E., Rouziou, M., & Bolander, W. (2023). More than Machines: The Role of the Future Retail Salesperson in Enhancing the Customer Experience. *Journal of Retailing, 99*(4), 518–531.
121. Barata, J., Cardoso, J. C., & Cunha, P. R. (2023). Mass Customization and Mass Personalization Meet at the Crossroads of Industry 4.0: A Case of Augmented Digital Engineering. *Systems Engineering, 26*, 715–727.

Index

Note: Locators in *italics* represent figures and **bold** indicate tables in the text.